On the Brink

Professor Peter Coaldrake has been Deputy Vice-Chancellor of the Queensland University of Technology (QUT) since July 1994. He spent four years in state government as Chair of Queensland's Public Sector Management Commission (1990–1994) and, before that, had held academic management positions at both the then QIT and Griffith University. In 1995 he was a member of the Higher Education Management Review (Hoare Committee). He is author of *Working the System: Government in Queensland* (UQP, 1989) and co-editor (with JR Nethercote) of *What Should Government Do?* (Hale and Iremonger, 1989).

Dr Lawrence Stedman is Principal Policy Adviser within the Chancellery at QUT. Prior to joining the University in 1995, he worked in the Commonwealth Department of Finance and the Department of Community Services and Health, where he was secretary to the Medical Research Committee of the National Health and Medical Research Council.

*This book is for Emma, Jessica and Lee Coaldrake
and for Dougal and Lucy Stedman and Robyn Baker*

On the Brink

AUSTRALIA'S UNIVERSITIES CONFRONTING THEIR FUTURE

PETER COALDRAKE
AND
LAWRENCE STEDMAN

University of Queensland Press

First published 1998 by University of Queensland Press
Box 42, St Lucia, Queensland 4067 Australia

Printed in Australia by McPherson's Printing Group

Cataloguing in Publication Data
National Library of Australia

Coaldrake, O. P. (Owen Peter), 1951– .
  On the brink: Australia's universities confronting their future.

  1. Universities and colleges — Australia. 2. Education.
  Higher — Australia. 3. Educational change — Australia.
  I. Stedman, Lawrence, 1960– . II. Title.

  Bibliography.
  Includes index.

378.94

ISBN 0 7022 3050 2

Contents

Acknowledgments

We would like to acknowledge the support and guidance of a number of colleagues and friends who reviewed draft material. Leigh Tabrett and Glyn Davis both perused the entire manuscript; their detailed comments and encouragement have been a great source of sustenance. A number of other people were generous enough to review individual chapters or early working drafts: Keith Leopold, Vicki Sara, Chris Fell, Ruth Dunkin, Carol Dickenson, Roy Ballantyne, Gail Hart, Dianne Peacock, Helen Williams, David Gardiner, Roger Scott, and Alan Cumming. Our thanks to all of them.

Special thanks to Sean Leahy, the *Courier-Mail*'s resident cartoonist, whose drawings hopefully will bring life to a number of the themes and messages buried in the text. We are grateful, too, to the *Sydney Morning Herald* for granting us permission to reproduce an editorial from an earlier era, and to the *Socio-Legal Newsletter* for permission to reproduce the cartoon on God and tenure.

Laurie Muller and Craig Munro, both of the University of Queensland Press, deserve special mention. They believed in the concept of the book, and gave us great freedom and constant encouragement. We also extend our appreciation to Maryann Martin, who edited the manuscript, for her excellent work.

Finally, we thank our respective partners, Lee and Robyn, for their love, patience and support. Emma and Jess have tolerated much more than their fair share of paternal distraction over recent months, while Dougal and Lucy had the good sense to arrive on the scene as the script was being completed.

Peter Coaldrake and Lawrence Stedman

CHAPTER ONE

Grappling With New Realities

There is a view held quite widely within our universities, and shared by many university leaders, that the changes which have taken place in higher education over the last decade or so have secured the future. The argument goes that universities have heeded the demands of government for institutions to lift the quality of their teaching, and upgrade the relevance of their research. Further, over recent years our universities have learnt to reach out into the broader community, and they have even learnt how to manage themselves. In any case, universities over the centuries have shown themselves to be extremely durable institutions, capable of adapting to changing circumstances while maintaining their traditional ideals.

But the reality of the circumstances facing universities is not entirely comforting. It is true that if Australia is to secure its economic and social future then it must increase the national capacity to produce and use knowledge. It is also true that universities have played a central role in providing access to knowledge, creating knowledge and fostering learning in students to enable them to use knowledge. However it is not true that the university is the only type of institution capable of undertaking these functions. Nor is it true that the approach taken by universities in the past can simply be scaled-up to meet the size and complexity of future needs.

Traditionally, the university provided the institutional form for dealing in knowledge for its own sake, both in education and research. We say traditionally, even though this ideal has evolved unevenly, and its expression in terms that encompass both research and teaching has only emerged over the past hundred years or so. Accompanying this ideal has been a set of rights and privileges extended to universities and individual academics in the form of autonomy, tenure, and academic freedom. These rights and privileges have been allowed on the often vaguely understood basis that universities were somehow unique and important, and that it was appropriate for universities alone to determine the basis on which they operated. The method of academic organisation which accompanied this was that of a medieval guild. The masters, or professors, *were* the university, and all were equal.

In Australia this tradition has existed uneasily. For many years governments and the public were indifferent to the ideal of knowledge for its own sake; from its earliest days Australia has been more concerned with pragmatic and short-term matters. Our universities have all been developed with professional and practical goals in mind, notwithstanding idealism on the part of some of their founders and the academics who came to them. Yet traditional academic methods of operation were able to hold sway - if not unchallenged - while universities remained small and of only marginal relevance to the country.

In the latter part of this century all this has changed. Over the past few decades universities in many countries have sought to adjust themselves to new realities. They have been encouraged to increase significantly their numbers of students, to make better use of their budgets, and to raise money from industry and the professions. Universities also have been forced to comply with new regulatory requirements, and exhorted to apply to their own activities the principles and language of business and industry. As a result, universities now operate more strategically. Many institutions express genuine interest in the contribution of degree study to the employability of graduates, and vice-chancellors talk about bottom-lines.

Universities even debate whether students should be regarded as customers or clients. This is a change in language from the idealised concept of students as participants in the scholarly community, and certainly a far cry from the long-held view of at least a proportion of university academics that undergraduate students were little more than a tiresome necessity whose presence had to be tolerated, mercifully for no more than seven or eight months a year.

We now have a university system that is vastly different in both size and purpose from the traditional ideal, and yet most universities are trying to act as if they can still organise their academic activities and manage themselves in the same way. The serious attempts by universities over recent years to lift their game should not be underestimated. Nor should those efforts be trivialised. Equally, however, there should be an appreciation of the extent to which our institutions of higher learning are struggling to cope with contemporary realities.

This struggle is occurring at all levels.

University students in many countries are paying an increasing share of their education costs, and a good number of these students are irritated, if not financially pressured, by this situation. They therefore tend to expect good teaching and a quality learning environment supported by the latest technology. Students also have a level of expectation that if they have paid for their studies, they should have better prospects of employment or, if they already have a job, that their career opportunities will be improved by their studies.

A very significant proportion of the senior academic staff in our universities have been in their posts for a long time. Mostly male, they were permitted in an earlier era to work very much at their preferred pace. Budgets were relatively secure, and not overly tied either to student numbers or published research output.

Things began to change in Australian universities about twenty years ago, when governments began to take a fresh look at how public money was being spent. There was particular concern that governments were beginning to be more intrusive about what was going on inside universities, notwithstanding the level of taxpayer support institutions were receiving. Academic staff did not appreciate the paperwork that was associated with new regulatory burdens. They also disapproved when large numbers of non-academic staff had to be engaged not only for a broader range of administrative duties, but also for an increasing array of activities associated with introducing new technologies or managing budgets.

As student numbers grew, more academic staff were needed, and the merger of institutions threw together different academic cultures. There was a perception - not a particularly accurate one, at least in Australia, until very recently - that university budgets were being cut. What was true, however, was that there was greater uncertainty in the university environment and budgets increasingly had to be earned. This meant, particularly in light of the industrial rigidities in place, that many of the new academic jobs which came on stream did so on a short-term contract basis. In turn, many of these positions went to younger staff, and a good number of them to women. The notion of tenure has democratically been broadened from a professorial privilege to an industrial condition to which most academics aspire. However, the lack of opportunity for tenurable appointment for many of those new staff has become a source of discontent.

Greater levels of uncertainty about career prospects have combined with growing resentment about the inadequacy of academic salaries. Over the years academic pay has deteriorated against salaries in comparable areas of the workforce. This has been a particularly sore issue in those disciplines allied to business and technology where graduate starting salaries were often equivalent to those of lecturing staff, and where salary packages available to graduates after two or three years in the workforce often exceeded those of their university professors. Uniform academic rewards have given way to enterprise bargaining, greater reliance on outside consulting income and the use of market loadings. The equal financial standing of the academic disciplines, one of the cornerstones of the traditional community of scholars, has been irretrievably broken.

Universities have sought to present themselves as useful to all comers. They actively seek out fee-paying overseas students, industry training contracts, and applied research opportunities; they emphasise the relevance of their degrees and the employability of their graduates; and they have drawn in a wider range of areas of study, such as performing arts, tourism and nursing. Increasingly, universities find themselves competing with private education and research organisations that operate without the restrictions in flexibility and cost that come from attempting to adapt traditional university practices to the demands of the marketplace.

It is perhaps little wonder that a large number of academic staff feel alienated. Yet it is of some concern that the plight of many universities, and the university sector in general, is more evident to those outside it than to many insiders. The most common reaction which is heard to the array of problems and challenges facing higher education is a railing against government, or a decrying of the apparent lack of understanding within the broader community of what is seen to be the self-evident value of universities to the well-being of society.

The problem with this externalisation of blame by universities is that hardly anyone outside the university sector is listening. In Australia this was most starkly exemplified during the 1996 federal election campaign when the country's Vice-Chancellors combined with the relevant industrial unions to demand from both sides of politics a set of guarantees regarding the taxpayer-supported funding of future salary increases. But neither of the major political sides blinked, and the universities were forced to fund sizeable salary hikes largely from existing income sources.

On the brink of a new millennium Australian society and its institutions are facing profound transformations arising from globalisation and developments in information technology. Institutions and organisations of all shapes and sizes need to be able to adapt quickly and

fundamentally, and sustain the ability to change and grow. This will require both an educated population capable of producing and using new knowledge, and organisations throughout the workforce which are able to manage continuing and large scale change.

Developing these capabilities will involve continuing major levels of investment in education services by governments, corporations, other institutions and, increasingly, by individuals. All of these players will expect that their investment is money well spent - that is, they will want research and education that are relevant and contemporary, delivered efficiently and conveniently.

Many academics pride themselves on the enduring nature of the university as an institution, one which provides almost monastic stability in a world of change. While there can be strengths in stability and tradition, universities cannot remain aloof from the expectations and needs of society. This is especially so now that universities are no longer catering for an elite, and are being weaned from an almost total reliance on government funding.

Universities, if they are able to deliver what is required, respond quickly to changing needs in a the workforce, and offer their services in a flexible manner and at a reasonable price, have an invaluable opportunity to cement their role and their importance in the life of the community.

This book argues that our universities do have an important future. It is a future, however, that depends on their ability to make a range of fundamental changes to the way they go about their teaching and research activities, as well as to the way they manage and present themselves.

CHAPTER TWO

Drifting Into Trouble

Universities trace their history back to the early years of the millennium. In 1980 a group of American educators noted that there are sixty-six Western institutions which were in existence at the time of the founding of the Lutheran Church in 1530 and which still exist today in recognisable form. Sixty-two of these are universities.[1] Despite the durability of the university as an institution, enormous changes have taken place over the years in what they do. Nevertheless, the medieval heritage in the form of values and traditions that date back hundreds of years continues to exert a powerful influence on universities today.

This book is about the pressures on modern Australian universities, and understanding why they respond to these pressures in the way that they do. To put this in context we have to look back to see how Australian universities came to be where they are today.

Australian universities have, of course, only been in existence for a relatively short time, the first being established in the mid-nineteenth century. Australia was shrugging off its convict past; the colonies were developing their own style and sense of freedom, driving back frontiers into an undeveloped continent. The discovery of gold in 1851 led to a trebling in the population over ten years, and sparked predictions of imminent nationhood. It also reinforced the materialism of most of the colonists as they pursued short-term wealth through the plundering of the continent's natural assets.

These developments in Australia coincided with a period when higher education was undergoing fundamental change in Britain and the United States. The ancient institutions of Oxford and Cambridge were Church universities, whose education was built on the classics and whose purpose was to preserve and instil civilised values in future gentlemen, professionals and the clergy. This mission was seen as all the more important in the early to middle years of the nineteenth century in an England that was caught in a backlash to the French Revolution and the Napoleonic Wars. English society was dominated by Church and conservative government, determined to preserve the status quo against the perceived depredations of new European thought and potential revolution.

Entry to the English universities required adherence to the Thirty-Nine Articles of Anglican faith, a barrier which served to exclude many of the ablest minds of the time. Prior to the Napoleonic Wars, Dissenters Academies were founded in England by such excluded scholars, who set about developing curricula in relevant subjects such as science and modern languages. These Academies did not survive in the period following the Wars, and Dissenters were forced to seek education elsewhere. They turned to some of the universities of Europe and to the more practically-oriented institutions in Scotland. Edinburgh University became known as the "Northern Athens" as it provided a gateway to new ideas from the Continent and offered a broad range of scientific and medical subjects for study. A similar tag was applied to Warrington Academy near Manchester.

Pressure for reform in England mounted and, in 1826, the "godless" University College of London was established, emphasising a practical education strong in science, medicine and engineering. By the time the first Australian university was being established in Sydney in the late 1840s, the breaking of the Anglican monopoly on Oxford and Cambridge was underway.

Thus while the colonies looked to Britain rather than the United States for inspiration, they could draw on models in the form of the University of London and the Scottish universities, which were more suited to the pragmatic and materialist climate which prevailed at home. Notable characteristics were that medicine and science were given early prominence, and Australian universities did not develop around the college model. Professors belonged to the university rather than to a college, and students developed a different association with the university and its professors than the more personal master-tutor relationship that characterised Oxford and Cambridge. Nevertheless, the new Australian universities were heavily influenced by "Oxbridge" and the Irish universities. Residential colleges were established, with names and rituals reminiscent of the English university tradition. However, these Australian halls of residence were never academically autonomous centres of learning. Although they did, and still do, offer some limited tutorial support for students, their function was and is primarily to house students. Nor did they cater for most of the student population, many of whom lived and worked outside the university and came from outside to hear lectures and take tutorials. A review of residential accommodation in Australian universities in 1990 found that the total stock of places amounted to around 10 per cent of the full-time student population.[2]

A non-denominational Sydney College had been founded in 1835 by dissenters and emancipists, though by 1841 it had taken on an Anglican flavour. Its closure in 1848, together with the opening of a NSW Bar which needed trained legal expertise, provided impetus for the first university in Australia.[3] The two early universities, established in Sydney in 1850[4] and in Melbourne three years later, were not the result of popular demand. The prevailing sentiment in Australia was one of money-making and practical economic development; most people in the colonies could become excited about feats of exploration, expansion of agricultural boundaries, and the beginning of the gold rush, but few sought to replicate the elite, remote and religious institutions of Oxford or Cambridge in such surroundings. A select group of leading citizens, however, saw the need to establish a university to provide professional education, to prepare youth for positions of leadership in the future, and to provide a civilising influence on the colonies.

While the ideals of the founding fathers of the early universities in Australia may have included more lofty purposes, those of the government and general public were pragmatic and ambivalent. The view of universities as primarily professional training institutions began from their inception in this country; it is a perspective which for many persists today. The models chosen for our universities were those of the secular and scientific institutions that arose from nineteenth century utilitarian reforms. For the first three, in Sydney, Melbourne and Adelaide (founded in 1874), the University of London and the Scottish universities tempered the influence of the old English and Irish universities. By the time the next three were established in Tasmania (1890), Queensland (1909) and Western Australia (1912), founders looked to the progressive regional universities in Britain and, particularly in the case of Western Australia, to examples from the United States.

The American influence showed itself in a commitment to wider access to higher education, and in a closer involvement between the university and the community. In 1862 in what Lord Bowden, a former UK Minister for Education and Science, described as "the most important event in the history of education in the Western world"[5], the Morrill Act was passed in the United States. That Act established the "Land Grant" colleges which later evolved into the American State Universities. These colleges combined liberal and vocational studies, emphasised community service, and provided access to higher education for the economically underprivileged. Initially looked down upon by the older universities, they came to exert a powerful influence on the shape of American higher education, and on universities in Australia.

For a time in the later nineteenth century, a strong base of scientific research flourished in the three Australian universities. The early group of professors were young UK graduates, finding opportunities in Australia that were more limited in their home country. The average age of professors before 1890 was only 33 years.[6] While Sydney drew its professoriate from Oxford and Cambridge, Melbourne was more enterprising, attracting eminent graduates from Irish and Scottish universities. These young men were firmly of the view that research was an integral part of a university. Some outstanding research was undertaken in the three universities in fields such as hydrodynamics, chemistry, anatomy and the physiology of marsupials.[7]

This Golden Era did not extend for very long into the new century. The generous private benefactions which helped to establish the universities were not ongoing and any enthusiasm on the part of State governments for the support of universities waned in the face of economic difficulties exacerbated by the end of the gold rush and prolonged periods of drought. In accordance with British models, the universities catered for an elite group of students (though elite in the sense of performance rather than in clear social terms). By 1895 the four universities of the time enrolled around one-sixteenth of one per cent of the population. This figure grew as two new universities were established in Queensland and Western Australia. By 1914 3,300 students, or just under one per cent of the population, were enrolled in the six universities.

Growth continued in the years directly following World War I, but by the 1920s the university system had entered a period of stagnation. The influx of bright new scholars from abroad slowed as the best minds sought to build on their reputations by "going home" to careers in British universities, and local graduates began to fill positions on the basis of length of service or on political favour. Popular opinion was often directed against the universities, with the press frequently criticising Australian academics for being too remote, failing to contribute to the national identity, and for providing education more suited to the British classical ideal than to the practical needs of the new Federation. To be fair to the universities, they had several times tried to be responsive by establishing more "relevant" courses. The University of Melbourne in the late 1890s and the University of Tasmania in 1902 attempted to introduce courses in mining engineering and metallurgy, but in both cases the efforts failed because of lack of public interest and government funding.

It was generally true, however, that the older universities in particular felt a natural affinity with the classical traditions of conservative Britain, rather than with the radical agents of change in England or the active nationalists in Australia. This may have enabled them to provide the civilising influence that to some is the hallmark and true value of a university - and to balance out the narrow self-interests of the new country[8] - but it also emphasised the remoteness of the university system from the aspirations of many Australians of the time. And it is this remoteness which laid the foundation for Australia's long-standing ambivalence towards its universities.

In the period between the Wars, no new universities were established in Australia, although two university colleges appeared in the regional New South Wales areas of Canberra and Armidale. University colleges (another British tradition) are fledgling universities, set up initially as offshoots of established institutions. Usually they do not have the authority to grant their own degrees, but in time they are expected to evolve into full universities. The six universities became more like one another, taking on the role of undergraduate teaching factories, preparing students for the professions or, if sufficiently academically gifted, for postgraduate studies in Britain. The Depression years of the early 1930s saw tertiary funding cut by the State governments, and by the time of the Second World War universities enrolled only 14,000 students, or one fifth of one per cent of the population. A little money had been provided for research; for example, in 1936 the National Health and Medical Research Council was established by the Commonwealth to provide a small amount of funding for medical research. By and large, however, there was very little original investigative work undertaken in the universities during the years leading into the Second World War.

*

World War II represented a turning point for the nation. It helped bring about a stronger sense of national identity, and established a prominent role for the Commonwealth Government which continued after the War with the retention of uniform taxation. Australian universities are, with the exception of those in the national capital and the Northern Territory, established under State legislation, and up to the time of the Second World War they were also largely under State supervision and support. In keeping with British traditions, however, they enjoyed an impoverished sort of autonomy. State grants provided just over a third of their funding, fees provided another third, while a mixture of endowment income and some Commonwealth grants comprised the remainder.

After the War Australia began a period of national reconstruction which provided a powerful stimulus for higher education. The most immediate impact was the introduction of a large cohort of students and, importantly, of Commonwealth money, through the Commonwealth Reconstruction Training Scheme (CRTS). Enrolments more than doubled just after the War (rising to nearly 32,000 by 1948) before falling back slightly as the CRTS cohort worked its way through the system. This post-CRTS dip was the last time higher education enrolments fell, at the system-wide level, in Australia.

It quickly became apparent that Australia's attenuated universities were not equipped to deal with a large influx of new students. Many academics were also concerned at the implications of the rapid growth. They saw, correctly, that the American trend towards mass participation in higher education spelled the end of elite British traditions, and would pose fundamental problems for our universities. Nevertheless, once the momentum for growth had begun, it could not easily be slowed. Demand was fuelled by a need for teachers for the "baby boom" generation and by a growing realisation on the part of government that higher education had an important role to play in national economic growth. Over the decade of the 1950s, enrolments grew by 30,000 and participation rates, the percentage of people in a particular age group who attend university, doubled.

In 1951 the Commonwealth provided the first direct grants to universities, signalling the beginning of an assumption of national responsibility for funding. The national government's role was more firmly cemented six years later, when Prime Minister Menzies established a Committee on Australian Universities, to investigate the growing reports of problems with overcrowded and underfunded universities. The Committee was chaired by Sir Keith Murray, the Chairman of the UK University Grants Committee, and its findings make interesting reading in the light of problems experienced by our universities today. Prominent concerns detailed overcrowded lecture theatres, high drop-out rates, lack of adequate infrastructure, poorly maintained buildings, and underpaid staff. The Committee's Report noted that in one English Department that they had visited, a "substantial proportion" of a class of 700 students was packed into a large lecture theatre, so that many were "quite unable to see the blackboard."[9]

The weak state of university research was also highlighted in the Murray Committee's Report. The need for tertiary-level research and postgraduate study had been recognised in the 1940s, when the Australian National University was founded as a national research-only institution. It was not until this time that the first PhD was offered, at the University of Melbourne. The Murray Committee found that research in Australian universities was hampered by limited staff and student mobility, lack of adequate equipment and funding, and by a culture in some areas, particularly in the technological departments, that saw postgraduate work as unrelated to their interests.

The Murray Committee's Report was not universally welcomed in Canberra. Treasury was sceptical because Murray recommended both substantial increases in expenditure on universities, and the creation of an Australian Universities Grants Committee, which could be seen to provide universities with privileged access to Commonwealth funding.[10] Nevertheless, the Government accepted the Report. It provided increased funds to the sector and formed an Australian Universities Commission (AUC), a name chosen by Menzies to emphasise its mandate to advise more broadly than on grants alone.

By 1960, Australia had ten universities which catered for 53,000 students. It was clear by this time that attention also should be directed to the other arms of tertiary education - the various State-based technical and agricultural colleges, institutes of technology, and teacher training colleges, which at the time enrolled around two thirds as many students as did the universities. These organisations had their origins in the mechanics institutes and teacher training institutions of the nineteenth century and, while lower in status than universities, shared with universities the problem of chronic underfunding.

In 1961 the Commonwealth commissioned a special committee to investigate the future of the whole tertiary education sector. The committee, headed by Sir Leslie Martin, head of the AUC, took three years to undertake its work. The main outcome of its report was the establishment of the so-called binary system of higher education, where universities would undertake research and provide education suitable for degree-level study, while colleges of advanced education (CAEs) would concentrate on vocational education up to the diploma level. As noted by some critics at the time, the rationale for the distinction was not clearly made in the Committee's Report, and was based in part on a dubious view that there were some students with practical minds and others with analytical minds.[11] In fact, the riding brief for the Martin Committee had been to find ways of expanding tertiary education that did not bear too heavily on the public purse. Invention of a new category of cheaper higher education institution was the answer, and the Commonwealth duly funded a rapid expansion in enrolments in the CAEs, so rapid that by 1980 enrolments matched those in universities, and exceeded them shortly thereafter. The CAEs typically provided courses that built on their institutional antecedents, specialising in areas such as teacher education, technology-related subjects, business and agriculture.

University enrolments continued to climb steeply throughout the 1960s, roughly doubling over the decade. The fuel for this increase, however, was not so much a wish by governments to increase the participation rates in universities, as had been the case in the 1950s. Rather it was the result of natural population growth in the 20-29 year old age group, with the "baby boom" cohort attaining university age. The momentum continued throughout the first half of the 1970s, although the level of growth was constrained by the Commonwealth through enrolment quotas in favour of building the colleges of advanced education. The pressure of student numbers led to the establishment of eight new universities, five in the first half of the 1970s alone. On the campuses of the older universities there was an active program of construction of new buildings to cater for the increase in student numbers; brick and concrete buildings sprung up alongside the sandstone.

The post-war growth period created a strong demand for university staff. Job opportunities within the university system and the education sector in general were relatively plentiful for university graduates. The Martin Committee noted that staff numbers had grown by 350 per cent over the previous decade, and it forecast that this growth would need to continue for at least another decade. However it observed that Australian universities were not well equipped to provide sufficient graduates for this purpose.

The typical complement of university staff a hundred years ago comprised a set of tenured professors, supported by lecturers, assistant lecturers and demonstrators. In the early part of the twentieth century as funding became more scarce, there was pressure to appoint cheaper grades of teaching staff on a short-term basis. At the University of Sydney, professors declined in relative numbers from around half of all full-time staff in 1900 to around one quarter by 1919.[12] In the 1960s a different set of pressures led to an expansion in cheaper forms of teaching staff, notably in the form of the tutor system, where postgraduate students gained practical teaching experience by providing tutorials to smaller groups of students.

The post-war expansion also placed great strain on the traditional ways in which universities were managed. In keeping with British traditions, Australian universities at this time operated as autonomous self-governing institutions, ruled by the professoriate. The typical organisational structure was a department comprising a handful of lecturing staff and headed by a professor. Key decisions about academic and resource matters were made by peak committees, particularly the Professorial Board or its equivalent, which were frequently overly large, interminably ponderous in their style of deliberation and not overly disposed to the task of making decisions.

The role of the Vice-Chancellor, as seen by the academic staff at least, was that of money-raiser whose rule was based on persuasion rather than authority. The first full-time Vice-Chancellors did not appear until 1927 at the University of Sydney and 1934 at Melbourne. Academic governance and management represented a limited form of collegiality, where power rested firmly in the hands of the "god professors", for most of whom administration and finance were lesser matters, unworthy of professorial attention. As a consequence, management procedures and authorities for decision making were often loose and unclear. This might have sufficed when universities were elite, small and impoverished, but real problems were encountered in the 1960s, particularly by the older universities, where traditions were more entrenched.

Writing in 1960, A.P. Rowe, the first full-time Vice-Chancellor of the University of Adelaide (1948-1958), painted a dismal picture of the management of university education of the time, at least within his university.[13] Vice-Chancellors were in an impossible position, hamstrung by "the two greatest evils" of "a departmentalism which tends to make a university into a number of isolated units, and an egalitarianism which assumes that all departments and all professors are equally worthy of support." There was a chasm between the licence afforded to the professors, and that of the lower levels, with administrative staff at the bottom of the heap. He saw at least part of the solution in raising the prominence of deans, the position of dean being that of a senior professor with management responsibilities across a group of departments. In his time, the position of dean was of low status, and was filled on a rotating non-appointment basis rather than with any consideration to permanency or particular flair for the job. Rowe looked to the United States, where Vice-Chancellors occupied the position of "president" with clear authority, and deans were of high status, chosen on the basis of merit on a permanent basis. However he could not resist recounting a story to show that even the American system did not always guarantee ability:

> A New York society woman wrote to the university president asking that a member of the academic staff should talk to a society of special interest to her and she stipulated that his status must not be less than that of a dean and that he must be a wit. The president replied that he had no dean who was a wit, but that he had two deans who were half-wits and that he would send both.

*

In the middle and later years of the 1960s, student unrest was having a profound effect on universities, particularly those in Europe, Japan and the United States and, to a lesser extent, in Britain. Demands for more "relevant" curricula and greater student participation in decision-making led to sometimes violent confrontations between students and university administration. The demands for greater democratisation filtered through to Australia, in the form of pressures for organisational change and participation in decision making by junior staff and students.

In the 1960s and 1970s the management problems of the older universities, coupled with the establishment of new universities, and the pressure for democratisation of decision-making, led to a widespread reform of university management structures. The membership of decision-making committees was opened up to include a wider range of staff, and consultative committees were established, chaired by student representatives, much to the chagrin of some heads of academic departments. Changes in organisational structure, including the more widespread establishment of schools and large departments, weakened the power of individual professors, shifting it to designated positions of authority. However these changes were not overly far-reaching; universities remained cushioned by growth. As F.J. Willett, at the time a Pro-Vice-Chancellor at the University of Melbourne and later Foundation Vice-Chancellor of Griffith University, observed in 1972: "with growth there is a capacity for creativity, innovation and experiment; the inevitable mistakes can be contained and by-passed without too much agonized reappraisal. A stable university, with its revenue growing little faster than wages and prices, must create a capacity for creativity and experiment which is the lifeblood of any university, by reallocating its resources, not by channelling new funds. Reallocations of this sort must hurt and may imperil morale."[14] The pressure for such hard decisions was to begin, albeit hesitantly in Australia, with the slowing of post-war growth in the late 1970s.

*

No one expected that universities could sustain indefinite rapid growth, but the check came rather more abruptly than many had anticipated. In 1974, the Commonwealth assumed full responsibility for funding higher education, and a few years later drew the two funding systems and the oversight of TAFE into one umbrella organisation, the Commonwealth Tertiary Education Commission (CTEC), which provided advice to government and was responsible for allocating among institutions the money provided by government.

This was a tumultuous time in higher education. Many academics were suspicious of the Commonwealth, believing it to have ulterior motives for taking financial control, and that this control would shortly extend to attacks on university autonomy. But when the crunch came it was one of funding, not of academic freedom.

In 1975, in a climate of political crisis and economic recession, triennial funding was suspended and clear signals were given that the growth in university enrolments was to be curtailed. Demographic pressures for increasing higher education places remained, but most of the growth was channelled into the cheaper CAEs and into technical education training, mainly through the State-controlled Technical and Further Education (TAFE) colleges.

Throughout the growth period of 1960-1975, funding that could be used for employing staff had kept more or less in proportion to growth in student load. Universities were able to maintain the ratios between staff and student numbers, although the government was not so generous as to enable them to decrease class sizes in any significant way. Between 1977 and 1979, student load in universities fell by 1.5 per cent, before returning to 1977 levels by 1981. Over this period, CAE numbers continued to increase so that overall higher education numbers did not fall. In the early 1980s the problems caused by static student numbers were compounded by a squeeze on funding, so that recurrent grants per full-time student decreased by 6 per cent between 1980 and 1984.[15] Universities were forced to impose freezes on staff replacements and there was an actual decline in the number of university academics in 1983, a situation reversed in following years as enrolments again increased.

The Fraser Government's 1981 Review of Commonwealth Functions, or "Razor Gang", confirmed that the financial constraints on higher education were no temporary phenomenon. The Razor Gang proposed replacing student assistance grants with loans, abolishing the commitment given by the previous Whitlam Government to "free" higher education, and set out a sweeping program of institutional amalgamations. The proposals relating to student loans and fees were blocked by the Senate, but almost all the amalgamations involving twenty-six teacher education CAEs, proceeded.

The convenient fiction that a hard and fast distinction could be made between universities and CAEs came under increasing pressure in the 1980s. A decade earlier, many CAEs had made inroads into degree-level education, and many of the mainly university-trained staff in those CAEs were involved in applied research projects. Universities had also expanded their range of vocational courses, for example drawing in the education of teachers and nurses, and extending their offerings in the business-related fields. The net effect was the further blurring of boundaries between the universities and the CAE sector.

The principal difference between the two sectors by the mid 1980s was that the older universities were better funded than CAEs, in that they enjoyed explicit provision for research activities. The 1986 CTEC Review of Efficiency and Effectiveness in Higher Education argued that the binary system should be retained on the grounds that it had served Australia well. However, the battle was already lost. Moves were afoot in various States to redesignate some CAEs as universities, and the end of the binary system was to come just two years later, with the so-called "Dawkins Revolution" ushered in by the Federal Government's 1988 White Paper.

The 1988 White Paper heralded a major change in the Australian higher education system. Unlike past changes, however, these were not driven by investigations and recommendations made by a formal body of eminent university experts. Rather, they were orchestrated by the Federal Minister and his department, albeit with some advice from a select group of senior academics, and were the result of pressures arising from the situation of higher education within the public sector and the broader movements of public sector reform. In essence this reform sought to bring about political, social and management changes which would focus public organisations on the efficient and effective delivery of particular planned outcomes, under government guidance. For the universities, this meant among other things that the sector would be streamlined, facilitating national supervision through a series of institutional amalgamations. The Federal Department would then negotiate a "profile" of activities with each university with regard to national needs and priorities, and fund the institution on that basis. The philosophical basis for the reform was a desire to see universities serve national economic ends, secured by much more direct steering by government.

Accordingly, CTEC was disbanded and a National Board of Employment, Education and Training (NBEET) was established to fulfil a purely advisory role. The task of amalgamating the former CAEs, either with other CAEs or with existing universities, took a few years to achieve, but was brought about relatively painlessly, with a couple of notable exceptions. The eighteen universities and forty-seven CAEs that existed in 1985 were reformed into thirty universities by 1991, and thirty-five by the end of 1994.

The effects of this regrouping have been far-reaching. Perhaps the most evident is in the redistribution of research funding. Former CAE staff were now in universities; many senior staff were reclassified as professors and sought out more active research roles. Some initial funding was earmarked for the new universities to establish suitable research infrastructure, but by 1995 this was discontinued, and all universities competed on the same criteria for public funding for research.

As is the case with many other university systems, Australian universities receive money for research through their block grants (over which they have control) and also through applying to research councils for grants on a competitive basis. At the conclusion of the binary system, some money was "clawed back" from the block grants of the universities to boost the competitive grants schemes. Not surprisingly, the established universities have seen this as a watering-down of research resources which they believed were rightfully theirs, notwithstanding that the older institutions continue to reap the lion's share of competitively-awarded funding.

*

In 1939 the Australian university system comprised fewer than 15,000 students in six universities. By 1960 it had expanded to 53,000 students in ten universities; by 1975, 148,000 students in eighteen universities; and by 1985, 175,000 students in nineteen universities. By 1997, with the collapse of the binary system, Australia had a total of more than 650,000 students enrolled in thirty-six public universities.

The rapid expansion of higher education in the post-War period was a worldwide phenomenon, at least for the Western developed countries (it was particularly marked in the United States). Roughly similar demographic forces and public sector reforms from the 1970s onwards dictated that the subsequent decline in growth and the squeeze on university finances became an international dilemma. Where Australian universities differed, however, was that there was a gradual erosion of funding in the period since the early 1980s rather than the type of abrupt cuts experienced in the United Kingdom and in some jurisdictions in the United States. In Australia, overall funding levels per student have fluctuated, but have been held fairly constant. Within this constancy, however, the resources available for employment of teaching staff have been eroded in favour of money for buildings and maintenance and for research. As a consequence, the ratio of students to academic staff has been significantly increased. In 1982 there were around 11 students to each academic staff member (in full-time equivalent terms); ten years later this increased to around 15. Writing in 1996, the then Federal Minister for Education made the rather surprising claim that since resources per student were constant, it must have been the universities' decision to increase student to staff ratios.[16] If it had been possible (leaving to one side for the moment whether it would have been desirable) for university management to divert money from building works and research to teaching staff, this claim would be valid. But the Commonwealth had already imposed clear directions on the purposes for which such funds were to be used.

In general, Australian universities have retained substantial control and autonomy over their operations. However, the Commonwealth has been able to exercise considerable influence through the direction of some university funds for specific purposes. Over the past ten years, separate funding has been provided for Aboriginal participation, special research, equity, industry placements, quality enhancement, teaching improvement, and building works. Such a list of line items illustrates both the government's need to reflect its priorities and its uncertainty as to the willingness and capacity of universities to match them.

In the 1990s, additional funding was provided for the quality assurance process. Three "quality rounds" were held, involving short institutional visits by a small group of experts. As an assessment of quality, the exercise was flawed and superficial, highlighted by lack of time, resources and uniform agreement as to what actually constituted quality at an institutional level. Nevertheless, the three rounds served to focus attention on market sensitivities in Australian higher education. The process also galvanised a remarkable degree of compliant activity in the universities as they sought to benefit from the prestige of a good ranking and from the relatively small pool of money that was available.

Funding has been just sufficient to enable universities to accommodate expansion without forcing major change. That is, it has not been generous enough to allow significantly greater diversity to develop, nor drastically cut to force fundamental reappraisal of approaches. The effect of this, together with the restrictions imposed on flexibility by the Commonwealth, has been to entrench a culture of incrementalism in Australian universities. Change from within has often been funded by small, limited-term grants, while change from without has been directed at national reform designed to achieve a coordinated and efficient system, supposedly responsive to national economic needs.

In more recent years, we have seen a repositioning of the relationship between universities and the Federal Government. Universities have been given greater discretion over their funds, many of the line by line grants have been folded in together, and market-based mechanisms in the form of student charges and fees play an increasingly important part in university budgets. Government is now positioning itself less as the patron and guide of the system, and more as a purchaser of higher education on behalf of the taxpayer. It seeks to define the appropriate base level of public subsidy and to focus on accountability and quality assurance.

In 1996 the Federal Budget imposed on universities so-called "efficiency dividends".[17] While new to the Australian university system, such cuts have been common practice in many other areas of the public sector for many years, particularly in government departments. Even more significantly, the Government refused to pay university salary increases derived from enterprise bargaining above a minimum "safety net" level. Again, this was in line with practices in the rest of the public sector. The effect of these decisions has been to squeeze university budgets in ways unprecedented over the past fifteen years: between 1997 and 1998 total Government-funded student numbers in higher education are expected to decrease, something not seen in this country since 1955.[18]

Australian universities are now at a critical point. The tidal waves of enrolments arising from the post-War boom and increased school retention have peaked, so future changes within the system will not be accommodated within a climate of sustained growth. These changes will be driven by Australia's need to shift from a resource-based to a knowledge-based economy, by reforms in the vocational education and training sector, by technological advances, and by a weaning of universities from government support. Universities must be able to demonstrate their relevance and quality in this environment and be able to adapt in ways which have hitherto been unfamiliar.

Some may think it an exaggeration to say that the situation in Australian universities is critical. Perhaps it is true that at this moment they are getting by, some more comfortably than others. It is also true that overall demand for higher education will remain high: demographic factors associated with the "baby boom echo", that is, the children of those born in the population surge in the 1940s and 1950s, will ensure that in some States there will be an upturn in school leavers seeking university education in the new millennium[19]. Upward drift of qualifications required for professional employment will also ensure a strong demand for both undergraduate and postgraduate education. However, our universities would be extremely unwise to overlook the changed situation which confronts them in the decades ahead.

Australian universities have been cocooned in the past by growth

and relatively generous funding, notwithstanding the occasional slow-down and the gradual attrition in support per student over the past fifteen years. The primary management concerns of the past have been how to manage growth within the prescriptions of national structures and policies, competition usually taking the form of institutions vying for larger pots of money.

This is not to say that universities have not had to face painful changes. Over the past half a century the system has been almost entirely re-invented, transformed from a ghostly colonial antique to a modern mass education system. In the process it has tried to reconcile the management of this change within traditional academic structures, practices and aspirations. Some of the structures have been changed, but many have not. Most of the changes that have been made have been vigorously opposed by various academic factions, some of whom invoke images of golden ages that have clearly never existed in Australia, or of lofty academic ideals and traditions that attempt to define the role and purpose of The University. From the earliest days of Australian higher education, it has been clear that Australians in general have seen the universities in different terms from those within university walls. The rapid growth in higher education in Australia was not a product of any acceptance by government of the civilising role of universities; it was always pragmatically based, vocationally focussed and sought to achieve its ends as cheaply as possible.

Universities, some have argued, should be self-governing collegial communities of scholars, their methods of operation and management *sui generis*, or unique, based on academic authority alone. If this was ever so, it was initially limited in scope to the professors, and only viable while universities were small. In any case this halcyon ideal was firmly laid to rest after the High Court decided in 1983 that universities were an "industry" for conciliation and arbitration purposes. Academic union and employers subsequently registered with the Conciliation and Arbitration Commission in the mid 1980s, and industrial employment relation and processes were thereafter entrenched in the university setting.

A striking feature of our universities is their centripetal tendency. Although founded with diverse intentions and structures, they have drifted towards one another. Before the Second World War this uniformity was probably most due to the lack of resources, limited academic mobility and parochialism. But it has also been a feature since then, all the more striking for the lack of variation in institutional form in the face of the enormous changes accompanying "massification". The Australian National University was founded in 1946 with a view to fostering research and postgraduate research training for national purposes, and shortly afterwards the New South Wales University of Technology, later the University of New South Wales, was established along the lines of the Massachusetts Institute of Technology. By the early 1960s, both institutions had assumed many of the features and aspirations of the other universities.[20] Dr J.A.L. Matheson, Vice-Chancellor of Monash University, commented in 1965 that he was one who had ".. tried - who indeed came to this country with the avowed intention of trying - to produce a university different in character from the other university in the city in which Monash is located. Instead of this I now find myself Vice-Chancellor of a University that is disappointingly like the University of Melbourne."[21]

Perhaps this trend to uniformity is driven by Australia's egalitarian tendencies and the local nature of our universities: if one institution offers a course in a certain way to a certain group, then the same should be available to all other groups. It also no doubt owes something to the limited mobility of students and staff between institutions, and to the dominance of the public sector in the provision of higher education. In particular, the Commonwealth Government over the years exerted a strong influence in the expansion of higher education in this country, often acting on the advice of senior academics trained in the British system.

However, we should not fall for the line promulgated by some of the older universities, that they represent the ideals to which other institutions aspire, and that the younger universities are "wannabe" sandstone institutions, mimicking the practices (and particularly the research cultures) of the more senior players. There is some truth in this, but it is equally true that the older universities are very different now from their earlier forms, and they have taken on many of the courses, methods of operation, award structures and markets of the newer universities. Both the old University of Queensland and the new University of South Australia chose the term "The People's University" in documenting their history.[22] Each university has striven to be all things to all people.

Over the past one hundred and fifty years, we have adapted a British elite system to a growing colonial society, watched it stagnate, then let it rapidly grow, leavening it as we did so with ideas from other countries, notably the United States. Universities are creatures of society, and as societal and economic needs change, so must they. For the past fifty years our economy has grown, in fits and starts, from an inward looking agricultural base to one that is increasingly international in outlook, reliant more on higher levels of skills and with a greater diversity of industries from manufacturing to information technology. Universities have been shaped by this change; we have needed a better educated and skilled workforce, and a growing body of basic and applied research. Along the way we have become more culturally diverse, and universities have played an important role in this.

Australian universities have evolved in multiple ways over the past fifty years; many of the worst aspects of academic stagnation depicted by Rowe as true of the 1950s have been overcome either wholly or in part. Movement of staff within the sector has been greatly improved, as has attention to the needs of students. Management is more professional and accountable, the processes of teaching and research within universities have been the subject of a great deal of research and improvement, and the range of studies at both undergraduate and postgraduate level has been greatly expanded.

However there is a long way to go. Many of the changes that have occurred to date have been marginal, reflecting attempts to marry old structures and practices with new imperatives. The traditional models and processes of universities can only be adapted so far, and they are under increasing strain. Society's needs are not static: they are changing rapidly and it is far from clear that our universities are well equipped to accommodate such change. Universities will need to deal with the implications of new environments for their full range of activities.

The idea of university and the very nature of academic work are under constant challenge. The usual approach of universities is to rush to the trenches to defend hallowed traditions and ideals, to reassert the relevance of timeless values in a changing world. Some of this will be of benefit. If universities do not defend what is worthy then there are few who will, but much of this reaction will miss the point. What is needed is not a model of the university that seeks to preserve the "glories" of the past, but a university that does what is appropriate and relevant for the future.

Academics occupy a peculiar position in the public eye. While many are respected for their opinions, echoes of Australia's pragmatic and egalitarian disdain for donnish attitudes remain strong. Universities are useful for training our necessary cadres of professional men and women, but are academics really useful for solving "real" problems? Oscar Wilde was expressing a view popular with many outside the universities when he quipped that professors "show a want of knowledge that must be the result of years of study".

There are several icons of academic life which are held by many to be of unquestionable status. These include the interrelated ideals of academic freedom, tenure of employment, university autonomy, the pursuit of basic research, the linking of teaching and research, and the right to decide who is taught, how they are taught, and what they are taught. This is not to say that these icons are not questioned - they are, and with increasing frequency. However, they are too often defended as ends in themselves, without which there could be no real university. The reality is that these ideals are not valued to anywhere near the same extent outside universities as they are within.

We opened this chapter with reference to the founding of the Lutheran Church. One of the triggers for this was a repudiation of the widespread practice of selling indulgences, whereby the Catholic Church allowed sins to be pardoned in exchange for money. Luther nailed his Ninety-Five Theses to a church door, proclaiming that repentance had to be a life-long activity and that divine grace could not be cheaply acquired. The modern challenge to the medieval institution of the university has turned about; universities find themselves faced with demands for life-long learning, but this time there are demands for education to be made available easily and cheaply, and sold to a commercial market.

The American sociologist Robert Nisbet has described the changes facing the modern university as a "Last Reformation":

> ... contemporary history is proving to be anything but kind to the role of professor, who is, after all, in academic dress no more, no less than a knight: a knight of the classroom, laboratory, and study, but not less a knight. He too is, or has been, the beneficiary of certain immunities and indulgences that the social order long since ceased to grant to other knights, other craftsmen, other guildsmen. But I know no better way of describing the contemporary Reformation in its impact upon the university than by saying that it is exceedingly unlikely that these immunities and indulgences will continue for much longer.[23]

The Australian university system, unlike its American, German and British parents, is a recent invention. It has never had a clear status and mission. Australian universities have evolved in confusion; shaped by major reviews dominated by British academics, and their academic staff aspiring to goals that were realised in their highest form in the older universities overseas. Each university has sought to combine the British ideals of the cultivation of intellect and the training of the academically gifted, with German traditions of research and academic freedom and the American influence of democratisation and community service.

As Nisbet pointed out, the medieval structure and privileges of the university were tolerated as long as universities were apart from society, and while they could command respect as institutions which dealt with knowledge for its own sake. This was never the overriding rationale for the Australian university, or if it was to those inside, it was never communicated to or accepted by the community or by governments. With the advent of mass higher education and, in the quarter of a century since Nisbet wrote, the reformation of the public sector and the imposition of an explicit market focus on universities, the potential role of universities as practical social agents has been driven home.

CHAPTER THREE

The Purpose of a University

S hould a university be a community of scholars or a degree factory? It is not unusual to hear Australian academics put this dichotomy forward as traditional universities struggle to come to grips with the mass education system and the many demands that are placed on them by stakeholders such as students, staff, government and business.

The "community of scholars" is an evocative and attractive ideal to most academics. It is associated with the life of autonomous professionals, who pursue knowledge for its own sake, who interact collegially, and whose authority is derived from academic expertise. Students come to this community to learn from the masters, and some go on to become academics themselves.

This ideal is often contrasted with that of the university as a large corporate identity, where major functions and resources are "managed" and where concepts of relevance and service are paramount.

To this dichotomy we might add a third contrasting view. This would see the large corporate university giving way to more flexible "virtual" structures, where the traditional functions of academics are split up and contracted out. Temporary alliances and joint ventures might be formed to exploit particular opportunities or to deliver education and training to specific markets. Proponents of the more extreme versions of this scenario have argued that the university of the future will be built on information technology, and that the physical campus will become obsolete.

These are more than just different viewpoints on structural or management aspects. The very purpose of universities is under question. Why do we need them? What roles can and do they play in modern Australia?

*

We live in a very different society to that of thirty years ago. We have seen fundamental changes in cultural mix, social aspirations and in our national identity. In the past Australia relied heavily on agriculture and mining for much of its national wealth, and we have accommodated the post-War population boom largely through expansion of low-technology manufacturing and service sectors, both of which depended on stability arising from government protection and public service delivery.

Yet over the past two decades there have been fundamental changes. There has been a swing away from full-time permanent employment towards part-time contract-based work. Jobs that seem straightforward and secure one year might disappear in the next, and expertise and skills need constant updating to keep pace with changing work requirements and technology. Government has been steadily retreating from many areas that were formerly considered as the exclusive concern of the public sector, and stability has retreated with it.

There are many labels used to describe the shifts in economy that have occurred, not only in Australia but in all developed countries. Typically these describe a move from an industrial economy to a postindustrial economy. The former is characterised by industries which relied heavily on labour, often unskilled, to produce standardised products, which operated in a fairly stable environment and which ran themselves along rigid bureaucratic lines. In contrast, the postindustrial economy is fluid, continuously changing to adapt to a more volatile external environment, which is international rather than local in nature, and highly competitive.

There are three main forces which symbiotically have brought about these changes. The first is what might broadly be termed "globalisation". Under this heading we can include the opening up of markets to greater international competition; the increased flow of people between countries; the influence of international forums, law and treaties; and developments in communications technology, particularly satellite telecommunications and more recently the Internet. Collectively these developments have radically increased the ability of companies and other organisations to operate across national borders and improve interactions between financial centres. A distinction should be made between the operations of organisations which operate in many different countries, but which tailor their work to the local environment, and the global operations of an organisation which can extend a coherent program world-wide.

We have not seen a wholesale breaking-down of national sovereignty or a transfer of power from nation states to global companies. Instead, what has mainly occurred is that domestic industries face competition from industries based in other countries, both at home and in traditional export markets. Our economy is now heavily influenced by regular movements in the economies of other countries and our industries are being shaped by the need to adapt to a variety of regulations and conditions in other countries.

Technology has also been a major force. Technology has not only replaced routine tasks performed by people, it has enabled work to be done in ways which were previously impossible. The effect of such developments has been evident for many years in the primary industry and manufacturing sectors, as labour-intensive processes became mechanised with a resultant reduction in less-skilled jobs. Products can be designed, ordered and delivered far more quickly and flexibly than before, with profound consequences for traditional industrial organisation and management. A more subtle transformation has been wrought in the "white collar" sector, particularly with the introduction of computer technology. Typing pools disappeared in the 1980s as word processors replaced the typewriter and became integrated with the personal computer. A new class of employee emerged in the form of data processing operators, whose task was to enter information into computer databases. In turn, the job of "DPO" has been transformed as techniques for transmission and manipulation of information are made more sophisticated. Replacement of routine office tasks by the introduction of computer technology, and the need to upgrade computers on a regular basis, has created a burgeoning industry in hardware and software supply and in computer training. The constant thread throughout is that technology has tended to lead to a reduction in demand for less skilled or routine specialist work and to create demand for better skilled workers. This new class are able to adjust to regular technological upgrades and can exercise abilities not readily replaceable by technology. These include personal interaction with clients, as well as the more advanced skills of judgement, reasoning, enterprise and creativity.

The third force is social change. The effects of such change on the way we live and work have been multiple and complex. In a review of Australian education between 1960 and 1985, Professor W. F. Connell of Monash University wrote:

> In the early 1960s, Australian society and culture were entering a period of substantial and rapid change. Twenty-five years later, in the mid-1980s it had become clear that the Australian cultural landscape had been modified in

several significant ways. To study the history of Australian education during that twenty-five-year period is to observe a fairly staid and unimaginative institution swept into the rapidly moving social and cultural pattern of Australian life, exhilarated, reconstructed piece by piece, and subsequently obliged by somewhat confused economic and conservative pressures to check the pace and restrict the extent of innovative change.[1]

In the period since the 1980s the pressures to which Connell referred have continued unabated, particularly as the size and role of government has undergone fundamental reappraisal. In more recent years there has also been a growth in consumerism. People have far higher expectations of choice, service and quality than in the past. As society has grown more diverse and demanding, the industrial framework that produced "one size fits all" has had to change. Pressures for flexibility in product and service have in turn put pressures on conditions and types of work.

Another characteristic of the changing workforce worthy of mention is the widening scope of professional status. The long-standing professions of medicine and law have held high social status and have usually been associated with university training. The evolution of various other vocations to the status of a profession was examined in a 1996 report commissioned by the Higher Education Council.[2] This considered a variety of definitions of professionalism, most of which had in common the requirements for a national body, a code of ethics and professional conduct, a specialised body of knowledge and ongoing training requirements. No less than twenty-eight fields laying claim to the title of "profession" were examined by the report, including vocations that traditionally have a more modest social status, such as nursing, school teaching and social work. As such vocations aspire to professional status, their presence is evident in the form of specialised university awards. Moreover, the level of award necessary to secure professional recognition and advancement has been increasing over the years. This phenomenon, known as "credentialism", is not unique to the professions; in general the "employment power" of a university degree is less than it used to be. However it ought to be acknowledged that credentialism is not just a matter of ratcheting up the status of vocations. For the reasons outlined above there are ever-increasing requirements for higher levels of education in order to survive and succeed in the modern workforce.

While these changes are occurring to our economy and society, the

Australian population is steadily ageing. The average age in 1971 was 31 years, and the Australian Bureau of Statistics estimates that this will rise to 37 years in 2005. The proportion of our population aged over 40 has increased from 34 per cent in 1971 to 40 per cent in 1995 and will reach 45 per cent in 2005. There are two important consequences for our universities. First, a system dependent on public funding will have to compete for the taxpayer's dollar with an ever-increasing call on public services arising from an older population. Second, educational opportunities for mature-age people will become ever more important in an environment in which the nature of jobs is constantly changing. This has implications for education and training systems traditionally geared towards young people entering the workforce for the first time.

*

The upshot of all of this is that national economic success is no longer guaranteed by the physical exploitation of assets in the form of natural resources or farming, but by the ability to create and use new ideas and knowledge.[3] We are moving towards what some have called the Information Society, but which has been better termed the Knowledge Society. In this environment, success will depend crucially on the ability of individuals to be adaptable, to learn new skills, and to make sense of the ever-increasing stockpile of information. This is not just a statement about individual needs; it has been recognised for some time that our chronic long-term unemployment owes something to redundancies in skills, and there are profound social problems that accompany such a situation.

There are clear implications in such developments for the nature of education, training and research in Australia, and for higher education in particular. The different conceptions of the university have a common underlying concern with *knowledge*. All too often knowledge is confused with information. There is vastly more information about today than ever before, and we have access to it far more quickly and conveniently than ever before. The Internet is a good example; it is a combination of encyclopaedia, gossip magazine, graffiti wall, and newspaper with a letter-to-the-editor page that is open to all. However the value of information obtained over "the Net" is often hard to validate, and it is often transitory, as Web pages appear and disappear.

Knowledge, on the other hand, is about understanding. It is

"information put to work ... it is what enables people to make judgements, create new products, solve problems and interpret events."[4] The role of knowledge is to synthesise, to make sense of facts and information. Sir Peter Medawar, arguing for a definition of "science" which is more in keeping with what we have termed "knowledge", illustrated the difference with an example of an examination question in Comparative Anatomy set by a professor from the University College of London in 1860:

> By what special structures are bats enabled to fly through the air? and how do the galeopitheci, the pteromys, the petaurus, and petauristae support themselves in that light element? Compare the structure of the wing of the bat with that of the bird, and with that of the extinct pterodactyl; and explain the structures by which the cobra extends its neck, and the saurian dragon flies through the atmosphere. By what structures do serpents spring from the ground, and fishes and cephalopods leap on deck from the waters? Explain the origin, the nature, the mode of construction, and the uses of the fibrous parachutes of arachnidans and larvae, and the cocoons which envelope the young; and describe the skeletal elements which support, and the muscles which move the mesoptera and metaptera of insects. Describe the structure, the attachments, and the principal varieties of form of the legs of insects; and compare them with the hollow articulated limbs of nereides, and the tubular feet of lumbrici. How are the muscles disposed which move the solide setae of stylaria, the cutaneous investment of ascaris, the tubular peduncle of pentalasmis, the wheels of rotifera, the feet of asterias, the mantle of medusae, and the tubular tentacles of actinae? How do entozoa effect the migrations necessary to their development and metamorphoses? how do the fixed polypifera and porifera distribute their progeny over the ocean? and lastly, how do the microscopic indestructible protozoa spread from lake to lake over the globe?[5]

Medawar noted that this was by no means the longest of eight examination questions posed by the professor.

At that time the mastery of biology was the mastery of facts. The triumph of Darwin's theory of evolution was that it provided a framework for understanding the bewildering complexity of life, and so it provided understanding and knowledge in ways that the encyclopaedic recital of facts could not. The modern university certainly requires students to digest a substantial amount of factual material, but it does so in the context of theory, which serves to organize and make sense of information.

Universities are in the knowledge business. For much of the history of the university, it has been the preservation and transmission of knowledge which has dominated; indeed the idea that new knowledge should be created through experimentation or radical thinking was often viewed as heretical. Since the nineteenth century the notion of research and pursuit of new knowledge has emerged as a major concern of universities, a role which has been vastly accelerated by the injection of funds since the Second World War.

But while universities have an important role in developing knowledge, they are not the only players. Knowledge is not fixed and unchanging; there are rapid developments occurring in frontiers outside the institutions of higher education. These frontiers might be in business, research organisations, public sector agencies or in some of the fluid and temporary alliances that are established between different organisations. Moreover, there are many organisations, in both the public and private domain, which provide some of the traditional services of the university in the form of education and training, research, or other creative activity. Many of these organisations are directed towards specific ends: they specialise in utility. While universities were involved primarily with abstract matters and apparently "useless knowledge", they could operate as an elite guild, with considerable autonomy. However, much of the transformation that has occurred in the relationships between universities and their external communities has centred around making universities more useful. The more universities sell themselves as delivering something relevant, important and useful, the more they will be held accountable and will need to compete in, and adjust to the needs of, different markets. As they do so, the underpinnings of traditional academic organisation and management are inevitably weakened.

*

Universities have never played the same discrete role in Australian society as they have in many other countries, for example in the United States, Germany or even in the United Kingdom. Most Australians, including most Australian politicians, see them as glorified training grounds for the professions, and as gatekeepers to individual economic prosperity. The importance of higher education has grown as an ever-increasing proportion of the public aspires to attend university, or to send their children there.

This focus on the immediately useful aspects of higher education is not shared by many within the universities, despite its prominence in public marketing rhetoric. Even within universities there is no universal agreement about purpose or strategy, other than in broad terms that refer to the holy trinity of research, teaching and service (usually in that order). Outside the walls of our higher education institutions, governments seek to describe universities in economic terms and, in Australia up to this point at least, as part of the public sector. There are inevitable clashes between those who seek to press higher education into the moulds that apply to other sectors of the Australian economy, and those who argue that universities serve a higher, wider and more nebulous social purpose.

It is this widespread confusion of understanding about what universities are, and what they should be doing, which is at the heart of many of the problems being experienced by our higher education institutions.

Despite the fact that the structure of universities, in the form of the nomenclature of positions and the guild organisation of academic work, has remained largely unchanged for centuries, there is little that is inherently timeless about their role. The modern university bears little relationship in purpose and in day-to-day activity to the medieval institutions that shared the name.

This is not to say that universities are infinitely malleable, and that no appeal to core values and traditions is valid. What it does mean is that we should know something of the nature of the university ideal, but we should place it within the context of the broader pattern of social and economic changes that are shaping Australian life.

*

Defenders of the university ideal frequently invoke two names: Newman and von Humboldt. The first is the patron saint of university teaching, the other of research.

Cardinal Newman was a former Oxford University man, who was instrumental in the founding of the University of Dublin around the time when the reform of the ancient universities of England was well under way. His published series of lectures, produced in 1852 and entitled, "The Idea of a University", set out eloquently the ideal of general education, where a young man could develop civilised values and a philosophical mind through the study of the accumulated wisdom of the past. The university was the realisation of this ideal. His view was strongly non-utilitarian; knowledge was valuable for its own sake, not for the uses to which it could be put. Newman's university quite clearly kept separate the study of vocational or professional matters and was not concerned with research. "If the object were scientific and philosophical discovery", he wrote, "I do not see why a University should have any students."[6]

What Newman described was essentially consistent with the scholastic tradition of the medieval university, where knowledge and culture, with pride of place given to classical Greek culture, was conserved and passed on. A major and influential break with this tradition had occurred some forty years earlier, with the foundation of the University of Berlin. The scholar and Prussian minister for education, Wilhelm von Humboldt, saw the university as an embodiment of national rebuilding in the aftermath of the Napoleonic Wars. This nationalism was built on ideas developed by Hegel and other German philosophers which saw a central role for the developed individual. Science and philosophy were the mainstays of the new university; teaching and research were combined, though teaching of the professions was not a central function. This formulation was built on departments and professors, with academic freedom as a keystone. Significantly, student freedom, *Lernfreiheit*, was also important, and German university education placed far less emphasis on the institution. The early practice was for students and teachers to move freely between universities, with students picking subjects from offerings at different places.

The German model of research and academic freedom had a profound impact on higher education, particularly in the United States. The concept of student choice and freedom did not catch on so quickly, at least in its broadest conceptions, although the American system of electives was a new feature inspired by the ideal. Indeed, student freedom of choice was modified in Germany during the nineteenth century, and in some respects it is only now seeing a resurgence in the guise of open learning.

Humboldt's university was most clearly epitomised in the establishment of Johns Hopkins University in 1876 which, as would be the case for our own Australian National University seventy years later, began as a graduate school with an emphasis on research. Around the same time, the Land Grant colleges were developing in the United States. As already observed, both models were to be influential in shaping the new generation of Australian universities.

The German notion of the university as a player in national culture was thrown into some turmoil in the twentieth century, heightened by tensions between universities and the State following the First World War. In 1923 Karl Jaspers published a book with nearly the same title as that chosen by Newman, *The Idea of the University*, a work he revised in 1946. Jaspers' formulation was based around the idea that the university could strive for independent seeking of knowledge and truth, through the efforts of a community of scholars. Jaspers gave a prominent place to the role of transmission of a culture based on critical enquiry, but also had room in his university for the task of professional education.

The influential American educationalist Abraham Flexner, a student of Johns Hopkins in the 1880s, wrote in 1930 of the *Idea of a Modern University*.[7] By this he meant an institution that combined the ideas of Newman and von Humboldt within a "unity of purpose" to pursue excellence. He deplored what he termed the "service station" role, where universities were expected to provide vocational education and demonstrate their practical usefulness to the community, and the proliferation of what he saw as much poor-quality research. Flexner's "modern" university represents an ideal with powerful attraction for many today, but it was an elite which had little place for the democratic aspirations of the United States and post-War Australia. As Clark Kerr, the President of the University of California, wrote in 1960, both Newman and Flexner were describing universities that had already ceased to exist.[8]

Developing the university theme, Clark Kerr wrote of The Idea of a Multiversity. This conception had the university as not one community but several; different communities of students, different communities of academics, and external communities of alumni, government, business and so on. The multiversity is a city, a "City of the Intellect", in which students and staff identify with particular subcultures rather than with the whole.

This identification of university subcultures came shortly after the novelist, administrator and molecular physicist C.P. Snow wrote of the "two cultures" of science and the arts.[9] Snow's complaint was that there was little common understanding or communication between these two cultures. Such a rift had been well recognised in academic circles for many years, if not as publicly articulated by Snow. In fact it was central to Jaspers' formulation of a university that it sought to draw together the fragments of disciplinary knowledge. Snow's preferences clearly lay with the sciences; his criticisms of the arts and his claims to have a foot in both camps infuriated his literary "colleagues". F.R Leavis, a literary critic and, like Snow, a Cambridge Fellow, penned a vitriolic attack on Snow's work. "The judgement I have to come out with is that not only is he not a genius; he is intellectually as undistinguished as it is possible to be", wrote Leavis, " ... He exhibits an utter lack of intellectual distinction and an embarrassing vulgarity of style."[10]

Leavis and like-minded critics did not take issue with the fact of cultural divide, more with the imperialist claims of one of the sides. Other criticisms of Snow's work argued that in fact a division into two cultures was a gross simplification - academic life was divided into numerous sub-cultures, which communicate fitfully if at all. In the late 1980s, two books[11] appeared which described these sub-cultures, or "academic tribes", in some detail. Both books portray academic tribalism as characteristic of autonomous professional intellectuals, something to be respected and even admired.

In itself there is not much wrong with this: universities should be expected to harbour diversity. Yet as David Damrosch, Professor of English and Comparative Literature at Columbia University, has pointed out[12], the fragmentation of academic work conflicts with the ideal of the "community of scholars", is at odds with the emergence of greater collegiality and team work in professional circles outside the university, and works against the design and delivery of a broad liberal undergraduate education.

In Clark Kerr's multiversity, the university that straddles these communities provides some coherence to the whole, so that wasteful duplication and needless complexity are minimised. The task of the president (equivalent to our vice-chancellor) is akin to that of the head of the United Nations; he must be "leader, educator, creator initiator, wielder of power, pump; he is *also* officeholder, caretaker, inheritor, consensus-seeker, persuader, bottleneck. But he is mostly a mediator."

The United Nations metaphor is also apt when considering the different mixtures that need to be reconciled in a modern university. In Clark Kerr's view "a university anywhere can aim no higher than to be as British as possible for the sake of the undergraduates, as German as possible for the sake of the graduates, as American as possible for the sake of the public at large - and as confused as possible for the sake of the preservation of the whole uneasy balance."

Clark Kerr was undoubtedly influenced by his presidency of the large, multi-campus University of California. His multiversity is certainly closer in conception to many of today's universities in Australia, the United States and the United Kingdom, in that it is large, many-faced and with multiple constituencies. However it is a *place*. If anyone is to write the *Idea of a Postmodern University* it will be to crystallise the current challenge to the conception of the university as a place, given the power of information technology to deliver the offerings of a "virtual university". There has been a great deal of talk in recent times about this concept, but relatively little clarity about what it actually might involve.

The curriculum

Clark Kerr's writings also said little about what was to be taught and researched within a university. This was of far greater importance to Flexner and Newman, for whom there was a clear mandate to concentrate on liberal education and research driven by curiosity rather than immediate application. If professional education was to have any place within the university, they saw it limited at best to medicine and law. The fact that those particular professions became a traditional part of the university has more to do with their social status than with any clear-cut logic.

In Australia, a professional and vocational emphasis has been a typical part of the university from the nineteenth century when applied science was part of the curriculum of the first universities. This applied aspect also has been central to how the broader community understands the idea of a university. In more recent times, as universities expanded in the era of "massification", they inevitably took on a wider portfolio of activities. We have seen a rapid growth in the range of subjects studied within our universities, and in the spectrum of professions that are taught at the university level.

In all of our universities, indeed in universities around the world, there has been a long-standing tension between vocational and "liberal" education, the latter meaning the sort of general education that seeks to pursue learning for its own sake, as championed by Cardinal Newman. As the modern university has grown more encompassing, it seems to satisfy neither those who value the elite and civilising roles of universities, nor those who wish to see universities serve the more immediate wants of students, government or business.

This situation is exacerbated by the growing climate of competition among universities, and the uncomfortable emergence of the view that universities are providers of a service to various clients. One of the more obvious groups of clients are students, but most Australian students go to university to gain a passport to a career. As higher education has been opened up to a mass market, this trend has intensified. Yet providing students with a university education that is too narrowly tailored towards techniques and skills related to a particular profession is not what universities are traditionally supposed to be about.

Australia, following on from the British practice, tends to allow early specialisation in undergraduate education. By way of contrast, the American model is typically to provide a four-year general undergraduate education, albeit one which can include vocational components, followed by postgraduate study directed toward particular professions. The Australian undergraduate degree can allow selection of major areas of study within awards that are specific to vocations. Professional organisations also have considerable influence on Australian undergraduate education. This influence usually takes the form of prescribed areas of study that need to be included, but at times there is pressure to diversify the range of vocation-specific undergraduate awards and to pack more professionally relevant material into the curriculum.

The concern is that undergraduate education is being forced ever further away from the form which supposedly marks it as uniquely belonging within a university. Too narrow an education is not in the interests of the student, even if that is what the student wants. The most pressing issues faced by society, for example the problems posed by AIDS or environmental degradation, are multidisciplinary in nature, while the professions require an ever-increasing breadth of knowledge and expertise.

This concern is reinforced by the fact that many graduates from professionally-oriented courses ultimately work in fields unrelated to that profession. It has long been accepted that many Arts and Science graduates do not go on to become academics or scientists, but now, for example, many graduates of Law courses work in non-legal fields, and only around one quarter of graduates in the natural sciences work as scientists.[13] A 1995 Federal Government report compared projections of the number of graduates in various fields over the next ten years with estimates of the growth in employment in those areas where they would normally be expected to work. They found that in areas such as Law, Engineering,

Education, Visual and Performing Arts and Building Design/Architecture many graduates would need to find work outside their professional field.[14]

All Australian universities have made efforts of one sort or another to address these problems. Some have established a set of compulsory subjects that must be studied by all undergraduates, with the intention of giving students a broader perspective. This is not practical for the larger universities, which instead offer "core" subjects at the Faculty level. Other initiatives include offering double degrees, which combine two undergraduate degrees and enable students to complete two three-year degrees in a more compressed period of time, usually five years. A third approach is to delay entry into professional streams for a period of time. This might be for either one or two years or, in some cases such as the new medicine course developed collaboratively between the University of Sydney, Flinders University and the University of Queensland, to move the professional component to the postgraduate level, along the lines of the American model. Such a trend in some respects harks back to the Newmanite model of higher education, where the real activity of the university is liberal undergraduate education, and the professional schools are separate. It also acknowledges the fact that relative to most other countries, the duration of university education is shorter and students are streamed into vocational courses early on. In the United States, students enter professional courses after completing a four year undergraduate degree, while in the United Kingdom and Western Europe, students enter university from one to two years older than their Australian counterparts.[15]

All of these approaches have their shortcomings. Compulsory subjects in the arts or sciences are often resented by students as being "irrelevant" and frequently provide superficial exposure to an area rather than any significant program of general study. Many double degrees combine two vocational awards, rather than supplementing general with vocational education. Delayed entry may mean that earlier years are dominated by prerequisites rather than being available for general education, while delayed entry and postgraduate professional study may also have to compete against other institutions offering more popular immediate entry into professional study.[16]

Universities are supposed to encompass a wide range of academic disciplines. The value of this approach is that students can potentially be exposed to a breadth of knowledge by practitioners whose professional lives are devoted to understanding and furthering their disciplines.

However, the problem is that disciplinary differences can be hard to integrate. The core subjects and double-degree programs may expose students to different areas of study, but these will not be properly integrated unless there is a genuine bridging of the academic disciplines. Two opposing forces have to be reconciled. Course designers in specialist areas often do not want discipline-based academics to teach subjects out of context; for example, they contend that the introduction to business ethics should be business-based rather than about general ethical theory. On the other hand, there is a danger that if breadth is sought within vocational courses by teaching a wider range of subjects within a particular faculty or school, some subjects will be taught by academics only tangentially "expert" in the relevant discipline. For example, we might find engineering academics teaching management theory in engineering management subjects, law lecturers teaching ethics, or media experts teaching history.

An education which could reasonably hope to encompass in any depth a significant range of the contrasting and in some cases competing fields of academic knowledge would last a lifetime. It is clearly beyond the scope of a three or four year undergraduate degree program.

The liberal education that educators had in mind fifty to a hundred years ago might have encompassed the study of great books, fine arts and music, history and areas of the sciences within one undergraduate course. Indeed, the first three or four professors of the University of Sydney and the University of Melbourne each covered the entire range of subjects offered by those universities.[17] Nowadays the best that seems possible is to design courses to enable students to develop particular skills, or academic competencies, such as critical thinking, problem solving, and communication within more narrow confines. Moreover, the pressure to expand professionally-relevant content, enhance student skills and broaden the educational experience is offset against increasing costs to the student and the taxpayer.

Another complicating factor is that many students are not school-leavers. They may be older people entering higher education for the first time, they may be already employed and seeking a career change, or they may be people who already have a professional qualification and a career path but who are seeking an upgrade to improve their prospects. Should people in the latter group be required to have the same sort of "liberal" component to their education as a school leaver? What credit should be given to existing qualifications, or to skills acquired on the job rather than through formal education? Should such people be required to attend a campus?

The modern mass higher education system demands a far greater degree of flexibility in course structures, content and methods of delivery than has been the case in the past. This is particularly important for universities in the context of "life-long learning". This term, which has been the subject of much discussion in higher education circles, implies a shift in thinking from education of young people as a preparation for life towards the notion that people need to adapt and learn throughout their lifetime, moving in and out of formal education where necessary and having the ability to derive knowledge from information for themselves. It has implications for the entire education structure, which has evolved in line with the view that a person is given an injection of education at a young age to last them a lifetime.

*

In addition to research and teaching, there is a third dimension to the role of the university that is usually referred to by the ill-defined term "community service". To some, this might include the extension of internal teaching and research activities to the external community on an informal basis, for example in the form of community lectures, performances or seminars. There is a long history of such activities, stretching back to the early years of Australian universities.

There is also a broader concept of the social role of universities which needs to be considered. Universities are nowadays more reticent than was the case in the past in putting the view that they have a place in transmitting some measure of national or other common form of culture. Such a role was central to the German universities in the nineteenth century and, in a different way, to Jaspers' formulation of a university. At the inauguration of the University of Queensland in 1911, the representative from the University of Sydney pronounced that "it was the function of a university to give civil society dignity and permanence." [18]

While some may still hold the view that the principal cultural value of a university, at either a national or local level, is as a counterbalance to parochialism and poor taste, there is a growing acknowledgement that the university can and should serve as a gateway that develops or "embeds" local activities within an increasingly international world.

This means more than the usual university rhetoric about striving for international excellence in all fields of endeavour, or the participation by academics in international collegial communities of their peers. Universities have links at local levels, within States or Territories, across the nation, and internationally. Some regional universities are major employers within their areas, but beyond this function they tap expertise and strengthen contact with the outside world. By connecting the local with the national and international, universities can bring national and international perspectives to bear on local problems, and conversely can contribute to the wider pool of knowledge and culture in unique ways.

As championed by Karl Jaspers, universities will also often highlight higher education's role as social critic, providing an independent voice through academic analyses of society and government. Putting a slightly different spin on this role, the Commonwealth Government's 1988 White Paper stated that higher education "promotes greater understanding of culture, often at odds with majority attitudes and, in doing so, supports the development of a more just and tolerant society."[19]

In some respects, these service and cultural roles should not be separately identified from teaching and research. The fact that they are arises partly from a view that there is something self-contained and inward-looking about the university, and that internal teaching and research can be distinguished from engagement with the community, or from the application of scholarly enquiry to the broader society. Nevertheless, there is an important distinction to be made between those activities of the university which are pressed into the service of society, and those which are independent.

There is one other social aspect to the university that deserves mention. In his State of the University Address given in 1995, Gerhard Casper, the President of Stanford University, reflected on two roles that have traditionally been an integral part of universities: social integration and a rite of passage. By social integration he meant the capacity of universities to draw together people across multiple social and cultural boundaries in a peaceful manner, something that occurs to a far lesser extent in most workplaces or at school. The American educationalist Ernest Boyer wrote extensively on the concept of the campus community.[20] What he meant by that term was a repositioning of the notion of the community of scholars to emphasise inclusiveness - students as well as academics - and active values of service. Community service was integral to this conception of a campus, not peripheral as is so often the case. Boyer emphasised the importance of intertwining service with learning for students, and engaging the work of academics with the problems of society. The purpose was to bring together the disparate strands of the university, and to develop a sense of belonging for all members of the university.

The rite of passage role is primarily concerned with, in Casper's words, "the function of furthering the process of coming of age, or growing up". In Australian universities, with our lesser reliance than the UK or US on residential colleges, this role is more passive, with students leaving school and coming for the first time into an environment where they must exercise responsibility for themselves, find new friends, and navigate their way through an unfamiliar environment. Universities nowadays have done away with the *in loco parentis* role, where they assumed a role which included setting and supervising rules and taking pastoral care for their students. Nevertheless, universities provide important opportunities for young people to develop their outlook on life and establish significant contacts and friendships.

These "socialisation" functions depend fundamentally on the educational context in which they occur; meeting and interacting at university provides its own setting. People spend considerable amounts of time with each other, exchanging opinions or discussing courses and teachers. This is an interaction free of many of the constraints found at schools and the workplace, and cannot be replicated by meeting at social clubs. Nor can it easily be accommodated in distance education programs, given the technological limitations likely to apply in the immediate future.

*

How well are our universities placed to respond to the needs of the Knowledge Society and demands for life-long learning? The case for the defence might observe that the best education a person could receive would be one where they learned *how* to learn, and that this is far more important than learning particular facts or techniques. Universities which provide a stimulating, broad and challenging education, for young people in particular, should be highly valued. The case for the prosecution might observe that education in the future will be composed of many markets, and that life-long learning not only requires a sound education for young people, but the capacity for older people to gain access to new knowledge and skills in flexible ways. Universities are not renowned for flexibility, either in delivery of their programs or in the structure of their awards.

Questions of flexibility and responsiveness become more important as higher education becomes more competitive, particularly as universities move into commercial areas of education. The effects of competition and quasi-market forces are only just beginning to be felt in our universities. At this stage, most of it involves competition for the best students among universities within a local region. However, we are moving inexorably to a situation where universities will find themselves less protected by government, and their traditional position as providers of higher education will be increasingly contested by others.

CHAPTER FOUR

The University Identity Crisis

A ustralia's university system is predominantly a public one. There are at present forty-three higher education institutions in Australia. Two of these are private universities, four are Commonwealth-funded colleges, thirty-six are public universities funded through the Unified National System and one, located on Queensland's Sunshine Coast, is a University College which hopes to secure formal university status as soon as it can do so. Under the relevant legislation the awarding of degrees is almost entirely limited to universities, and institutions seeking the title of university or to offer higher education award programs must be accredited by the relevant government.

The private universities are small, particularly in terms of Australian students. This situation is hardly surprising given the spread of publicly-funded universities and the fact that government subsidies for higher education are given directly to those universities that participate in the national system. Many smaller incursions have been made into higher education by private providers. The Australian Council for Private Education and Training cited data from State accreditation agencies to the effect that in 1997 there were "forty-nine private institutions offering some 186 accredited higher education programs leading to awards including those at diploma, graduate certificate, graduate diploma, bachelor, masters and doctoral levels. These courses cover a wide range of subjects in such discipline areas as education, arts, nursing, theology, music, science, management, engineering, physical education, design and hospitality."[1]

Since our universities are mainly public sector institutions, they have been profoundly influenced by changes that have been sweeping through government and public sector organisations over recent decades. We will postpone for the moment consideration of the effects upon universities of trends in public sector management, and concentrate instead on the effects of changes in the *role* of government in Australia over recent years.

The heyday of higher education growth occurred in the period between 1960 and 1975, although expansion in student numbers began from the years of early post-War reconstruction. The focus was national (even though the Federal government did not assume responsibility for full funding until the end of this period) and expansion driven by the view that providing citizens with university education would somehow boost the national economy. This accorded with the popular view that government had a rightful place in stimulating the national economy through large-scale investments, subsidising industries, or directly providing many basic services. However it is worth qualifying this observation slightly; when the Whitlam Government came to power in 1973 it had a mission of social reform. Education and economic development were central goals, equity and access the keywords, and "free" education the initiative of 1975.

Certainly the view at the time was that government could and should play a central role in national development, whether economic or social. Education, including higher education, was a key tool in this endeavour. The public sector played a dominant role in society, and the Commonwealth seemed to be expanding indefinitely; by the mid 1970s, nearly one in every fifteen workers in Australia was employed in the Commonwealth public sector.

During the 1960s challenges to the role of government had been mounted in some countries, particularly in the United States. While rarely stated explicitly and systematically, such challenges filtered through to the Australian context as a number of factors converged through the mid 1970s and early 1980s. Perhaps the two most important of these were concerns about the sustainability of government finances, brought to a crisis point in 1975, and the growing recognition of the effect of the global economy on Australia. The latter manifested itself in a worsening balance of trade situation and the clear lack of international competitiveness of our protected domestic industries.

Governments, both Labor and Liberal, were not entirely blind to the consequences of social and economic reliance on the state. It was clear that an ageing population and widespread expectations of social welfare were going to pose problems in the years ahead. These might have been accommodated, as those on the left in politics still maintain, within a view which gives a dominant role to government. Instead, we have seen the emergence of a view which sees the public sector as "crowding out" the private, and which strives to place primacy in the individual rather than the state. The emphasis nowadays is on individual choice, where, so the theory goes, services are provided on a competitive basis in order to ensure that they meet the customers' needs and not those of the provider, with the result that customers obtain better and cheaper service.

The negative image of government as a provider of services was reinforced in Australia both by the financial problems of the Whitlam government and by the misfortunes of State-owned business enterprises in the 1980s. At the Commonwealth level there were no such acute business crises in the 1980s, but even the Hawke Labor Government had a commitment, in the shape of its Budget "trilogy", to reduce the size of the public sector. This commitment reflected a trend in many other developed nations, which reacted to the imperatives of global competitiveness by attempting to reduce government expenditures and national debt as a proportion of gross national product. The motivation was pragmatic; there were economic problems to solve, and solutions were offered in the form of reductions in public debt, freeing-up of markets from government regulation and the introduction of competition into the public sector. These solutions were not accepted wholeheartedly, they conflicted with generations of political tradition, and they were applied selectively. Financial markets were de-regulated early in the life of the Hawke administration, but industrial relations remained closely controlled.

In recent years we have the seen the gradual ascendancy of the "contractual" view of government. This shifts the focus of government from being a provider of public services and infrastructure to that of a "purchaser" on behalf of "clients" of the various services those clients need. The agencies that actually provide these services might be publicly funded, but they might (and many advocates of such arrangements argue that they should) be privately-owned. This "purchaser-provider" separation came to characterise many of the British reforms under Margaret Thatcher in the late 1980s, and has been a notable feature of public sector reforms in New Zealand.

The contractual view of government represents more than a change in the management of public services. It goes to the heart of the way governments relate to citizens. Rather than the traditional political and legal relationship, we see instead the emergence of a contractual one. As Griffith University political scientist Glyn Davis put it: "Electors become clients, their rights and expectations encapsulated in a 'citizen's charter' or, as in some Australian states, a 'guarantee of service'. This contract binds the state to produce certain levels of service, and specifies penalties for compliance failure. The model of principals and agents, their mutual obligations spelled out in writing, becomes an organising ideal for public life."[2]

These developments have implications for the universities. The most obvious impact is financial. From the early 1980s there has been a gradual erosion in funding, offset by some extra money for new buildings and growth in research grants. Between 1983 and 1996, government funding available to spend on teaching each student (when expressed in full-time terms and taking inflation into account) fell by nearly thirteen per cent.[3] It is worth noting that this impact has been more gradual than that experienced in Thatcher's Britain or in many American States. Nevertheless, the decline in funding for university teaching is clearly reflected in a steady increase in the ratio of students to staff, which shows itself in larger class sizes and greater use of part-time and casual teachers. More money has been made available for research, particularly money for research projects allocated through competitive grant schemes. However even when research grants have been secured, the funding provided has not been sufficient to cover fully their costs, which in turn has led to further pressure on university finances.

Until the early 1990s universities were able to cope with funding pressures as the environment was one of continued growth. In 1998, for the first time in many years, there occurred an actual reduction in the level of public university funding.

Another impact has been the re-introduction of charges on students. This began in 1987 with the levying of a $250 administrative charge, later replaced by the Higher Education Contribution Scheme, followed by fees for overseas students and fees for some postgraduate students. These moves addressed both the need to save taxpayers' money and also the view that education was at least in part an individual benefit and responsibility.

Throughout most of the post-war period, and certainly since the late 1980s, governments have sought to balance the conventions of university autonomy with a desire to shape the sector and take a close interest in the working of higher education institutions. The Commonwealth Government has intervened at different times to control the provision of distance education, to prescribe the mix of students proceeding to universities, to encourage the introduction of new technology, to promote staff development and improved quality by allocating extra funding, and in various other ways. If in the years ahead government pursues the "contractual" path, we are likely to see less direct intervention from the government and the relevant Federal departments and more focus on matters of output, accreditation and quality assessment. If universities do not adopt better practices, then that is their business and they will suffer the market consequences. Improvement of providers will not be a priority for the government. To take an extreme example of the consequences of a contractual relationship, one might imagine what would happen if government took the view that it was contracting with the community to produce a certain number of graduates. It might partly fund universities according to how many graduates were produced, instead of the number of students enrolling. This would undoubtedly focus the minds of university management on student drop-out rates.

Of course we are already seeing some moves in this direction. In recent years the government's discretionary funds, which are used, usually in a haphazard manner, to stimulate new directions in universities, have been reduced and consolidated. Staffing levels in the Higher Education Division of the Commonwealth Department of Employment, Education, Training and Youth Affairs (DEETYA) have been cut back, and the Commonwealth has signalled for some time that it would like to examine ways in which it could allocate funds on the basis of performance rather than on student enrolments.

Perhaps the most concrete indication of the Commonwealth's desire for a more distant relationship with universities was the decision of the Keating Government, later confirmed by the newly-elected Howard administration, not to bankroll the cost of salary rises for university staff above a "safety net" level. This decision was not, of course, specific to universities; it applied across the whole of the public sector. However, it came at a time when pressure was building for university salaries to rise, and the cost of any salary hike had to be borne within existing budgets. This placed far greater pressures on the sector than the publicly-visible "efficiency" cuts to government grants.

In recent years the Commonwealth has indicated that it also wants a less intrusive relationship with universities, the trade-off being greater accountability. In the first Howard Budget, it was stated that "The Commonwealth's objective is to secure high quality outcomes for the public investment in higher education while limiting its own direct role in the management and delivery of specific purpose programs and streamlining reporting and accountability requirements for institutions". This rhetoric has been challenged by the vice-chancellors. When the first draft of DEETYA's new procedures and requirements for determining educational profiles (which are used to determine university funding) were issued, the vice-chancellors complained that the new arrangements were in fact more intrusive rather than less. Nevertheless, we can expect to see a steady change in the relationship between governments and universities which sees government more concerned with what the universities do rather than how they do it, and which sees funding channelled in different ways which will allow competition from other providers.

The other major development has been a move to introduce greater elements of competition and contestability into the education sector, including those that remain publicly-funded. This can be seen most clearly in research, where public funds are provided in two key ways. One is through the block grant to universities, so institutions themselves decide how much of it should be spent on research, and where it should be spent. The other is through grant schemes, where university researchers compete by lodging applications for funding. Such schemes may be directed towards specific areas of priority. In some cases, schemes are more widely contestable, so that non-university researchers also are eligible to apply. In the case of teaching, moves towards a more competitive environment have begun with the quality assessment exercises of the early 1990s, the setting by government of enrolment targets (and penalties for failure to meet those targets), and the introduction of fee-paying categories of students. The effect of even limited market mechanisms on the universities has been profound. We have already drawn attention to the fragmentation of academic conventions and processes as universities come under pressure to be more overtly useful.

The divide between those individuals who are successful and those who are less successful in competition is growing greater, and the imperative for competitiveness is driving fundamental changes in the way academic work is organised and managed. US higher education scholars Sheila Slaughter and Larry Leslie recently published a study of higher education systems in Australia, Canada, the United States and the United Kingdom. Their findings reveal that these trends are common across all four systems, although to a lesser extent in Canada.[4]

It is worthwhile considering whether the trends towards a "hands off" approach and smaller government will inevitably continue. There are many factors which come into play. Perhaps the most important is finance. Australia is a relatively lightly-taxed country in comparison with most of its OECD partners, but there is a very firm opposition to taxation increase from almost all walks of life. It is hard to see how public sector debt could have been managed, not only at the level of expenditure relative to tax income that applied in the past, but also at the level likely to be generated by future demand, particularly as the population aged. It is also hard to see any scope for a major expansion in the public sector in the years ahead.

Another factor is the rise of individualism. The rhetoric of individual choice, of the need to have flexible and tailored services, and of self-reliance, is particularly seductive for a country like Australia. Our icons are the "battler" and the "man on the land", where there is a paradoxical relationship between independence and invisible reliance on government support. Many Australians are happy to use "public servant" as a term of disdain and the promise of less taxation and better service through competition can be seductive.

There are other factors, including those of internationalisation, social change, and the impact of technology, which certainly have an impact on public sector management, but do not in themselves suggest directions for changing the scope or role of government. What is probably most important is the interaction between politics, pragmatism and ideology. New ideas about government come and go. The extent to which they influence a country like Australia depends on many things, but if they are seen to solve problems arising from previous government actions then they will gain some currency. The extent to which they spread throughout the economy will depend on political decisions. We see a different approach to the role of government, for example, taken by the Liberal Party in Victoria under Premier Kennett compared to the National-dominated coalition in Queensland under Premier Borbidge. It may also be the case, as Martin Painter from the University of Sydney has suggested[5], that such reforms are discarded if or when they create their own problems.

Writing in 1989, Christopher Hood (at that time also from the University of Sydney) observed that practical limitations on contractual government are more likely in areas that affect public safety or lie in the traditional domain of government, such as policing, prisons, foreign affairs and defence. Contractual government will be ongoing in the social services, including education and health, because they are less closely allied with political power, they are more stable, and "because (in some areas of these services, at least) opportunism is checked by a tradition of voluntary-service ethos."[6]

In many respects Australian universities remain among the last of the big public sector monopolies. The awarding of degrees is protected by law, institutions are funded directly rather than through their "clients" and, as we have seen, only a few small private sector providers operate. Such a situation is at odds with the paradigm of contractualism and competitiveness.

The hegemony of the public universities is already under attack. There are several scenarios which have been put forward:

- prestigious overseas universities will extend access to Australian students using advanced information technology;

- major media corporations will enter the higher education market, either establishing their own universities or brokering access to the best university teachers and courses using advanced information technology;

- new "universities" will develop within Australia, possibly franchised versions of overseas institutions, which operate flexibly and offer tailored education using advanced information technology; and

- existing or new vocational education providers, particularly some of the more aggressive private providers, will extend their activities into the university sphere.

Proponents of some of these scenarios, particularly the first three, claim that they potentially spell the end for our existing universities, and that they herald the era of the "virtual university", where physical campuses and buildings will be obsolete. The common thread is that of the enabling power of advanced information technology. The short-to-medium term likelihood of some of the claims, particularly those that include the interests of media corporations, has been examined in a 1997 report commissioned by the Commonwealth Government.[7] This report suggests that it is simplistic to make sweeping claims about the impact on higher education: there are real threats in some areas, but less likelihood in others.

Nevertheless concrete action will take place in fields of activity that can potentially generate commercial returns. Universities are exposed to risk to the extent that they wish to expand their activities into these commercial fields, yet remain bound by practices that inhibit their flexibility.

One major area is that of education and training for working adults, either at undergraduate or postgraduate level. Most universities provide some "off-the-shelf" programs of continuing professional education or community education, along with particular programs for specific workplaces. Some private companies, unhappy with the responsiveness of universities, are establishing their own training "universities". Others are contracting with conventional universities or new providers to deliver education into the workplace. These examples usually focus on tailored vocational education delivered at low cost. However, one major player, the University of Phoenix (a large, private for-profit institution) also caters for a broader mass market, providing standardised curricula to working adults across several States in the USA. Phoenix has physical campuses as well as a "virtual campus". It keeps costs low by employing only part-time teaching staff and by avoiding the usual university overheads associated with research and other scholarly activity.

At another level, established universities are moving some of their more commercially attractive courses onto virtual formats, particularly using the World Wide Web. The most visible area of activity is in the MBA marketplace, where there is widespread use of the Internet. There is also notable variation of the cost and quality of these offerings. These developments will be examined later in some detail, but it seems clear that there will be different impacts on the elite market, where competition is for the top students and access to the highest status degrees, and the mass market, where the emphasis is on access, cost and flexibility.

Private non-university organisations have already made some inroads in the provision of higher education at various levels. These relate closely to the linkage between education provision and the needs of the workplace. At one level, the distinction between universities and other players would seem to be straightforward: universities are involved in longer, more reflective education, which is not tied directly to particular vocational needs. Yet it is clear that this distinction is not a rigid one; some university courses are closely allied to particular professions, while some non-university providers are seeking to incorporate more analytical perspectives. Indeed, it is hard to imagine how a vocational role for universities could be avoided if universities are expected to foster the translation of research into practice and if the workforce of the future needs graduates to maintain and update their work-related skills.

To place these matters in context we need to consider the wider range of post-school education. In Australia that means what is known as the Vocational Education and Training (VET) sector.

Other pathways, other problems

The VET landscape is dotted with numerous providers, of variable quality and size, dominated by the Technical and Further Education institutions which are run by the State and Territory governments. The non-TAFE providers include private colleges, adult and community education organisations and diverse providers of professional and industry training. A fair amount of what could be considered vocational education and training is also provided at the upper levels of secondary schooling. The principal purpose is to provide students with what they need in order to secure a job, although there is a stream in TAFE, catering for around one third of all students, which provides recreational education and training in "hobby" and special interest areas.

There has been major reform in this sector over the past ten years. During the 1980s State and Commonwealth governments made a concerted effort to lift the numbers of students staying at school until Year 12. In 1983 the proportion of students doing so was around 38 per cent; within ten years this percentage had doubled. This rapid increase drew attention to the unsatisfactory nature of school preparation for further study. Secondary schools were seen to be placing much attention on preparing the highest achievers for university while inadequately preparing the majority of students for alternatives. In fact, the phrase "preparing" is overstating the case for those who aspired to university; what actually predominated was a focus on securing the required prerequisites for gaining entrance to university courses.

By 1988, for every 100 students who completed school, 63 had completed Year 12. Of those 63, around 22 (or 35 per cent) would go on to university and 17 (27 per cent) would pursue VET education. All but four of the remaining 24 would go straight into work. For the 37 who did not complete Year 12, 16 would go into VET education, 15 would find work and the other six would be out of the workforce or unemployed.

Thus while university was an important destination for school leavers, it only catered for 22 per cent of that population. VET education catered for another one third of all school leavers and the rest had no further education and training after school. In addition to this, VET was of clearly lower status to university, and was seen as a destination for those who "couldn't make it" to university.

Clearly some modification to this system was warranted. Australia needed more school leavers to proceed to further education, and it needed to make the non-university education sector more attractive and responsive to the needs of the changing economy. A further imperative was that lifelong learning required a variety of flexible avenues for pursuing post-school education, and this was most acute for the growing group of workers retrenched by economic change. This latter group was typically older, male, blue-collar and with low education and skill levels.

Change came in the early part of the 1990s with the development of what has become known as the education and training reform agenda. This agenda was advanced by Commonwealth and State governments with close involvement from industry groups and the unions. It has largely taken place at arm's length from the universities, though this is not for want of trying by VET reformers. Schools and TAFEs fall far more clearly under State control than do universities and, as a consequence, there is much greater opportunity to develop national reform agendas driven by government and industry. Universities strongly resisted moves to apply such agendas to them.

A key step in the reform process came with the 1991 Finn Review of post-compulsory education and training. The Finn Report proposed national targets for participation in education and training, and recommended that education and training should be based around providing key "competencies" for students and should involve better coordination among the various providers. The competency approach followed similar moves overseas, and adopted principles that closely resembled those used in the United States during the 1970s and the UK in the 1980s.[8] The aim was to restructure education and training in such a way that systematic judgements could be made about whether or not a person held particular skills that would be of value in the workplace.

The nationally-agreed system to support national education and training reform followed five themes[9]:

- nationally consistent competency-based training;
- national recognition of competencies (however attained);

-     an open national training market;
-     equity and access to VET; and
-     an integrated entry-level training system.

Competencies have been drafted both at both industry and generic level. The latter "key competencies" were drafted in 1992 by a committee drawn from industry, education and training sectors (the Mayer Committee) and intended to apply to all levels (schools and VET). They comprised:

- collecting, analysing and organising information;
- communicating ideas and information;
- planning and organising activities;
- working with others and in teams;
- using mathematical ideas and techniques;
- solving problems;
- using technology; and
- cultural understanding.

The last of these, cultural understanding, was originally proposed by Finn, deleted by the Mayer Committee, and provisionally reinstated by education and training Ministers in July 1993.

Clearly these attributes are desirable not only for vocational education and training but for education in general, including university education. The issue is not so much the actual competency the students are supposed to have acquired, but the level at which that competency has been achieved. It is also important to understand how that level will be assessed.

The Finn Report drew attention to the phenomenon of the "convergence" of general and vocational education. "Convergence" is a term that is recurring with increasing frequency in education circles. It simply means that as society becomes more complex, old distinctions between categories are harder to sustain. As we have seen, the issues of "lifelong learning" and the ever-increasing need for knowledge, as opposed to job-related fixed skills, are breaking down the walls between broad education and the transmission of techniques necessary to obtain a job, and between obtaining a job and learning. Learning is now a skill that is needed for workers to adapt to changing circumstances.

＊

From the outset it was recognised that securing national agreement on VET reform would not be easy. A system was needed that would coordinate the activities of the Commonwealth, the State and Territory governments, schools, TAFEs, other VET providers, industry and unions. In 1993 the Keating Government established the Australian National Training Authority (ANTA) to help achieve this coordination.

Its premise was the development of national frameworks in a hitherto fragmented area. Of the five themes mentioned above, the first two - structuring the system around national competencies and putting in place a national recognition system - are the core of the matter. Defining the competencies was the easier task; more difficult was to somehow embed these into the maelstrom of VET. The task was threefold:

- to establish national frameworks for qualifications along with complementary standards;
- to change curricula in schools and VET providers consistent with the national qualifications and standards frameworks; and
- to establish a national system of assessment so that competencies could be measured, both within the workplace and externally. This would allow students - defined to include recipients of training - to move easily between the different sectors and providers within each sector.

It is a very ambitious program, complicated by the decision to adopt market-based approaches to delivery within a project environment which lacks clear priorities or coordination between different themes. Progress has been sporadic, with most success centred on establishing industry standards.

While results have been patchy, one important development has been the establishment of what is known as the National Framework for the Recognition of Training (NFROT). The purpose of NFROT was to develop an overarching structure across the various providers that would mean each would recognise what others were doing, and which would provide a basis for accrediting courses and registering private providers. Its main work so far has been in the development of an Australian Qualifications Framework, which seeks to define the various types of awards that could be offered by schools, TAFE, private VET providers and universities.

The universities provided a stumbling block for this process in the form of an Associate Degree, a qualification widely used in American community colleges. This is a two-year vocationally-oriented course which may earn credit towards the usual three-year undergraduate bachelor degree. The provision of the award is a bone of contention. VET providers see universities as trespassing on their turf, while the universities contend that they can offer awards as they see fit.

Disputes also remain about the traffic of students between the sectors. Universities and TAFE find it difficult to recognise the learning that students develop in each other's system. Despite the passage of many students from universities to TAFE to add a more vocationally-relevant diploma to a bachelor degree, the traditional perception of universities as being "above" TAFE remains. Differences in processes widen this chasm - TAFE entry and assessment is based on competencies while the university system is most often based on academic grading and ranking. VET providers are concerned that universities have not offered adequate credit for non-university awards; conversely, universities criticise the adherence to competency standards in TAFE admissions.

While it would be counter-productive to separate the two sectors structurally, there is a clear need for some better frameworks to underpin a more flexible system. Specifically, a Qualifications Framework should desirably be matched by a national system of credit accumulation and transfer, so that students can obtain proper recognition in one sector of work they have undertaken in another. The Australian Vice-Chancellors' Committee agreed in mid-1997 to a scheme of credit recognition for TAFE study; however its implementation was hampered by a refusal to participate on the part of a number of major universities. Whether or not a national scheme is feasible in an environment where universities wish to protect their autonomy and the status of their awards, and so might wish to strike individual arrangements on a case-by-case basis, remains to be seen.

The decision to adopt an open training market has been a key characteristic of the national reform program. Such an approach is, of course, entirely consistent with the prevailing approach by government to service delivery. The moves towards market-based provision of VET have not been uniform, relying very much on initiatives from each State and

Territory. Nevertheless, the trends are very clear and are already having a profound effect on the operations of TAFE. The most obvious effect is that to become more competitive TAFE has had to become more flexible in its operations, including the delivery of education programs. Flexible delivery is in many ways further advanced in this sector than in universities, but further progress is countered by its traditionally rigid employment award conditions. Private providers are nowhere near as constrained as the TAFEs in terms of limitations that arise from industrial awards.

During 1997 there were clear signs that industrial disputes in the TAFE sector were gathering momentum, compounded by moves in some States to rationalise TAFE institutions and to squeeze TAFE funding. In Victoria, the tertiary education minister announced a review in the aftermath of the 1997 Federal Budget to examine further rationalisation of TAFEs and the feasibility of merging some of them with existing universities. Rationalisation had already occurred in several other States over the preceding five years, leading to the creation of large TAFE institutes, with a broad range of activities. These developments have led to speculation[10] that another binary system may be emerging, driven not by national policy but by a hierarchy of VET institutions. In this scenario, the "upper levels" of VET become drawn into the university arena, initially emulating the role of the former CAEs and then, like their predecessors, aspiring to become universities.

At the other end of the spectrum of VET, the "entry-level training" agenda (advanced through the development of apprenticeships and traineeships) has continued to be problematic.

Apprenticeships have long been part of the Australian industry scene. However, numbers have fluctuated with changing economic circumstances and have been affected by a decline in employment in sectors such as manufacturing, which traditionally have employed apprentices. Apprenticeships have also been criticised for discriminating against women. In 1985 a new system of traineeships was introduced which provided shorter (usually one year) training as opposed to the four-year contractual commitment involved with employing an apprentice. Traineeship numbers have steadily risen, although not as quickly as was originally hoped by government.

The Minister then responsible for vocational education and training in the Howard Government, David Kemp, enthusiastically sought to develop entry-level training. The Government announced in the 1996 Budget a new scheme which would provide incentives for employers to hire apprentices and trainees, where training would be provided in an openly contested market. The scheme would link into Years 11 and 12 at school, providing "new pathways" for young people who did not go on to higher levels of education.

Whatever the merits of encouraging industry to seek more training for young people in the workplace, critics have pointed out that the scheme has several shortcomings. Clearly it depends very much on industry demand, and Australian industry has never been terribly strong on providing training for its employees. This particularly applies to small business. Most of the training industry is based upon individuals choosing to pursue education and training opportunities that are made available by the VET providers, much of which in turn depends heavily on government funding. The VET sector has been hit particularly hard by the transient nature of government "job schemes", which subsidise training opportunities for young people to deal with high youth unemployment. It will find it even more difficult to accommodate an industry-driven scheme.

Another major criticism has been that too little attention is being given to lifelong learning opportunities in favour of short-term training for school-leavers who manage to find employment. Youth unemployment is certainly high, but significant numbers of older people are also out of work, and periods of unemployment for older people tend to be much longer than for teenagers.[11] Many people who need and use VET are self-employed or seeking to change jobs. Employer-driven training will not help these people.

Another binary system?

We know that an increasingly wide range of vocational education has appeared in universities. The Chairman of the Howard Government's Review of Higher Education Financing and Policy, Roderick West, has expressed his own predilection for a return to Camelot, but vocational education in universities is here to stay. We also know that the convergence of general and vocational education is a major issue for the VET sector, notwithstanding the fact that more action seems to have occurred at the shorter training end of the spectrum. Evidence suggests that general skills, such as the generic "key competencies" outlined previously, cannot just be taught on their own and be expected to be applied in the workplace. What is needed is some context against which the skills are taught. Thus, rather than being taught a unit on "using technology", students should learn how to apply technology in the course of learning something else. In this way technology is seen to solve particular problems and be adaptable to specific situations.[12] This would suggest that "generic competencies" might be most effectively implemented in VET if the sector broadens its educational reach, which some have argued could well include the development of the kind of disciplinary study that occurs in universities.[13]

How robust can and should distinctions be between universities and non-universities in these circumstances? Certainly there are some profound structural differences between universities and VET institutions: TAFE institutions are much more subject to government control, VET is fee-based without a HECS mechanism available to students and, in the area of entry-level training, VET is being pushed to become industry-driven. Nevertheless many students move between the sectors despite the many barriers placed in their way.

Some observers are concerned that if VET, and TAFEs in particular, adopt a broader education mandate then they will inevitably aspire to become universities, and will lose their focus on their skills-based mandate. Yet if general skills are best taught in the context of a more general education, keeping VET to a narrow path is not in the interests of either the students, employers or of the community as a whole. If we are concerned about the quality of education rather than its cost then we cannot and should not try to separate artificially the general education components of VET from related undergraduate components of universities.

One model that has been put forward[14] is that of the higher education college which spans Years 11 and 12 of secondary school, VET, and the first year of undergraduate university education. Partial examples of such colleges already exist, mainly straddling the latter years of school and TAFE, while some colleges in remote areas deliver first year programs under cooperative arrangements with a university. In some instances, universities provide accelerated programs for higher performers in schools, although these arrangements have little structural implication for the two sectors and remain focussed on fast-tracking the top students into selected universities.

Objections to the higher education college model are that it might reduce the quality and viability of some schools, and provide less guidance and care for students who need it, particularly at Year 11 level. It has also been suggested that such arrangements would detract from the need to develop networks between the sectors, rather than find solutions in institutional arrangements. Nevertheless, it is hard to see why such a move could not be developed in such a way as to recognise the different needs of students at different stages of their life, nor why it could not be a useful way of encouraging innovative solutions to sectoral problems that might then be used by others. Indeed, is it too hard to imagine a variety of institutional forms that pay little regard to existing sectoral boundaries and which provide a range of educational opportunities from general VET education through to full undergraduate university degrees, and which might engage a mix of regular staff and outside "freelance" staff who supplement the teaching effort?

The enhancement of general education within the VET sector is desirable. The transformation of TAFEs into our current conception of a university is not. The solution will lie partly with changing institutional forms, to allow greater cross-over between undergraduate university education and other post-school education and training, and partly with improving links between our existing institutions. Such links will need to include better recognition of learning that has taken place elsewhere, development of "packages" that combine university and VET awards, and more cooperative teaching arrangements. But for these things to work, we need to change our conceptions of universities, both as "higher" institutions, and as places where learning is bound up in tightly-defined limits.

Considerable progress has been made by some universities in the area of making entry more flexible, including through recognition of previous TAFE study. However many others remain reluctant. It is notable that the older more prestigious universities have tended to move more slowly than the newer institutions in this regard.

*

"It has, however, become a question" wrote Flexner in 1930, "whether the term 'university' can be saved or is even worth saving." He wrote this long before the appearance of such august bodies as

McDonald's Hamburger U. or Mastercard University. The pressures at work are clearly stretching the definition of what a university can and should be. For some, the solution lies in further pigeon-holing the university system. Professor David Pennington, a former Vice-Chancellor of the University of Melbourne, has proposed a formal grouping of universities into "major research universities", "universities of technology", "regional universities" and "generalist metropolitan universities."[15] His purpose was ostensibly to "recognise" diversity, but it was in reality a policy agenda disguised as a taxonomy, the agenda being that of the older universities with large research programs, which we will consider later. In any case, such a categorisation can only be useful as a snapshot.

At the time of the establishment of the New South Wales University of Technology in 1949, an editorial in the Sydney Morning Herald, reproduced on the next page, cautioned the government not to confuse the new institution with a "university in the real meaning of that word". The place of the newcomer was to relieve the University of Sydney from "the burden of routine instruction", thereby allowing "more original research, social leadership, and free discussion and interchange of ideas at the senior institution." Nine years later, the University of Technology became the University of New South Wales, an institution which is now one of Australia's premier research universities.

Categorisation of the universities would also do little to address the fundamental issue of how best to accommodate lifelong learning. It has to be addressed in a cross-sectoral manner, that is, the solution cannot lie with university policy alone. For too long we have allowed questions of institutional structure and tradition to override questions of educational need. There are some concerns about "institutional creep", where new institutions of higher education might aspire to become research universities. However, some of this is scare-mongering by the older universities, who have seen some of "their" research money and good staff go to the new institutions. Aspirations to develop a research profile are not the problem. It is of more concern when aspirations to take on the paraphernalia of traditional academia work against innovative approaches to education.

The modern Australia university is a hybrid. Echoes of its origins with the medieval academic guild still can be heard in the rhetoric about communities of scholars, while traces of the aprentice/journeyman/

The New University Of Technology

While the Sydney public has become somewhat blase about foundation-stones, the laying of one this afternoon merits respectful attention, for it marks the formal beginning of what is to be called the University of Technology. This institution is dedicated to a quest for high efficiency in industry and applied science, and there is no doubt that a constructive and useful life awaits it in the State which holds the lead in Australian industrial life.

While welcoming the expansion which this new foundation will bring to the resource of tertiary education in New South Wales, the thoughtful citizen may still maintain some reservations. The first doubt—and a disquieting one in view of the parsimony succeeding Governments have exhibited towards the University of Sydney—is whether the existence of two centres of higher education may not leave us, in the end, with two emaciated bodies, too starved for funds to discharge their functions with the required vigour. The second is whether the newcomer may not be over-favoured by its governmental parent at the expense of the first-born. Governments have attempted, hitherto with indifferent success, to bring the University of Sydney to heel, but the composition of the council of the University of Technology shows that no chances are being taken there. That body is overwhelmingly composed of Government nominees, which could lead to an enforced and unbecoming servility.

The very name of the University of Technology suggests there has been confusion in the Government's mind about the relative functions of the two seats of higher education. A place where technical training is given in properly equipped surroundings is necessary in an industrial society. But no matter how well such an organisation discharges its function it is not, and cannot be, a university in the real meaning of that word. One aims to produce men highly qualified in their chosen calling, while the other aims to produce fully educated citizens. Mechanics, no matter how superb, cannot displace the humanities, and awareness of this is reflected in the fact that the most famous overseas centres of technology call themselves "institutes"—although some of them outrank many universities in prestige.

If the distinction is properly understood, the new technological centre may well aid and buttress the University of Sydney. By taking over much of the burden of routine instruction, it can open the way for more original research, social leadership, and free discussion and interchange of ideas at the senior institution. But if both are to play their full part, it is necessary that the distinction between them be clearly realised by those who provide their finance.

Sydney Morning Herald, 25 February 1950

master role of the student survive in the lecture format and the shape of bachelor and masters degrees. These themes hark back to the era when universities were designed to instil cultural values in an elite group of young men through the study of classical texts. The culture and structure of the university, which exalts the autonomous and isolated academic, drives towards ever greater specialisation in an age where team work is assuming ever greater importance in the "real" world and where society's problems are of a multidisciplinary nature.

The university design has great difficulty in dealing with a mass education system in an egalitarian democracy, where higher levels of learning are needed throughout a person's lifetime to adapt to a rapidly changing social and economic environment. As universities have grown larger, the notion of an academic community has been harder to sustain and the curriculum has come under pressure, in one direction to include more vocationally-relevant material, and in the other to reflect the broader social and disciplinary aspects of university study. Policies of selectivity, directing resources towards areas of "core business" or strength, or rewards for performance or earning capacity by academics outside the university, represent major sources of concern for many academics.

These difficulties are harder to avoid when resources are squeezed on one side by the government and on the other side by industrial pressures. Governments assume that whatever the cost, the same activity can be done just as well next year with a few per cent less. On the other side of the equation, unions argue that whatever staff are paid in one year, they could be paid a few per cent more in the next without major budgetary disruption.

The traditional university is already experiencing a limited form of competition among local universities, and some competition at a national and international level among universities for excellent staff and students as well as for overseas students. There is every prospect that this competition will be extended, particularly as the power of information technology expands, and that some markets will be contested by new players who can operate more flexibly and cheaply. Universities will have to come to terms with this new climate in an environment in which government cannot be relied upon to provide additional funding to promote innovation. In most cases change will have to come from within, and some activities may have to be wound back to make way for others to develop.

The outlook for universities is not entirely bleak. They have advantages in terms of local reputation, links with industry, research expertise, accredited status and social acceptance. A substantial number of domestic Australian school leavers will still want to go to an Australian university, and demographic factors will ensure a continuation in demand from this group in some States for the next several years. Even a liberal university education is, as we have noted, entirely justifiable in practical and work-related terms, as society will need flexible, creative and adaptable people to meet future needs.

Some universities are, however, better placed than others. Some have strengths in particular fields of study, some in relationships with industry, and some in the delivery of education at a distance. Some universities rely more than others on fee income, for example from overseas students, and would be more greatly affected by eventualities such as an assault on the South East Asian market by US-based "virtual universities", or by volatility in Asian currency movements.

In the future all education institutions will have to be more selective about what they do, as competition grows and resources continue to be tight. We will see less national uniformity in the university sector, as each institution seeks to identify and build on its own areas of advantage. Greater blending of universities and vocational education and training can be expected. This blending will be accelerated if and when the VET sector tackles the broader issue of implementing key competencies and lifelong learning, which to date has been overshadowed by process matters and attention to workplace training.

Signs of fragmentation in the "university community" are becoming increasingly apparent as competitive pressures take hold. The Australian Vice-Chancellor's Committee (AVCC) was established in 1920 to promote coordination and the collection of information. Over the years the AVCC has developed into a national lobby group, now representing the interests of 37 member universities at the national level. However the diverging interests of member universities are making the achievement of consensus increasingly difficult. In recent years the older more research-intensive universities (the "Sandstone Seven" or the "Group of Eight") have made plays for greater shares of research funding, while five of the newer universities with a technological background have formed the Australian Technology Network to advance areas of common interest. In April 1997 three Australian universities joined with ten other universities from around

the world to form Universitas 21, a so-called "super league" of universities designed to foster interactions between universities with a strong research base. Speaking at the launch of Universitas 21, the Vice-Chancellor of the University of New South Wales, Professor John Niland, said "there is no point being in a cloister, we would welcome our AVCC colleagues establishing similar societies. The 21st century will be a period for strategic alliances for universities - critical for survival and growth."[16]

In October 1977 the AVCC resolved to adopt a regulatory role in relation to the overseas student market, including the use of sanctions for breaches of its code of conduct. Shortly afterwards, the University of Melbourne Council adopted five resolutions proposed by the Vice-Chancellor aimed at asserting the independence and autonomy of the university from the AVCC. These resolutions rejected the "moral or legal authority" of the AVCC to act as a watchdog, and stated that any precedent for regulatory intervention would raise "the danger of elevating system-wide conformity over the imperatives of institutional diversity and internationalisation."[17] Clearly the AVCC, while able to coordinate activities and sponsor programs of common interest, will have difficulty in speaking with authority on behalf of the universities as a whole.

In years to come the crucial distinctions between institutions may well be phrased in terms of diversity of *external* relationships, rather than by different balances of teaching and research or professional and general education *within* the university. Different universities can play different roles at local, State-wide, national, Asia-Pacific or wider international levels. Across these levels, a variety of relationships can be struck between the individual university and the community, government, large corporations and small businesses. These relationships may well be transitory, and may well be conducted outside the formal regulatory apparatus of the university.

Despite technological and social change, the demise of much of the familiar university structure is not imminent. However, it is entirely possible that many of the current functions of the university, particularly the immediately useful and commercial functions, will be contested and assumed by new providers, operating either independently of, or in conjunction with, established universities.

We will now examine more closely the implications for the major activities of the university, teaching and research, and also consider the changes that are needed in the way universities manage themselves.

CHAPTER FIVE

Teaching: From Side Show to a Main Event

The Australian government and public have one thing in common with Cardinal Newman when it comes to their views of universities. The main name of the game is teaching.

People outside the higher education sector, and many within, could be forgiven for thinking that this is not the view of most universities. Full-time student numbers are counted as "load" on the university, and many academics seek "teaching relief" in order to pursue research. Academics need specific qualifications for research, but not for teaching. Despite revisions to promotions procedures, most academics believe, and the outcomes support the belief, that research carries greater weight than teaching in the career paths of academic staff. Many students have minimal personal interaction with university staff, and many complain about insufficient feedback about their work.

The post-War expansion of higher education certainly produced a qualitative change in some areas, notably in research. However, at the risk of oversimplification, traditional university teaching methods and structures were largely expanded and stretched, rather than re-invented, to meet the new mass market.

The situation is well appreciated by many who work inside universities. At present, universities are undergoing a painful transition between industrial and postindustrial education methods. In many ways, however, we are only at the beginning of this process. The great bulk of university education still occurs through fixed courses, delivered at fixed times in fixed places, and which proceeds at the same pace with few concessions for different student characteristics or needs. Changing a course structure is usually a lengthy process, involving prolonged scrutiny by various committees over many months or even years. On the next page is a depiction of the way in which much undergraduate university teaching is conducted in Australia. We are leaving to one side for the time being the many innovations that have been implemented around this model, since fundamental change to the mainstream has been small. Anyone who has

The reality of undergraduate students' experiences of teaching

The typical method of delivering a university course involves lectures, tutorials, assignments and examinations at the end of each semester.

The mainstay of university teaching is the lecture. It defines the job classification of most teaching staff: lecturers and senior lecturers. Students gather at a designated time and place to hear the lecturer speak, usually for an hour. Questions are discouraged, these are reserved for tutorials. Lectures can be very large. In many universities in Australia, particularly in the larger faculties and in the first year, hundreds of students may fill the lecture theatre at one time. An undergraduate student who is enrolled full-time might expect to attend around a dozen of these each week for twenty-eight weeks in the year.

Complementing the lectures are tutorials. These are smaller groups, where questions may be asked and problems worked through. With the rise in student numbers compared to staff numbers over the past decade, tutorial class sizes have also been rising. Opportunities for interaction between student and teacher in these circumstances become fewer, and for many students tutorials become another form of lecture.

Assignments, particularly those for first and second year undergraduate students, are usually on set topics with set questions that apply to each student. Under good conditions, assignments are read and marked promptly and returned to the student in time to remain relevant to their subject of study and with detailed feedback from the assessor. Under poorer conditions, assignments may not be returned at all, and if they are returned they might only have a score and no further feedback.

Those students who attend a campus also have the option of visiting their lecturer to discuss particular problems. Lecturers post timetables on their office doors indicating the hours they will be available for such meetings, but with ever larger student numbers and competing demands for time of academic staff, these opportunities are becoming more scarce.

been to university will recognise the main components of the lecture, the tutorial[1], the assignment and end-of-semester exams.

Such a system is best suited to an instructional, as opposed to an educational, approach to teaching. In the words of the eminent Australian education researcher, Professor W. F. Connell, the characteristics of an instructional process are "transference of information to a pupil from an authoritative source, dependence on textbooks, and orderliness of procedure."[2] Whether the student learns well or not depends on both the skills of the lecturer and tutor and the motivation and ability of the student. A good lecturer not only transmits information, he or she inspires students by imparting some measure of enthusiasm and energy for the subject. Poor lecturers also make an impact, but not one that aids learning. Charles Darwin, attending medical school in Edinburgh in the 1820s, encountered the lectures of Alexander Munro III, whose manner was described by one student as "unimpassioned indifference" and whose classes degenerated into riots.[3]

Not all students attend a campus. "External" or "distance" education has long been a part of Australian higher education. Around one in ten university students are enrolled in this way. Usually distance education involves the same entry requirements as on-campus study and parallels the on-campus methodology, the difference being that instead of lectures and tutorials, students receive material to read. Educational material usually comes through the post, and for many years distance education was known as the "correspondence course". It became particularly popular in the 1970s as many teachers' colleges became CAEs and sought to reach wider markets. It was also a feature of most of the regional CAEs and those universities that serviced a widely distributed student population.

The most notable feature of the standard university teaching arrangements is that they are highly structured and designed more to suit the needs and convenience of the institution and the teacher, rather than the student. Opportunities for interaction between students and teachers and for helpful feedback on student progress are limited, and becoming more limited as the system expands under financial constraint. Annual national surveys of graduates[4] show that nearly half of those graduating for the first time report that feedback was mostly in terms of marks and grades, around 40 per cent feel that staff do not put a lot of time into commenting on their work, and nearly one third disagree with the statement that "teaching staff normally gave me helpful feedback on how I was going". In such circumstances it takes an able and committed student to succeed and remain motivated.

Many do not. Student drop-out rates, formally referred to as "attrition", have been high for as long as reliable records have been kept in Australia. The allocation of Commonwealth funding allows for one quarter of an incoming group of full-time students to drop out each year, which would mean that only 56 per cent would last three years and 42 per cent would last for four years. In fact attrition rates are often higher than this, and are at their highest in the first year of study. It is not uncommon for 40 per cent or more of students to drop out in first year, and in many cases the majority of students who enrol in some courses never go on to complete them.

Attrition is not always a bad thing. Some students withdraw from one course to enrol in another, sometimes at another university. Others may leave because they feel unsuited to the course, to have children or for other personal reasons. However, many withdraw because of disillusionment or inability to cope with the program of study. It is easy to blame this on the student. Certainly there are many students in higher education today who would not have gained entry in the past on the basis of school performance. This is a characteristic of many countries, due to the transitions from elite to mass higher education coupled with shortcomings in secondary education. In the United States, a recent study found that 29 per cent of first year college students were taking remedial classes in mathematics, reading or writing. Nevertheless, attrition was identified as a major problem by the Murray Committee some forty years ago in Australia, before the advent of mass participation.

High drop-out rates suggest that a great deal of effort is being wasted by students and by universities, wastage that can be ill-afforded in the current climate. Some degree of attrition will always be expected because of student-related factors and if high standards are to be maintained. Put bluntly, there is a view that some students studying at universities are not up to the challenge. However, part of the problem undoubtedly lies with teaching methods, and with the difficulty in providing students with education that suits their own particular requirements and abilities. The least interactive form of university education, the correspondence course, has always had a far higher level of attrition, particularly in the first year of study.

...AND I THOUGHT THIS UNIVERSITY DIDN'T PROVIDE DISTANCE EDUCATION !
LEAHY.

The first year at university often represents an abrupt transition from school. Young people experiencing the benefits and drawbacks of becoming an adult, with attendant freedoms and responsibilities, are thrown into an often impersonal environment. They have to cope with large and complicated university administrative systems and navigate their way through complex course structures, all the while balancing personal and academic challenges, without the guidance or attention which might have been available when they were at school. Older students, particularly those who have previously studied at university, tend to do better, achieving higher grades and with lower rates of attrition. Nevertheless, this group has its own diverse set of needs; some may be less familiar with computers than school leavers, many are in the workforce and studying part-time and many have family responsibilities. They are more likely to be paying a substantial amount of money up-front for their education and to have higher expectations of quality and service. The number of "mature age" undergraduate students has risen rapidly over the past few decades, to the point where they outnumber the school leavers in undergraduate intakes at some universities.

Student diversity has many dimensions other than just age. There are nowadays more women students, students from different ethnic and cultural backgrounds, overseas students studying in Australia before returning to their home countries, students with disabilities, students with lower levels of English proficiency, and so on. Each of these dimensions is need-specific.

The increasing complexity of university education is more than just a matter of an increasingly diverse student body and a need to improve the quality of student learning in that context. As previously noted, the very nature and purpose of university education is under pressure. There are tensions between specialist and general education, and a pressing need to provide an adequate framework for life-long learning. These factors are driving change in what needs to be learned at undergraduate and postgraduate levels, and also in the way teaching and learning need to occur. They mean allowing multiple pathways of entry and exit, recognising prior knowledge of students and giving credit where this is appropriate, crossing the bridges between vocational and general education, and providing opportunities for learning "on the job".

A great deal of research has been undertaken in recent years to investigate the factors which enable students to learn. The main conclusions are not in themselves surprising; students learn more effectively if they are actively engaged, if they can relate new material to what they already know, and if they receive regular feedback. Learning is influenced by individual ability and motivation, as well as the parameters mentioned above. Not all learning requires teaching; students can learn from one other, using diverse sources of information, from undertaking practical classes, and from investigating specific problems. Learning arises from a mix of student characteristics, teaching methods and institutional factors, such as the provision of good libraries and equipment.

One of the fundamentals is that good teaching and learning is an interactive process. Interaction between a single lecturer or tutor and a large group of students is difficult, although there are ways of improving on the norm. Perhaps the most visible pressure for change in recent years is that arising from developments in communications technology, which holds the promise of enabling better and broader types of interaction. These can include interaction between teachers and students, both within the university and outside, such as link-ups with experts in other countries; between students, for example in discussion groups or in mentoring relationships; and between students and IT-based "learning programs."

The introduction of technology has transformed other sectors of the economy, most clearly through the mechanisation of routine tasks. Technology has also been pressed into service in education, from the days of radio and the "Schools of the Air", which supplemented correspondence courses for school children in remote areas[5], to television and video. Until the Open Learning Initiative was developed in Australia - an innovation we will consider shortly - television and video were used sparingly in higher education; mainly to supplement distance education programs and to provide additional resources for use in appropriate courses. Technology has also entered the lecture theatre, most obviously through the widespread use of the overhead projector. More elaborate presentation technologies have been introduced into many lectures, turning the lecture into a multi-media event, sometimes "beamed" to overflow venues or other campuses.

Broadcast media such as radio and television are suitable for delivering one-way messages to a wide audience. The obvious limitations - lack of flexibility, high cost of production (in the case of television) and minimal interactivity with the student - meant that there were relatively few incentives to move away from print as the central medium. Other media such as telephone and videoconferencing provided opportunities for interaction, but they remained expensive.

During the 1980s, computing became steadily cheaper, more powerful and easier to access. The personal computer provided a reasonably friendly "interface" with technology, and programming grew ever more flexible and simple. Greater volumes of information could be stored and handled by computers, particularly with the advent of CD-ROM technology in the 1990s, which could provide sound and pictures to accompany text. In recent years, computers have been linked together within organisations and across the world in the form of the Internet. The power of networks to transmit information, and of computers to process such information, has grown to the point where sound, pictures and movies can be moved over widely distributed networks. We are witnessing yet another convergence, this time of computing and telecommunications. Despite the almost relentless hype that bombards the mass media, this convergence has not yet been fully achieved. Ordinary phone lines cannot transmit the volume of information needed for a fully networked multimedia experience, and the "hardware" in the form of computers, and modems needed for computers to communicate with one another, is still developing. Nevertheless, we are already in a situation where vastly more information is accessible than ever before, and where computing and telecommunications technology can enable students to enjoy far richer experiences at a distance.

The imperative to use technology goes further than its application in the delivery of educational programs. People are using computers and information technology in all walks of life, and the ability to be "literate" in using information and technology is fundamental. Information and technology literacy are part of the key generic competencies defined for the VET sector and are just as important as attributes for university graduates.

As government moves away from a controlling and planning role in higher education and more towards one which focuses on outcomes and accreditation, the performance of universities in relation to teaching and student satisfaction will become the subject of increasing public scrutiny. For more than seven years, an independent publication, *The Good Universities Guide*, has published and analysed the various information which has been available on courses, quality and student ratings. Launching the 1997 edition of the Guide, Senator Vanstone, then Commonwealth Minister responsible for higher education, made clear her view that teaching was the "backbone" of the university, and that this backbone needed to be stronger. At that launch she announced three measures to provide impetus to this: a "hotline" would be established to receive complaints from students about the quality of their teaching; a range of prizes would be awarded to outstanding university teachers; and a national survey would be undertaken of the views of undergraduates on the quality of their education. These measures reveal a clear lack of faith by government in the ability of universities to give teaching its due prominence; however, they could reasonably be seen as window-dressing and administratively complex. Indeed the hotline initiative, dubbed "dob in a don" was dropped by Senator Vanstone's replacement as Minister, Dr David Kemp, within a couple of months of its original announcement.

The need for change in the way students learn in universities thus involves a conjunction of influences. There are educational influences, which relate to improving the quality of the educational experience, and to the changes in style and delivery necessary to respond to demands for workplace-based education and life-long learning. There are student influences, concerned with increasing the accessibility and flexibility of education. There is the technological influence, where greater potential is emerging for the design and delivery of more flexible education. And there are operational influences, arising from public pressure and accountability and moves to reduce the cost of higher education, increase access and equity, and compete with other providers.

*

The abolition of the binary system in the late 1980s brought a large number of institutions into the university fold which previously had been primarily concerned with teaching. While the older universities have deprecated the research aspirations of these newcomers, it must be said that the newer players injected a long-overdue focus on teaching, particularly the teaching of undergraduate students.

In recent years considerable efforts have been made to lift the quality and status of teaching in universities. Long overdue, it is now commonplace for the views of students to be sought on the quality of teaching and on the delivery of particular subjects. This feedback is usually sought at the discretion of the teacher and not made available to "management", as it is considered useful for the teacher's development, but not so useful that the institution should employ it to judge the teacher's performance.[6] Feedback is also sought on a nationally-consistent basis from graduates, shortly after they have completed their study. The results of this evaluation relate to whole courses, rather than individual teachers, and are used widely by institutions and others as providing one measure of quality. All universities contain units devoted to the study and improvement of teaching, and to assist academic staff with improving their teaching.

Some degree of flexibility in delivery has long been a feature of Australian higher education. In the latter half of the nineteenth century, low levels of interest and declining enrolments prompted some universities to offer part-time study and evening classes. Moreover, a significant part of Australia's service delivery, including education, has been shaped by its geographic and demographic characteristics. Most of the population is urban, clustered in cities by the coast and separated from one another by great distances. But many live in rural and remote areas. Such conditions encouraged the early adoption of distance education which, while ostensibly aimed at regional areas of Australia, has also been a convenient and popular option for many students who live in urban areas. The University of Queensland established a Department of External Studies in 1915, now closed, and many of the newer non-metropolitan universities incorporated such methods from an early stage. Equally however, external and part-time education have been seen over the years as the poorer cousins of full-time on-campus study; some would argue that in many universities today this is still the case. Many external and part-time students are older, they are already in the workforce, and many find such study demanding. Drop-out rates for external and part-time students have always been high, particularly in the first year.

Delivery of education by these off-campus methods was not part of the British tradition, which was based on full-time study in residential colleges. However they suited many Australian students, although sitting uneasily with many academics, including those eminent British experts who periodically reviewed our system. The Murray and Martin Committees confirmed that the "massification" of Australian higher education was permanently entrenched. Yet such a change was not easily reconciled with the British tradition of elite universities, and there were inevitable conflicts with idealised notions of what a university should be and how it should operate. Both Murray and Martin were steeped in the British perspective, and sought to preserve it in Australia in the face of rapid change and in the face of demands for greater flexibility and relevance.

Rather than seeing in the high drop-out rates a suggestion that traditional university teaching should change to suit such students better, many academics believed that they confirmed the unsuitability of external and part-time study for a university. Both the Murray and Martin Committees recommended, for universities at least, winding back these more flexible modes of higher education delivery in favour of full-time and residential study.

Governments of the day did not heed this advice, and external and part-time studies continued to grow throughout the period of university expansion in the 1960s and 1970s. By the time CTEC examined the situation in 1985 as part of its Review of Efficiency and Effectiveness, it noted that external enrolments had increased faster than on-campus enrolments over the previous decade, and that nearly one in eight students in higher education was studying externally. CTEC was concerned that external studies were spread across many institutions, and courses with fewer than 50 students were "likely to be very inefficient" given the various mixes of start-up and teaching costs. Similar analysis was not directed to on-campus study. The CTEC Review recommended that only a limited number of institutions should provide external studies, a recommendation whose grounds of efficiency appealed to the Federal Government, and which became policy shortly after the establishment of the Unified National System. In 1990, eight institutions were designated as Distance Education Centres (DECS), and others which wished to operate externally had their funds reduced and channelled to the DECs. It took less than two years for the government's main advisory body, the Higher Education Council, to advise that these arrangements were no longer justified. An unfortunate side effect of this policy was that the development of more flexible modes of higher education delivery was retarded in many universities.

Another approach to the freeing-up of higher education has been the use of summer schools. These have been trialled for some years, though again the numbers involved, and the range of subjects offered, were small.

Summer schools and external or part-time study have been in essence extensions of the on-campus instructional style to other places and times. In this respect they represented a response to the operational and student-driven influences for change which did not threaten the professional roles and practices of academics.

There have been waves of educational reform in the past, for example in the 1920s and 1960s, that have sought to move towards greater "student-centredness" at all levels of education. However, these have had relatively limited overall impact. Over the past twenty or so years, the need to shift from an instructional mode to one that is more conducive to student learning has gained momentum at all levels of education, from schools through to universities. In some ways, universities have more scope to experiment, enjoying the freedom to design their own courses and to deliver them as they see fit. On the other hand, universities are more bound by traditional practices and beliefs than other educational institutions. Autonomy can also work against innovation, as it is exercised at the individual as well as the institutional level. Academics who are not persuaded of the need to change cannot be forced to alter their ways, while at the other end of the spectrum an institution cannot afford to support a free-for-all approach to innovation by those who are keen to experiment with new approaches.

Important advances have been made in workplace-based education, which usually takes the form of a work experience or fieldwork component inserted at various stages of the course. In some cases, joint industry-university courses have been developed which are delivered largely at the workplace. Elaine Martin, from the Curriculum and Academic Development Unit at RMIT, investigated a variety of such programs and found that while they were on the increase, there was considerable variation in quality and limited awareness of what constituted effective practice.[7]

Information technology has also been used both to enhance traditional teaching methods and to develop new ways of promoting learning. The enhancement of traditional methods can include equipping lecture theatres with high-tech equipment such as projectors that work from computers, or using videoconferencing links to "beam" lectures or tutorials between campuses. Another major area of activity has been the development of computer-based teaching programs, which can act as infinitely patient, if sometimes rigid, tutors. Such programs often come with varying levels of "interactivity", usually meaning menu choices, to guide a student through simulated problems or question-and-answer steps.

New approaches to learning have been made possible with enhanced processing capacity and the communications capabilities of computer networks. Students can now be linked together in on-line discussion groups, where the teacher plays the role of moderator rather than instructor. Information can be provided through a Web site, or a student can be directed towards available information from all around the world and only guided where needed. Three dimensional visual computer simulations can be made of laboratory environments, animal dissections, chemical reactions and a host of other activities that previously either had to be imagined or directly experienced at high financial cost.

These innovations have consumed large amounts of staff time and money. In some areas they have made a considerable impact; in others they have withered as money ran out, or technology moved on to render the development obsolete. Some ground-breaking work is occurring in Australia and overseas on using computer communications, including the World Wide Web, in a wide variety of situations. At present these uses are hampered by poor infrastructure, both inside and outside the university setting. Despite the almost relentless hype, the capacity of most computer networks to deliver multimedia experiences is, for the time being, limited. The litany of frustrations is familiar to anyone who has used the Internet: slow response times, remote sites down or poorly maintained, and periodic network crashes. The failure of technology to perform as expected has bedevilled many a presenter at conferences designed to showcase the future educational potential of this or that application. Recently, a conference held in Melbourne entitled "The Global University - A 21st Century View" set up an international videoconference link between vice-chancellors from Edinburgh, Hong Kong and New South Wales. A report in the *Campus Review* noted that "if this was intended to show the marvels of modern communication, and how interactive seminars could link people across the globe, it proved something of a failure. The sound was poor and the jerky transmission made those overseas look as if they were suffering continual spasms."[8]

Enthusiasts await the golden age of the Information Superhighway. Meanwhile, the mainstream of activity remains much as it was; campus-based institutions still lecture and run tutorials, and distance education institutions rely heavily on the post.

Nevertheless, the conjunction of influences described above has intensified rather than faded away. Impetus has been added by computer companies such as IBM and Microsoft actively promoting the use of technology in teaching, while aggressive for-profit non-university providers are emerging to cater to growing commercial markets.

All universities are publicly acknowledging the need for change in the teaching and learning area, although many seem confused about why or what it is that should change. At conferences, within academic publications and in the general media, university staff are barraged by a stream of exhortations to adapt or perish.

There are many examples of inspiring changes introduced by teachers who are committed to their work and to their students. A recent compilation of professional experiences was prepared with the aid of Commonwealth government funding. Entitled *Reflecting on University Teaching: Academics' Stories*[9], it provides 44 examples of innovative approaches, many of which do not require large costs or use of new technology. The academics who provided these examples clearly found good teaching personally rewarding.

So why has it proven so difficult to reform the "mainstream" of university education?

Barriers to change

Significant change requires a commitment of resources. Pressures for greater flexibility have, however, coincided with those for institutional efficiency, in particular, resources for teaching have become tighter. Looked at in one way, considerable productivity improvements have been achieved. Between 1985 and 1996 the number of graduates produced has grown by 52 per cent, while academic numbers have grown by 35 per cent and funds available for teaching by 39 per cent. On the other hand, the pressure to produce greater output has made it more difficult to focus resources, the most expensive of which is the time of academic staff, on matters of improving quality. In some cases, the tighter funding situation is leading to more lectures, and less work with smaller groups. Many academics find it difficult enough to cope with existing tasks, without finding the time and energy to examine ways in which things might be done differently. Indeed given the high start-up costs associated with developing computer-based learning, it could be argued that mass lectures are a cost-effective alternative.

A particular problem facing universities is that of providing reliable computer networks and support, such as from a computing "help-desk".

Demand is growing at a phenomenal rate. Around the world we are seeing what some call the "support service crisis".[10] Some institutions are dealing with this by using students in various technical support roles, others are decentralising support across the different discipline areas of the university. In any case, each university has to cut its cloth to fit the types and extent of reform (particularly technology-based reform) that it can afford.

Much of the change in teaching and learning has occurred at the level of the individual rather than the institution, driven by academics who have the energy and commitment to push through a new approach. This is clearly a necessary part of change, but it has its drawbacks. The directions chosen by enthusiasts may not coincide either with the infrastructure choices of the university or with the directions of other academics or general staff within the institution. A fragmented approach can also spread resources thinly over many small areas without achieving substantial strategic change. In many cases, the product has been an expensive "bolt-on" to existing teaching, consuming considerable amounts of time and money in the process.

Different methods of teaching will also require different university procedures. Many places still use ratios of students to staff to determine the allocation of resources, usually with the implicit assumption that teaching methods will not change, and most of the non-distance education universities measure staff workloads in terms of face-to-face contact hours, meaning lectures and tutorials. University procedures for changing courses can be labyrinthine, with committee after committee considering vast amounts of paperwork to ensure that every possible aspect has been subject to external scrutiny. These processes can result in periods of two years or more between initial proposals and final approval of courses.

One legacy of former styles of academic management has been that academic matters and financial matters were for many years treated entirely separately. This has changed in most universities, but unhelpful separations remain widespread between academic and technical matters and between systems for academic and general staff. These separations retard the integration of technology as a tool for teaching and learning change, and do not help the development of team approaches across the range of jobs necessary for effective reform.

Australian universities have long adopted management styles best suited to stable or expanding environments and a mindset that values uniform treatment of all areas and expansion in size and scope. If universities are to be successful they must adopt greater variety and flexibility in what they do, which in turn means being more selective. Selectivity can be quite confronting to cherished academic icons of collegiality and the notion that all academics should be treated equally. Universities will be unable to be selective unless there is widespread acceptance from its academic staff of the need to change. For academics to change their minds, they need to be persuaded, either at their own initiative or by others, that change is worthwhile and they need to see educational change as important compared with other academic priorities.

The most pressing clash of priorities comes with the long-standing interrelationship of teaching and research in universities. All academics, particularly those who aspire to the levels of senior lecturer or above, are expected to undertake active programs of research. Most are very willing to do so, indeed for many years one of the main problems has been the higher status of research over teaching in the university. Research output, in the form of publications, is easier to quantify than is the case for teaching, and its quality can be assessed through peer review. This is not the case with teaching, where outcomes cannot be readily linked with individual teachers and where the interaction between students and teachers is treated as a private matter that should not be assessed in any systematic way by others. This situation serves to reinforce the highly influential position of research performance in decisions about career progression and promotion. The effect is to distort the balance of activity away from undergraduate teaching towards research, even for those academic staff who are poor researchers or have no interest in being active researchers.

A typical lecturer might spend around ten to fifteen hours a week in "student contact time", meaning lecturing or running tutorials, the balance being spent in preparation time, informal contact with students, assessing work and in research or service activities. As one moves up the ranks, the "burden" of teaching is usually diminished in favour of increased research time, to the point where most professors spend only a few hours a week in direct teaching, and many have entire days with no teaching responsibilities. In 1995, the *Campus Review* newspaper drew attention in its "Graffiti" column to an advertisement from Nagoya University of Commerce in Japan for a Professor of English Language, with an attractive salary of $A117,000 to $143,000. However Japanese expectations of employees, the newspaper noted wryly, were "somewhat greater" than those in Australia. The advertisement stated that "professors normally teach eight 90 minute periods per week. Monday to Friday."[11]

Research has the added attraction of visibly drawing extra money. Indeed Slaughter and Leslie in their book *Academic Capitalism* suggest that the diversion of effort from teaching to research is a rational response to resource changes, and that these external signals are probably more influential than changes in the inherent preferences or attitudes of academics or signals from promotions or other reward structures.[12]

Until recently, enrolling extra students above the number that the government was prepared to subsidise did not bring in any extra money, and merely meant extra work. By contrast, gaining extra research grants attracted more grant money and publishing more papers earned a larger share of the grant pie served up by the Commonwealth Government. However, these incentives may change, particularly now that some small compensation is paid to those universities which enrol extra students. Moreover, bringing in extra research grants often requires substantial subsidisation of the project from university resources, since research projects are rarely fully-funded. However, despite arguing that external resource influences are to blame for the shift to research, Slaughter and Leslie acknowledge that internal academic attitudes will also play a significant role:

> Research money is a critical resource for universities because universities are prestige maximisers. Since most faculty teach, and many faculty perform public service, but fewer win competitive research funds from government or industry, research is the activity that differentiates among universities ... if faculty were offered more resources to teach more students, it is not clear that they would compete for these moneys with the same zeal with which they compete for external research dollars targeted for government priorities or commercial endeavours.[13]

The link between teaching and research is for many the defining characteristic of a university. It is not sufficient that research and teaching take place in the same institution, or that researchers are available to contribute to the teaching of students. For some it is axiomatic that good university teaching *can only* be done by active researchers. A Review of Engineering Education in Australia, undertaken on behalf of relevant academic and professional interests, endorsed the view that "research is essential for the delivery of most undergraduate engineering programs.

Unless most of our teaching staff are engaged in research and current scholarship engineering education will fail to maintain contact with rapidly changing technologies and may in time be teaching superseded technology. If this happens we will fail to inculcate the graduating engineers with the enthusiasm required to keep challenging the established ways."[14] Most other disciplines would probably endorse these sentiments. The difficulty is, the evidence to support this contention is far from clear. A recent international survey of university professors found a fairly even split between those whose interests tended towards teaching and those who tended towards research. A notable exception was the United States, where more tended to have interests in teaching, perhaps reflecting the greater diversity in higher education in that country, with many distinguished institutions focusing primarily on undergraduate teaching. It was also interesting to see that nearly one in three Australian academics stated that they felt under pressure to do more research than they would actually like to do.[15]

Most academic staff have received no formal education and training in university teaching. They have in effect learned "on the job". Within universities the dominant qualification needed for academic career progression is for research: the PhD. A study of the qualifications of Australian academics noted that the Australian PhD, like the British, is a highly specialised form of research apprenticeship, lacking the coursework elements found in the American model which might make it a better preparation for the work many graduates will enter, including tertiary teaching. The authors of the study commented that:

> In these circumstances, it is difficult to convince oneself that the three quarters of Australian academics who have PhDs or research Masters degrees, actually need them for their academic role of teaching and scholarship. Perhaps the case can be made for the science based disciplines and some of the social sciences, but overall it looks very much like rampant credentialism which is driving the growth in the proportion of doctored academics.[16]

The eminent American educationalist Ernest Boyer proposed that academic scholarship should be considered more broadly than just teaching and research. He put forward four categories of scholarship: the scholarship of *discovery*, which is what most academics mean by research; the scholarship of *integration*, which covers the act of drawing together, interpreting and giving meaning to knowledge drawn from across the various academic disciplines; the scholarship of *application*, whereby knowledge is applied, and developed further by being applied, to particular situations; and the scholarship of *teaching*. There are good grounds for expecting that university teachers should take a scholarly approach to their work, meaning that they should keep abreast of the latest research, use new findings to illuminate their teaching and contribute in various ways to new knowledge within and across the disciplines and to teaching itself. However, this does not imply that they should all be actively engaged in the task of uncovering new knowledge for its own sake. As one commentator put it:"I found myself much in sympathy with the view expressed at one institution where it was pointed out that in the field of music a conductor was not without prestige or status because he was not a composer. Nor would it be suggested that a conductor did not exercise creativity in the presentation and interpretation of the works which he presented."[17]

The scholarship of discovery rules the academic roost. Yet it is the scholarship of integration that universities, and those who use them, most need. We need to cross the divides of the academic tribes, not deepen them by shoe-horning all academics into specialist disciplines. Much greater value needs to be placed on scholarly integration if universities are to improve the quality of undergraduate education and to tackle effectively the multidisciplinary problems that face society. We will have more to say about research and teaching at a later point, but for now it is relevant to observe that the balance of priorities towards research is widely perceived as being detrimental to encouraging innovation and quality in teaching.

The issue of integration also raises questions about another aspect of academic life that is relevant to the question of developing teaching, that of teamwork. Teamwork, despite widespread university rhetoric about scholarly collegiality, is not an outstanding feature of academic life outside the discipline within which academics work. Yet the ability to work in teams is highly prized in most areas of employment, and time and again it has been shown that effective extension of research and teaching outside the university requires a team-based approach, for example in providing effective workplace-based education.[18]

As the task of innovation grows ever more complex, so does the range of skills and expertise that is needed. The range of functions involved in university education can encompass:

- assessing students' credentials and giving credit for entry;
- designing and coordinating units and courses of study;
- designing and developing resources used in learning. These might include textbooks, videos, and computer packages;
- assessing resources for quality;
- navigating and advising students through choices of study options;
- delivering instruction, for example, by lecturing or demonstrating practical work in laboratories;
- acting as guide and mentor to students either singly or in groups;
- assessing, evaluating and providing feedback on student progress; and
- certifying completion of award programs.

Separation of some of the above tasks has been a long-standing feature of distance education, and it is being driven further as information technology and resource-based learning make an impact on campus. Some of these functions can and are being performed by non-academic staff, and some by people who work outside the university. Effective progress often requires teams of both academic and non-academic staff. This trend is becoming more prevalent as new cross-disciplinary fields are emerging, where expertise does not necessarily reside in academic departments, and where education is delivered in professional or commercial settings.

Some academics are not comfortable with this situation, nor with the notion that they need further training to become better teachers. These tensions become particularly noticeable as teaching and learning reform leads to more explicit separation of the above functions. The use of new technology may require input and support from specialist general staff with expertise in computer networks, CD-ROM production, graphic design, copyright law and the input of instructional designers - people with expertise in the design of teaching materials for particular groups of learners. In some cases, the academic is relegated to the less-than-central position of "content expert".

The factors that underlie the acceptance by academics of the need for change are complex. There are good reasons for being wary of change for its own sake, and of uncritical enthusiasm for using new technology. However, even the most sceptical lecturer will acknowledge that the current teaching and learning situation is far from ideal for dealing with today's needs for higher education. For some, everyday life is a matter of accommodating more urgent priorities, such as research or the need to teach large classes with fewer resources. For others, as we have mentioned, the will to do things differently is there, but not necessarily to do things the way others might wish.

Individual academic autonomy is highly prized. In the case of teaching, it is usually cast in terms of control over what is taught and how it is taught, although such autonomy becomes more problematic when the teaching is "sub-contracted" to graduate students and part-time staff, who have far less ability to exercise such control. One manifestation of this is the generally poor progress of open learning, in the sense of student control over what they should be learning.[19] Another is the reluctance of many academics to incorporate resources produced elsewhere into their courses. This has been dubbed the "Not Invented Here Syndrome". Such an attitude may seem incongruous, given the long-standing practice of using textbooks written by experts from all over the world. One difference is that extracts can be plucked from textbooks at the will of the teacher, but computer-based packages tend to come as a whole.

The world of academic work is changing. As the traditional academic functions are divided according to considerations of expertise and cost, rather than an all-encompassing job description of "academic", the concept of an academic community is further weakened. We are already seeing this in the mass-delivery distance education systems, where some staff specialise in providing core expertise in the development of learning resources, others in instructional design, and others are engaged solely as tutors to guide students at a distance.[20] As these tasks become specialised and as the staff undertaking them are engaged more and more on a contractual basis, the idea of "academic" as a job description becomes less meaningful. There are also profound implications for the university. The long-standing ideal of the university as a community of scholars, with organisational policies and procedures that flow from that base, is far removed from a core organisation that hires specialist staff on a contractual basis.

Not surprisingly, some academics see the push to reform teaching and learning as threatening. Some see it as an affront to their professionalism, driven more by the desire to be competitive and to save money than to improve student learning. There is often hostility towards what are seen as approaches imposed from "above", meaning at some level of organisation, whether a department, school, faculty, university or government.

Government involvement

Governments have recently taken a strong interest in promoting changes in teaching methods within universities. This stems in part from a desire to see greater productivity, meaning more graduates for the public dollar. Governments also doubt the quality and relevance of much university teaching; they want to see universities respond in appropriate system-wide ways to the various influences outlined earlier, particularly those that relate to expanding cost-effective equitable access to higher education. Over the past fifteen years the major involvement of the Commonwealth government in changing teaching has been to rationalise, and then de-rationalise, distance education; to provide grants for academics to experiment with new approaches; to attempt to provide a national infrastructure for network technology; and to sponsor the Open Learning Initiative.[21]

We have already mentioned the intervention by government, consistent with advice it received from universities, in the provision of distance education. Legitimate concerns with quality and cost led to an attempt to regulate the providers, rather than a distributed effort to improve quality that could take into account the general need for greater flexibility. One legacy of this intervention is that the status of distance education remains uncertain in several universities.

One way the government has fostered some productive change is through the use of grants. Grants have the attraction of being a quick means of producing visible activity in designated areas. A large number of projects experimenting with new approaches to teaching and learning flourished under government sponsorship in the 1990s. Most of these involved the use of computers and other technology to design "learning packages". Some major initiatives were also sponsored, the most significant being the establishment in August 1995 of five national "clearinghouses" for educational materials, known collectively as UniServe. These were given a grant of $1.1 million through the Commonwealth's Committee for the Advancement of University Teaching (CAUT) for the first three years of operation, and were supposed to provide ready access to educational materials, including those produced from government grants. The intention was to make these available at "cost price" only;

however, many details remained unclear. How could materials produced from a variety of funding sources be made available in such a way? How would costs be spread over the "lifetime" of a software package? How would quality control and peer review work?[22]

The two main drawbacks with any grant scheme are, first, that it is hard to take a systematic approach which will have a major influence, and second, when the money stops so does the activity. This observation applies equally well to grant schemes run within universities. Governments also tend to embark on schemes with the hope that in the future they will become self-funding. This is something that rarely happens in Australia. In the case of UniServe, plans for expansion were well under way at the time the first five centres were launched, and the Chair of the government's grant-giving committee was already referring to the $1.1 million as "seed money". "Now the seed is planted", he remarked, "a little bit of fertiliser would not be amiss."[23] As it turned out, the clearinghouses did not live up to the high expectations that accompanied their inception. The successor to CAUT, the less euphoniously named Committee for University Teaching and Staff Development (CUTSD), chose not to continue funding of the initiative.

Another key Government initiative in reforming teaching and learning was the Education Network Australia, or EdNA. Ministers were sure they wanted to do something to bring the benefits of the Internet and other technology to schools and universities, and they were fairly sure that it would be a good idea to establish some sort of network across the sectors. There were also thoughts about creating something like UniServe, to provide access to various educational resources. "The scope of this initiative is extremely open," said one member of the Commonwealth's EdNA task force with masterly understatement at a conference in August 1995.[24] A senior academic at the same conference described it as "very interesting, very confusing, and very worrying". Looking back in April 1997, a former Commonwealth Minister for Education, Peter Baldwin, commented that:

> The EdNA concept seems to have been overtaken by events - in a remarkably short period of time. Lest it be thought that I am implicitly criticising the then ministers (and bureaucrats) responsible, I have to acknowledge that the same point applied to an initiative of mine to create an electronic network for tertiary Open Learning students - this had the misfortune of coming into being just before the most useful technology - the World Wide Web - became widely

available.[25]

One final example of major government involvement in reform is that of the Open Learning Initiative. Open learning is a term frequently confused with distance education. In fact it means something a good deal wider, encompassing much more open entry to university courses and greater student control over the parameters of learning. It is a modern reformulation of the principle of *Lernfreiheit*, or student freedom, established as a parallel to academic freedom in the German university reformation of the early nineteenth century.

Open learning has more of a history in the United States than in Australia or the UK. Flexner made disapproving reference to it, when he wrote in 1930 of the ad hoc mix of subjects that students could choose to study at some universities, noting that some universities offered subjects by distance education for which they themselves would not grant credit towards an on-campus award, and that some universities waived entrance standards for off-campus enrolments while not wishing to do so for on-campus study.

In the early 1990s the Labor Government was faced with a situation where the demand for university places outstripped the number the Commonwealth was prepared to supply. The time was ripe for an experiment which would increase access to higher education, do it cheaply and at the same time introduce some innovations in flexibility. Building on some earlier trials, the intention was to use television as a broadcast medium in conjunction with various other technologies and print, to provide "a 'taste' of higher education . . . for those in the community who would not normally consider enrolling."[26] The term "open learning" was used to reflect the fact that entrance standards did not apply, and there was considerably more flexibility in regard to which units a student could choose to study.[27] Thus the Open Learning Initiative came into being at the start of 1992, effected through the Open Learning Agency of Australia Ltd (OLA). The OLA was established by Monash University and involved several other universities. The following year students commenced study under the Initiative.

OLA students are admitted freely, without reference to prior educational attainment, and can study units which give them credit towards awards at participating universities. These units are provided by various universities, and delivered by the OLA. Programs are broadcast nationally by the ABC in fixed time slots several times each week.

One unstated purpose of the Initiative was to deal with unmet demand without incurring high costs, while overt objectives had to do with widening access and promoting collaboration and credit transfer between universities.[28] As a broker rather than a university in its own right, the OLA was able to charge fees; indeed the intention was to cover its operating costs this way. The fee was set at the HECS rate of the time, which meant that it cost the student around the same as a university enrolment, but cost the government nothing for each extra student, because OLA enrolments were not counted as "load" which attracted normal grant funding. In effect, the running costs of OLA were structured to be around one quarter of the cost of a student enrolment in a public university. As the years have passed, the pressure arising from unmet demand has eased due to a combination of demographic factors and a slight fall in school retention rates. The OLA is now approaching self-supporting status, and has moved to widen its market by offering its service to overseas students and to the VET sector. For the time being it remains inexpensive, setting its fees at the HECS level that applied before the increases introduced in the 1996 Federal Budget. Whether it can sustain itself at that level in a competitive environment remains to be seen. Its role is now that of a commercial education broker which despite its description by executive director Tony Pritchard as a "virtual university"[29], does not offer its own degrees, but provides access to the awards of other institutions.

It is important to recognise that these initiatives have not arisen solely from the views of government ministers or Commonwealth public servants. Concerns about the proliferation of external education, and recommendations that it be regulated, were first voiced in the late 1970s and early 1980s by the government's advisory bodies, consisting of senior academics. Similarly, government intervention of one sort or another has been frequently advised by academics acting in an official or unofficial capacity. Nevertheless, the choice to accept such recommendations, and to pursue them in particular ways, remained a government prerogative.

There are good reasons for being sceptical about future government involvement in promoting teaching and learning reform. First, the direction of public sector reform has moved away from active involvement in "provider issues", as we noted earlier. Second, the track record of government intervention has been less than impressive, as exemplified in the experience of EdNA and the regulation of distance education. A cynic might observe that it is all very well for governments to exhort universities to employ modern technologies in what they do, but when it comes to running their own affairs, government departments are hardly shining examples of how to use information technology. Government policy on IT implementation has never been clear, and departments have lagged considerably behind both universities and the private sector in the use of electronic mail and the Internet. Third, system-wide top-down approaches will never be likely to succeed in a sector that adheres to traditions of academic independence and professionalism, and which is subject to forces which are moving it towards greater diversity. Governments and government officials tend to see higher education as being much more uniform than do those within universities, creating an inherent tension as government desires to rationalise and promote mass-production are frustrated by academic aspirations to specialise or tailor courses to local conditions.

*

If system-wide approaches have problems, and the work of motivated individuals does not cumulatively produce a sufficiently strong response, and if resources are tight and many academics mistrustful or sceptical, how should universities best respond to the winds of educational change?

The first point is that they should not all be responding in the same way. The prevailing influences call for greater diversity, not less. It is also likely that major cross-institutional programs will only be successful for a limited time, until technological and other developments lead institutions to seek more tailored solutions and to develop particular areas of advantage to them and to their student base. This is not to say that collaboration does not and should not occur, only that collaboration will need to be fluid and responsive to changes in technology and strategic direction.

The issue of rewards for academic staff who are good teachers, or rather the lack of such rewards, is frequently raised in discussions of promoting change. Typically, these mean extrinsic rewards, such as prizes and career advancement, as opposed to the intrinsic reward of a job well done. Prizes or awards for outstanding achievement may have a symbolic value, and promote debate about the subject, but the likelihood is that those who receive them would be those who would do well anyway. A more mainstream impact could be achieved by system-wide approaches, particularly to recognise good teaching in promotions and appointments. All universities say that they do this, but convincing the bulk of academic staff is no easy task.

However, rewards can only ever be one part of the picture. A major issue for any university is the need to take a fresh approach to the ways in which teaching and learning are organised. Most are burdened with the view that these matters are primarily academic responsibilities, subject to the individual academic as an autonomous professional, and distinct from the work of general staff and the functions of information technology.

The romantic notion of the university as a community of scholars, and little more than the sum of its academic parts, has worked against the idea that a university should focus on levels above that of the individual academic or, at best, the academic department. There is widespread resentment of corporate approaches to university management, resentment that is often justified by the often heavy-handed and cumbersome approaches taken to strategic planning and central oversight of academic activities. We will say more about this in a later chapter. However, if sustained and widespread innovation is to take hold in university teaching, it needs a focus on programs and courses as well as the encouragement of individual academic staff.

Most universities have attempted to promote innovation by scattering money to individual academics, who then engage in ad hoc and often unsatisfactory relationships with staff who are responsible for university computer systems or central production facilities. These systems and facilities, for example the purchase of major network upgrades or the provision of student access to the Internet, in turn proceed with relatively little academic input or clear relationship to the teaching and learning directions they are supposed to support. Meanwhile, separate staff development programs for academic and general staff reinforce these divisions, as do separate organisational and planning structures for teaching and learning development and the development of information technology.

The separation of technology from academic concerns serves to reinforce the erroneous idea that technology is somehow separable from the other considerations that accompany teaching reform. It allows academics to claim that change is being driven by technology, and it allows technical experts to accuse academics either of being Luddites or over-enthusiastic amateurs. Proponents of converting teaching to the World Wide Web can proceed in blissful ignorance of efforts by other arms of the university to adopt other innovative approaches to teaching and learning.

Staff development plays an important part in all of this. Training, assistance and other forms of development are needed to investigate different options, to become familiar with new technology and to share information. Communication and integration are the keys to successful staff development programs, and help to break down barriers between the various staff groupings.

It is also worth noting that the education and training of staff can suffer from precisely the same problems that were outlined earlier for ordinary students, and can also create some new ones. Large staff training groups become lectures, or series of short lectures, which do not cater for individual needs, while smaller groups and workshops often only attract the most interested staff. Professional staff do not like being told what to do. Instead, forums are held for "reflection", "sharing of ideas", "brainstorming" and other distributed pastimes. Unless carefully planned and managed, the outcomes of such events can be unsatisfying.

Whether staffing and technology support should be centralised or distributed around the university, and whether all components are provided by the university or some are contracted out, is a matter for each university to decide depending on its own strategic choices.

Strategic directions

One way of looking at strategic choices in this area was provided in a recent report undertaken for the Commonwealth Government by Phillip Yetton of the University of New South Wales.[30] He proposed three strategies for using information technology in teaching. While these are only about technology, and do not distinguish between different markets and different needs, they represent a useful starting-point for thinking about strategic directions in teaching:

- a value-added strategy, supposedly best suited for older "brand name" universities. This would aim to provide an individually customised high cost experience using a variety of systems for an elite market;

- a "cost-based" model, which aimed to provide standardised, high volume, centrally supported programs to a mass market; and

- a hybrid, which had a mix of centralised and decentralised support. Each area would seek to develop flexible responses within a powerful and standardised framework supported by the university.

The first approach is one that is most compatible with the traditional university mindset. It would rely on decentralised academic initiatives aiming to enhance quality, while drawing on the university's resource base and pulling power to sustain the higher costs involved. The obvious drawback is that it might work well for a wealthy elite university, but few if any of our universities have proved themselves immune to the tight financial climate, particularly since institutions cannot as yet set their own fees. In the United States some of the wealthier private universities have begun to move down this path, particularly in the field of professional education, which in the US is more at the postgraduate level than is the case here.

The second approach typifies the thinking behind the Open Learning Initiative. It makes explicit the idealised response to the operational influences, mentioned earlier, concerning cost and competition.

The third provides some sort of compromise, where efficiencies are realised by maintaining a standardised framework, but scope is allowed for areas to tailor approaches to suit their own markets.

It is useful to examine these matters a little further, not least because they are central to the current debate about "virtual universities" and the apparent threat created by the Internet and globalisation to Australian universities. In particular, a great deal of the attraction of the cost-based model hinges on the assumption that a quality university education can be delivered at low cost without the need for regular interaction with a teacher. How valid is this assumption?

Cost and quality

Thirty years from now the big university campuses will be relics. Universities won't survive. It's as large a change as when we first got the printed book. Do you realize that the cost of higher education has risen as fast as the cost of health care? ... Such totally uncontrollable expenditures, without any visible

improvement in either the content or the quality of education, means that the
system is rapidly becoming untenable. Higher education is in deep crisis ...
Already we are beginning to deliver more lectures and classes off campus via
satellite or two-way video at a fraction of the cost. The college won't survive
as a residential institution.

These apocalyptic comments came from Peter Drucker, a prominent
management guru.[31] Related sentiments were expressed by Eli Noam, in
a widely discussed article in a major science journal in 1995:

... a curriculum, once created, could be offered electronically not just to
hundreds of students nearby but to tens of thousands around the world. It
would be provided by universities seeking additional revenues in a period of
declining cohorts, though probably not at first by elite colleges, which guard
their scarcity value.[32]

Both authors were drawing attention to potential parallels between
what could happen to education and what was happening with other
sectors of the economy, particularly the manufacturing sector. The ability
to produce quickly and cheaply high volumes of customized product, using
new technology both in manufacture, advertising and distribution, has
been bringing about revolutionary change in the structure of many
manufacturing companies. Some see this as leading to the emergence of
the "virtual corporation", which will have flexible management structures
and will consist of temporary alliances designed to capture changing
markets.[33]

The parallel with the "virtual university" is interesting. Most people
use the term "virtual" for universities to mean that much if not all activity
takes place on the Internet, without needing a home location. Yet, as
previously mentioned, it is entirely possible that a "virtual university" will
emerge which is not only independent of a physical location, but operates
in a completely different way to the traditional higher education institution.

We should acknowledge that one version of a virtual university is
already here, in fact it has been in operation for many years. The Open
University in the United Kingdom is a large "virtual" university which
delivers its programs through distance education, and in that sense is
independent of physical location. However, it is an industrial model of
higher education, delivering mass product to a mass audience. This is very
different in structure and conception from the university as a virtual
corporation which is flexible, tailored to individual or corporate needs, and

fluid in structure.

As we mentioned earlier in this chapter, some fledgling examples of such virtual universities are emerging, some of which operate in ways entirely alien to the traditional academic culture. Most notably the traditional academic roles in teaching and research, encompassing a wide range of functions, have been separated, with only a small core of permanent staff concerned with overseeing the programs and the detail of course development and delivery contracted out to staff employed on a part-time and contract basis.

Conventional universities have also sought to cope with funding pressures by employing part-time teaching staff. In addition to staff who are employed on a contractual basis to teach part-time, many universities use graduate students as teaching assistants, and bring in people who work in relevant areas to lecture on a part-time basis. Nevertheless, the core of teaching staff are full-time; they are expected to undertake research, and there are constant industrial pressures from staff unions to reverse the trend towards part-time teaching.

There is a common assumption that delivering education through the use of materials and technology will reduce costs. This is based on the idea that conventional teaching is labour-intensive, with high ongoing costs spread out over the year and with costs escalating with the number of students. Conversely, resource-based and technology-based teaching will have relatively high start-up costs, but can accommodate a large number of students fairly cheaply. This may well be true, but it needs to be qualified.

To begin with, extra mileage can be squeezed out of existing systems by filling up any spare capacity in teaching spaces and by not increasing teaching staff in direct proportion to student load. This has in fact been the pattern over the past couple of decades, as teaching space has been used more effectively. Second, the cost of delivering education by way of a piece of software or print needs to take into account not only the cost of developing the package in the first place, but also constant updates to keep content relevant and to cope with regular technological change. Third, there are significant costs associated with what is known as "intellectual property". Quite a deal of good teaching material has been made available free of charge in the past. However, as universities and academics become more commercially canny, and as it costs more and more to produce such resources, this situation is unlikely to continue.

A fourth point in relation to costs is that ongoing student contact time will still be needed if conventional notions of quality are to be maintained. To some extent tutorial functions can be programmed into packages in the form of a "virtual guide". This programming will, however, increase the complexity and cost of packages and will have inherent limitations. Programmed communication is not true interaction; the student is still only selecting from a limited range of responses. Costs will vary considerably depending on the extent to which a human tutor is available, either contactable directly or via some delayed mechanism such as electronic mail.

The most tangible cost savings would come from the balance saved by "infrastructure costs". Whereas a physical university has the cost of lecture theatres, tutorial rooms and laboratories, the "on-line" university costs involve machines, networks or satellite links. However, when considering costs, it is also worth keeping in mind that the commercial providers do not supply students with computers; they are assumed to have the required equipment. Some American universities now require all their students to rent laptop computers. Others are charging for the computing infrastructure that is provided through the university. Most Australian universities will be following suit.

Ultimately, costs need to be considered on a "lifetime" basis, and will depend on the way that educational reform is structured. Harking back to the three strategic directions for information technology, universities might choose to follow a value-added, cost-based or hybrid approach depending on their student market.

On-line does not necessarily mean lower cost, particularly if the institution involved is able to charge a premium for convenient access to prestige. Duke University charges $82,500 for its on-line Global Executive MBA, with almost half the students enrolling from other countries, compared with $50,000 for the on-campus version.[34]

However, it is possible to deliver education cheaply by employing part-time staff, and delivering standardised material to a mass market. Provided sufficiently large numbers of students are involved, the main costs are those to do with paying only for the time teachers are actually involved in the process, and for development and maintenance of materials. Costs can be held down further by minimising the interaction between students and tutors. Such a scenario already exists for the many commercial providers of workplace-based adult education and training.

However there will be great variability in cost depending on the technologies used and the student numbers involved.

Some existing universities have tried such an approach, accommodating change within their existing staffing structures, although these are coming under strain for financial reasons. Some are competing in the workplace-based professional education market; others are offering general and vocational education to a mass market through on-campus and off-campus delivery. However, whether or not universities can achieve cost savings by these means and compete with non-university providers is far from clear, given their more rigid staffing arrangements and greater overhead costs.

In the case of the Open Learning Initiative, costs were kept artificially low. Its future role in the higher education sector will depend very much on whether it is either sustainable or accepted on a commercial basis, and what degree of personal interactivity is proposed to take place with students. One interesting proposition was put forward in April 1997 by the former Labor Minister responsible for universities, Peter Baldwin. His proposal was for a new paradigm for post-school education, reasserting the role of government in actively intervening in provision. This proposal would have government overseeing the development and provision of educational materials, made widely available at low cost, and associate this with a "learning account" that would put funding decisions in the hands of the student. The proposal amounted to "many OLAs". It is a very different proposal from the trends of the past, but its success would rely crucially on several difficult and questionable propositions. One of these - that educational materials can readily be produced and distributed at low or no cost to students - we have already found reason to question. His plan also relies on allocating learning accounts to prospective students, yet it is far from clear who would receive them, how they would be administered, or what value they should be. These questions will be considered later. One final point is that a return to active government involvement in the provision of education flies in the face of the trend towards contractualism that was noted earlier.

Other universities are following the "value-added" strategies outlined above, mixing technology with other approaches to develop higher quality on and off-campus learning experiences for students. In these instances there are more signs of higher costs rather than lower. This is particularly the case if resource-based learning and technology are used as an addition to "normal" teaching. Diana Laurillard of the UK Open University has modelled scenarios of the impact on staff time of different mixtures of face-to-face teaching and resource and technology-based learning. She noted that there would be high calls on staff time in the early years of change, with long-term implications depending very much on a wide range of variables, particularly the amount of materials that were brought in from outside.[35] Two American higher education writers, William Massy and Robert Zemsky, tried something similar. They modelled costs of a mixed approach, and concluded that it is possible to reconfigure the way teaching is conducted within a fixed funding level so as to reduce staff time costs and to increase student involvement in learning through use of resources.[36]

Effecting such change is not entirely straightforward. Courses designed for delivery on campus for one group of students cannot simply be transcribed onto paper or onto the Internet to suit another group of students learning by distance education. In 1997, one commercial company, RealEducation Inc, advertised its services to universities in creating "on-line campuses". The company made the remarkable claim that "course conversion will take a professor 2 hours a day for three weeks if they have taught the course on campus before. If it is a brand new course it will take about twice as long. Our people would not need to be on your campus for more than 5 days as the rest can be done over the Internet." By contrast, the UK Open University offers an 80 hour course designed to help people convert to the Web courses that are already structured for distance education. Nevertheless RealEducation has generated considerable interest and by the end of 1997 they were involved with 20 institutions and the development of an on-line associate degree program across the Colorado community-college system.[37]

Of course, lowering costs in any area of endeavour is usually possible by compromising quality. Is there any evidence of the effect on learning of the various changes in higher education practice? Unfortunately there does not seem to be any clear answer to this question. There are many studies indicating instances where students perform better under different systems, but the improvement is not attributable to any one aspect. Technology in itself does not lead to greater productivity. Students who have unrestricted access to the Internet may spend more time playing games, surfing for trivia or looking at pornography than deriving educational benefit. Better results may be due to the way the course was structured to suit the needs of the student, with problem-solving exercises, group work and greater individual attention, rather than the fact that it used particular technology or was delivered at a distance. Some students, either from innate ability, motivation, or because they have been well educated, are better able to cope without close interaction from a teacher. Others need more help.

Distance education is not necessarily of lower quality than on-campus education, particularly the type of minimally interactive lecture-driven program that is experienced by many undergraduates in Australia. Indeed many studies show that some students do just as well with notes delivered through the post and minimal interaction with tutors. There are no absolute measures of educational quality. A student's intellectual development depends on what he or she brings to the educational institution, what the institution provides by way of learning experiences, and how the student learns from it. The quality of *any* form of education will depend on the extent to which it is well designed, suits the needs of the students, challenges them to learn and apply knowledge, and provides useful interaction and feedback. Factors such as location or use of technology are secondary.

We have described in this chapter a variety of factors that can hamper the traditional university in embracing more effective teaching. It is clear that the quality of learning experience that an institution provides is inevitably constrained by the level of resources it has available. And this is far from being the only constraint. Under current Australian higher education funding mechanisms, universities cannot set their own resource levels by charging fees except in limited areas; instead they are more or less uniformly funded. Moreover, the level of funding is being progressively tightened, pushing universities to seek cheaper methods of teaching. Such a system works against fostering diversity in teaching methods. In the United States it is possible to find institutions like Swarthmore, a small, prestigious private college which specialises in general undergraduate teaching, and boasts a student to staff ratio of 9:1. The college employs no teaching assistants and instead requires all its full-time staff to contribute significant amounts of their time to teaching. This contrasts to the approach adopted by the University of Phoenix which, as we have noted, employs no full-time teaching staff but offers a considerably cheaper education. Deregulating the financing of higher education would undoubtedly encourage greater diversity, but would also raise complex questions about access and equity and have profound consequences for the future of some Australian universities. These matters are examined later.

Flexibility

Flexibility is the education buzz-word of the 1990s. Sceptics will point to the fact that we have always had some sort of flexibility in higher education, and that past predictions of revolutions brought about by technology have proved groundless.[38] They might also say that we have had waves of "fads" sweep through higher education that are now more peripheral, for example Total Quality Management in universities and institutional amalgamations. The hope of many academics is that if they dig themselves in and wait until the latest fad passes, then all will return to normal.

This, of course, will not happen. The pressure on university education comes from fundamental changes in Australia's economy and society, changes that are ongoing. Most universities recognise this, but none have progressed as far as they would have liked. A great deal of work has been done on mapping the issues, holding conferences, arguing, debating and quibbling over terminology. A great deal of money has been spent experimenting with new approaches.

Part of the difficulty with educational change comes from the labyrinthine nature of universities. Part of it comes from confusion about what should change and why. Some years ago, the dominant terminology was "flexible delivery"; it remains the term of choice for TAFE. However, many academics felt that this suggested a transmission model of education, implying change was only needed in what teachers did. The preferred term was "flexible learning". Then some people pointed out that it was students who did the learning, and a university can only set the conditions for learning, not make it more flexible per se. Perhaps "flexible education" is a more appropriate phrase. But what does it mean? Does it mean putting a course in distance education mode? Using CD-ROMs? Does it mean delivering fixed courses in more flexible ways, or does it mean being able to develop or re-design courses quickly to suit changing circumstances?

In fact "flexibility" covers four distinct purposes: convenience, quality, cost and choice. Distance education can be more convenient for students but, in its traditional form, can mean lower interaction and quality, and does not necessarily provide students with any choice. Students can be provided with a greater variety of options in on-campus study without greatly increasing the convenience for those who have to work and study part-time. Some academics remain sceptical about the extent to which quality can be reconciled with choice, particularly for students who are new to higher education. Harking back to Flexner's criticism of the "smorgasbord" university, the Commissioner of the Texas Higher Education Coordinating Board recently commented that:

> Those of us in higher education have learned some lessons from past experiments; for example, allowing students to design their own degree programs and granting college applicants academic credit for work or life experience. Students generally should not be permitted to design their own degree plans, because they don't know what they don't know. Nor do many people in the course of their jobs perform tasks of such breadth or intellectual substance that the work should be deemed adequate to constitute a university credential or credit toward such a credential.[39]

The four purposes of flexibility are often run together, the agenda based very much on particular contexts. Arguments about an all-embracing terminology are fruitless.

The shape of things to come

There are many pressures on universities to change the way they teach; many universities have made some progress towards beneficial change, but for the most part things remain much as they were decades ago. As more attention is focussed on teaching and learning, and as information technology exerts an ever greater influence on the process, profound implications are raised for the future of academic work. In particular, the link between teaching and research at an individual level is increasingly being called into question. The functions of teaching are being separated out and in some cases undertaken by non-academic staff or being contracted out; and the terms of engagement of academic staff are changing.

We mentioned earlier the hype about apocalyptic scenarios, where "Microsoft University" or "Disney University" is confidently predicted to emerge within a few years and render "traditional" Australian universities obsolete. Alternatively, doomsayers predict that within twenty years, the physical buildings of the universities will be obsolete, as all higher education will be conducted over IT networks.

It is easy to overestimate as well as to underestimate the threats posed in reality. There is likely to be considerable interest and competition in those areas of higher education that represent a potential commercial return, such as overseas students and some areas of postgraduate education and continuing professional education. As in all areas of commercial endeavour, providers will need to know their markets well and establish "niches" that build on their strengths. In other areas, notably in the domestic undergraduate market, competition is likely to remain, in at least the short to medium term, among existing universities, given the considerable advantages they enjoy in terms of established reputation and local relevance.

Information technology will change the way universities teach. Universities can no more afford to ignore the potential of developments such as the World Wide Web than they could afford to stick to typewriters and ignore the impact of computer-based word-processing. But the future, again at least in the short to medium term, does not necessarily lie in distance education, and in most cases, the missing ingredient is not computers. *It is interaction between students and teachers.* There is enormous potential for information technology to enhance interaction both on-campus and off-campus, but predictions that buildings will be obsolete within ten or twenty years miss the point. A variety of approaches can and should be adopted which take into account what students want, not just what "visionaries" can project. In many cases, students want to come to a physical campus and meet other students and practising academics. The socialisation aspect of university education, for undergraduates in particular, cannot be lightly dismissed, nor readily separated from the educational context in which it occurs. It will take many years, if ever, before "virtual" experiences provide a more than adequate replacement for, as opposed to supplement to, real life.

Having said this, it is clear that existing universities cannot afford to be complacent. Their survival depends on the ability to show that they can in fact offer the answers to contemporary challenges, in a unique environment and at reasonable cost.

The higher education market of the future will include both high-cost and low-cost education. Some areas of the market are amenable to the type of course that can be segmented, relying on mass-produced materials delivered cheaply at the students' convenience. Higher costs can be charged for greater degrees of interaction with tutors, for example for those who are experiencing higher education for the first time, and for access to "brand name" degrees. The emphasis would be on flexibility of course design as well as delivery. This type of education will particularly suit those who wish to obtain an award while still working, or those with family commitments. It will also be attractive to industries wishing to implement tailored on-site education and training programs for their staff.

Flexibility will also be suited to an environment where education brokers operate. Brokers of one sort or another are likely to grow in importance in the future, as they can provide customised response without the "baggage" that comes with a broader institutional mission, and they are well-placed to respond to a contractual environment. Brokers might seek tenders for the development of particular programs which universities would then bid for, as is the case for the OLA, or they might provide gateways for access to particular university programs, as is the case with the US-based National Technological University and the private JEC College Connection. The first is a private non-profit organisation that awards its own engineering and science degrees based on courses provided by participating universities. The second is a private for-profit organisation offering remote access, via satellite and other means, to courses at participating universities, but does not grant degrees itself. Its tag is "courses and degrees from recognised universities delivered right to your home or office".

Some courses are more suited than others to this sort of approach. Typically, on-line courses are in areas such as business, engineering and information technology.

In addition to mass education, some institutions will offer higher education that provides a more focussed interactive experience. This will incorporate both on- and off-campus study, mixing face-to-face work with independent study undertaken by the student using material delivered by information technology and, when appropriate, with guided placements in the workplace. It may also incorporate higher-cost uses of information technology that are more advanced than those which are likely to be available to the student at home. This might include complex interactive 3-D simulations of laboratory environments or "virtual" manipulation of materials. This educational experience will be more suited to students who are prepared to pay for higher quality over convenience, and for those undertaking certain professional courses which incorporate greater elements of specific professional requirements and practical work, such as medicine or engineering.

It is entirely possible that universities will combine both approaches, in much the same way that some offer courses in distance education mode. However, the delineation between distance education and on-campus education will not be so rigid; instead, distinctions will be based on the degree of interactivity and cost that is involved in developing and delivering a particular course, whether or not it involves on-campus study.

Collaboration in the production of learning materials will be important to ensure costs are kept to manageable levels, particularly in the "mass" situation. This collaboration could emerge more from informal than formal government-driven exchanges, and would occur both between different universities and between universities and other organisations. Some materials may be produced with government funds and made available at no or low cost. It is more likely that government will not wish to subsidise such activity indefinitely, and the production and exchange of resources will be a commercial activity with quality assurance and payment taking place on a case-by-case basis.

There is also likely to be an effort by many universities to extend higher education internationally to capture a greater share of the overseas student market. One approach might simply be to offer overseas students access to the local mass market education that can be delivered using information technology. Assuming that overseas students have access in their home country to the necessary technology, such an approach will face an increasingly competitive market, particularly in the light of the rapid development of competent and cheap commercial "virtual universities" in the United States. There is also the likelihood of on-line access to some courses, particularly in business and information technology, from prestigious universities around the world. Tony Bates, from the University of British Columbia in Canada, highlighted a number of factors that need to be taken into account in successful international delivery.[40] These included cultural and linguistic barriers; difference in degree structures and lengths; availability of suitable communications infrastructure; and the costs of development, maintenance and delivery. To this list might be added difficulties arising from time differences and exchange rates and the task of administering and assessing applications. Clearly, the internationalisation of higher education will not be as straightforward as some have supposed.

Flexibility will be needed in design as well as delivery, particularly for those institutions which wish to compete in more volatile markets such as workplace-based education and training or delivering education to overseas students where accreditation requirements may be less stable. This will require major shifts in the way coursees are designed and approved in most universities.

Such niches may well be characterised by mixes of types of education. These types include award or non-award courses at various levels; general or vocational education at undergraduate level; and research or professional education at postgraduate level. Within each of these fields, different strategies may be pursued to attract the target catchment of students (whether local, regional, national or international). Universities may wish to emphasise quality, convenience, professional relevance, staff-student interaction, the social benefits of a campus life and so on. It is likely that many universities will hope to cover all these bases, but in practical terms the intake, cost and delivery will vary according to what is achievable.[41]

Depending on the context, some courses may well be amenable to being broken up into modules that can be delivered flexibly and linked together. At postgraduate level, for example, a university might develop a suite of offerings that commence as short components for graduates in the workplace to update their skills, and progressively build through accumulated credit into Graduate Certificates, Graduate Diplomas and Masters awards. Some or all of these could be delivered electronically and cross-credit might be given to awards from other institutions. At the undergraduate level, similar arrangements might apply, but it will be important to ensure that a coherent program of study is assured that imparts a proper measure of breadth and depth.

These changes are already happening, albeit slowly in Australia. The structural and attitudinal barriers mentioned above remain formidable. Yet even under the weaker form of competition that characterises the current Australian situation, where diversity is dampened by more or less uniform funding and where resources are allocated on the basis of institutions rather than students, universities are moving to position themselves to respond more effectively to different segments of the educational market. It is likely that in years to come they will receive even less government support to do this, and they will face even greater competition from other education institutions within Australia and from overseas, particularly in areas where there is a strong commercial demand. This will have profound consequences for the revenue base of most universities.

It is worth repeating that major changes are in train for academic work. The various functions of academics are being "unbundled", some offered as contracts or on a part-time or casual basis and some being undertaken by non-academic staff. Expertise will no longer be taken as a given; it may be the case in the future that some form of formal qualifications in teaching will be required of teaching staff. More and more, academic staff are being asked to work in teams which may include non-academic staff. This is more evident as universities move into areas that rely on information technology. Under these circumstances the traditional lines of academic authority and ownership are changing. A major challenge for universities will be to ensure that their processes continue to provide rewarding and productive environments within which academic and non-academic staff can work.

Redefining the place of teaching and learning within the university will mean challenging some of the most cherished traditions and practices of university life and will raise hard questions about the place of research and the most effective methods of managing change. In the next two chapters we will examine some of these questions.

CHAPTER SIX

Research: Making it Count

Fifty years ago there was little research occurring in the existing Australian universities. Today, research dominates higher education and it is widely accepted in university circles (if not enshrined in national policy) that all academics should be researchers, and that the mark of a true university is the production of research and the output of PhD graduates.[1] Research work is prestigious and influential in decisions about academic appointments and promotions; its outputs amenable to measurement and readily open to judgements about quality through peer review.

At the outset, it is worthwhile examining further what we mean by research. To most, "research" means what Ernest Boyer called the "scholarship of discovery", that is, the uncovering of new knowledge. In keeping with the distinction between knowledge and information maintained earlier, research should mean more than the uncovering of information. To some, research includes the use of surveys to establish opinions, or the description of clinical symptoms of a new disease. To others an activity is only research when part of a larger program of analysis, or where a particular hypothesis is being tested. Academics in the humanities would include new interpretations of existing texts as research, while new challenges to the definition are being posed by the entry to universities of fields such as the Visual and Performing Arts. Some people may draw a distinction here between research and creative expression. Borders may also be blurred between research and intervention programs in cases where researchers are working with communities to deal with problems of public health.

Nevertheless we will use the term to encompass a broad range of activities, held together by the idea that research in the university setting is the professional extension of one academic discipline or more, whether this be biology, history or the performing arts.

It is understandable that research is attractive to many academics. Universities are, after all, places of the intellect, and the pursuit of hitherto unrevealed knowledge is one of the most satisfying uses of the intellect. It enables academics to participate in international communities and, if successful, to achieve the respect of their peers and recognition and standing in their chosen field. As Slaughter and Leslie observed, research is also prestigious, particularly externally-funded research, because it is an activity that differentiates among academics and universities. But why should it be important to the broader community and, if it is important, who should decide the nature of this research?

The importance of research

A person or organisation can only deal effectively with change if they have some understanding of what is changing and why. New knowledge is needed to adapt to new circumstances, whether we are talking about a new disease, changes in economic conditions, or developing social issues.

We know that research and development are essential for economic development. Manufacturing firms which sustain innovation, particularly in the low and medium technology fields, are likely to be more competitive in the export market. This in turn is strongly related to the amount they spend on research and development. Around the world, there has been a long-term trend towards increasing trade in high-technology products, in industries such as aerospace, electronic equipment and pharmaceuticals, which depend heavily on research and development.[2] The Australian Science and Technology Council estimated in 1996 that if Australia increased its total investment in research and development effort from 1.7 per cent of GDP to 2.5 per cent of GDP (or around 2.5 billion dollars per year), then within ten years our national income would be $60 billion higher.

Some have argued that while it is undeniable that research is necessary to create new knowledge, benefits come from the application of this knowledge rather than from its creation. AIDS, for example, is a disease of international scope, and massive research programs are being undertaken in Europe and the United States on funding a vaccine or cure. Why should we try to duplicate this? Would not it be better to wait until results became available and then assimilate these findings? Since short-term profitability and competitive edge come from product improvement and change, rather than the higher-risk strategy of branching out into entirely new fields, proponents of this view argue that we should be directing most of our effort to industrial research and development or, at best, into translating offshore research into products.

There are several reasons why these views are misguided. Research results from overseas will not come to us free of charge. These results - and often the developed products - will be overseas-owned. Further, there has been an ongoing trend towards commercial involvement in research. The results of these endeavours are not available in the public domain, as the commercial sponsors seek to recoup their investment by patenting findings. We will either need to pay directly or by way of licensing arrangements for the "intellectual property" of others. As partners in research, Australians will be better placed in pricing arrangements, and also to take earlier advantage of new findings. Scientists often refer to this partnership as "the seat at the table"; it might include access to candidate drugs for clinical trials, or the opportunity to enter into international industrial collaborations.

A strong level of domestic research expertise is also necessary if we are to make best use of knowledge that has been developed overseas. We cannot build on what others have done if we do not have a body of skilled people trained in research in the first place. In addition, as the Harvard economist Michael Porter has observed, firms which rely for innovation on overseas technology will be always a generation behind, and will lose competitive advantage.[3] Finally, Australia needs to conduct research on matters that are unique to Australia. In the case of AIDS, for example, overseas research will be of little help in combatting spread of the disease in Aboriginal communities.

Japan appears to have recently accepted many of these arguments for basic research. For many years it relied on high levels of industrially-driven applied research, but in 1997 the Japanese government announced that it would seek to lift research and development expenditure from 0.6 per cent to 1 per cent of GDP. An editorial in the international journal *Science* noted that at its currently low level, "the vast majority of Japanese scientists, especially in the basic sciences, have not had the opportunity to participate in rapid developments in scientific research".[4]

At one level the situation is clear. If Australia is to be economically competitive then it needs to conduct its own research and development to foster innovation in knowledge-based industries. Research is also needed to maintain and improve our quality of life, for example in the fields of health and environment, and to enable informed decisions to be made about social issues, such as economic and welfare policy.

But what sort of research should we be doing? There is a constant tension in all countries that undertake substantial amounts of research between "applied" and "basic" research. The application of research to real problems presupposes an existing body of fundamental knowledge. It is said that a former chairman of the Commonwealth Government's medical research funding body carried about with him a paper which he would brandish in the face of any person who questioned the importance of basic research. The paper reported a study which traced back the key research contributions to diagnosis, treatment and prevention of heart disease, and found that two-thirds of those contributions derived from basic rather than applied research.[5]

Basic research is sometimes defined as the pursuit of knowledge for its own sake. But there is something of a problem with this formulation. Society might accept the need to pay people to uncover knowledge which might not in itself have immediate or short-term application, on the understanding that this knowledge provides a base for practical application at a later time. Society may be more reluctant if this task was portrayed as an activity that should be supported because it had intrinsic merit (in the same way that a country might have publicly-funded arts programs). Do we need to support in the same philosophical and pragmatic way, research into medieval European literature, the functioning of the human immune system, or astronomy?

There are some who argue that universities should be places where research without practical applications is protected. But there is a world of difference between arguing that some research is needed for which no use can be assigned, and arguing that impracticality is a virtue in itself. Sir Peter Medawar argued this point strongly some years ago, when he criticised the elevation of the term "pure" to describe basic research: ".. we make a special virtue of encouraging pure research in, say, cancer institutes or institutes devoted to the study of rheumatism or the allergies - always in the hope, of course, that the various lines of research, like the lines of perspective, will converge somewhere upon a point. But there is nothing virtuous about it! We encourage pure research in these situations because we know no other way to go about it. If we knew of a direct pathway leading to the solution of the clinical problem of rheumatoid arthritis, can anyone seriously believe that we should not take it?[6]"

Unfortunately, there are no reliable criteria for determining whether the results of research may ultimately prove useful. There are plenty of examples of research which was at one time considered useless, and which later proved to be important. Nothing could seem further removed from application than the study in the nineteenth century by several mathematicians of how geometry might work on curved surfaces, yet it laid the foundation for Einstein's general theory of relativity in the early years of the twentieth century. Radio waves were cited in an 1892 Grammar of Science as an example of a discovery with no apparent usefulness.[7] Even myrmecology, the study of ants, has turned up some practical applications in the mining industry, as these insects have proven to be useful "bio-indicators" of environmental regeneration after mining.

The definition of "useful" also deserves some consideration. The term implies that research leads somewhere that we want to go, that it contributes to some goal that society or a particular "user" wants. It is easy to see this in terms of economic goals, particularly given Australia's pressing needs to enhance the knowledge-base of its industries, or in terms of finding solutions to the many immediate social problems facing the country. However, society's goals may include enhancement of culture and social understanding. Like millions of others around the world, many Australians were fascinated by the landings on Mars in 1997, though this offered no obvious social or economic benefit. We support research into fields such as archaeology, astronomy and literature even though it could be argued that we would be no worse off materially if we knew nothing of dinosaurs, or of the "big bang" and if we left people to make their own minds up about literature.

We should not pretend that all basic research will eventually "pay off" in social, cultural or economic benefits to the Australian community, or that all research has equal potential. But it is of enormous importance that a solid foundation of basic research is supported in Australia, a foundation that cannot be laid on the basis of judgements about the usefulness of the research being undertaken. It comes as something of a shock to incoming governments and their advisers to find that basic research funding cannot be allocated on the basis of tidy cost-benefit calculations. In practice, the costs are straightforward, the benefits diffuse.

This does not mean that it is impossible to distinguish between different disciplines, or that there should not be some clear basis for making decisions about the amount of money which funds, for instance, medieval European literature, immunology or astronomy. What it does mean is that these decisions about basic research are not amenable to

objective assessment, and that judgements are best made by a community
of researchers, within parameters that are understood and accepted by
government and the community.

Nor does this mean that those outside the universities cannot and
do not have a say in research priorities. We will consider later some of the
means by which this is achieved.

The role of universities in research

Universities play a central role in basic research. Organisations
which have specific missions (such as private companies or government
departments) usually do not have the resources or the forward perspective
to conduct sweeping programs of basic research. The outcomes of these
programs are unpredictable, and may not in fact be "captured" by the
organisation that instigated them. Instead these organisations, to the extent
they undertake research, focus on the application of research in ways that
meet their missions, whether this is to gain competitive advantage in the
marketplace or to implement government programs.

Not all the research undertaken in universities is basic. Plenty of
high quality research is positioned at various points on the spectrum of
applicability. Australian Bureau of Statistics research data for 1994 show
that "pure basic" research, or research with no particular application in
mind, comprises around 36 per cent of university expenditure on research.
Another 25 per cent is "strategic basic" research, which is directed towards
particular ends but not of immediate applicability. A further 33 per cent is
"applied research" while the remaining 6 per cent is experimental
development of research results.[8] At various levels, universities play the
role of competitor or collaborator with other organisations undertaking
applied research. Basic research is not, of course, the exclusive preserve of
universities. Some larger companies support in-house research that is
longer-term; there are numerous institutes and centres, particularly in the
field of medical research, which conduct high quality basic research and
which are separate from universities.

A wide range of organisations is involved in the knowledge creation
business. Indeed, nearly three quarters of Australia's research and
development activity takes place outside the universities, in places such as
industry, government departments, and the CSIRO.

The principal role of the universities is to act as a resource base for this effort, including the production of trained researchers, and to enable an interaction to occur between research and teaching. There are two questions that arise in relation to this role. How good is the quality of this base, and how effectively is it tapped?

Our national report card

At one level, the question of quality is constantly asked and answered by researchers themselves. Grants for basic research are usually awarded on the basis of scientific merit, where proposals are scrutinised by peers along with the past performance of those submitting the proposals. Large grants such as those which are made to research centres and institutes are under regular review, usually every five years, by panels which include eminent overseas experts. The results of research are usually made available for all to see. The process of allocating research funding - particularly under a competitive grants scheme - tends to be more open to scrutiny, competitive and externally-evaluated than in many other endeavours, for instance, teaching. Peer group review of quality may seem incestuous, and has been criticised for being conservative, overlooking innovative research that does not fit the prevailing disciplinary mould. However, no satisfactory alternatives have been found for allocating limited amounts of research money for basic research.

Grant-funded research accounts for most of the research undertaken within a university. This was not always the case, but over the past two decades there has been a steady shift from funding research through the operating grants given to universities (and which they may use at their discretion), towards paying for research by way of competitively-awarded grants. This has certainly assured quality - as determined by peer review - for an ever-increasing slice of the university research pie. Some academics, however, maintain that this has been at the expense of government control, and loss of the ability to undertake ground-breaking research that goes against prevailing wisdom. We will consider these propositions later.

The most recent attempt to measure research strengths in a national and systematic way was undertaken by the Bureau of Industry Economics (BIE) in 1995.[9] The BIE measured both the inputs (the funding and staffing of research) and the outputs (publications in scientific journals, the number of times other scientists referred to those publications, patents, and links with industry), and compared the results with other developed countries. It should be kept in mind that systematic results are only available for scientific research, rather than research in the arts and social sciences.

The BIE found that Australia contributes just over 2 per cent of the world's scientific publications. This is higher than would be expected on the basis of our population and income. Moreover, since 1988 Australian scientists have increased their rate of publication in leading world scientific journals. The positive impact of Australian papers is suggested by the fact that they are widely cited by other scientists, having the third highest citation rate among APEC countries, behind the US and Canada. The BIE also found that Australia publishes across a broad range of scientific fields, and maintains high quality across that range. Our main areas of publication are in medical and biological sciences, chemistry and plant and animal science. The highest rates of citation occur in the fields of molecular biology and genetics, immunology, neuroscience, astrophysics, biology and biochemistry. There is some evidence that we are falling behind in terms of the relative impact of our papers in several fields, including immunology, chemistry and materials science, and while hypotheses abound the reasons for this remain unclear.

In general Australia is considerably stronger in basic scientific research than in applied technology research and development. Imports of high-technology goods and services are double our exports in services and four times our exports in goods. One positive sign here is that the growth rate of high-technology exports exceeds that of other manufacturing exports.

These patterns make sense in terms of our funding of science and technology. Most our total research and development (R&D) funding comes from government[10], and most of that goes to government research agencies (including the CSIRO) and to universities. Research supported by public funds, particularly university research, tends to be less directly applied and technological. Universities account for around one quarter of all R&D spending in Australia, which is a higher proportion than most other OECD countries. In terms of levels of R&D spending compared to size of the economy, Australia ranks around the middle of OECD countries for government spending, and near the bottom (better only than New Zealand, Canada, Greece, Spain and Portugal) in terms of business expenditure. Our business expenditure on R&D has improved over the past decade, probably as a result of government incentives which we will consider later.

As a measure of productivity, the BIE compared our rate of patents, publications and citations with inputs in the form of total R&D expenditure and the number of research scientists and engineers. Among OECD countries, our performance per dollar was well above average, while performance per person was in the middle range. This might suggest that we spend less on our scientists and engineers than do other countries, and indeed this is the case. A 1995 government report[11] found that wages for researchers and scientists in Australia are considerably lower than in other developed countries and the rapidly developing Asian countries (with the exception of Indonesia and Malaysia). Australian scientists are paid about 90 per cent of their UK counterparts, 68 per cent of the US rate and 37 per cent of Japanese scientific salaries. This situation was presented as a comparative advantage by the BIE: Australia should be an attractive ground for business R&D because we have abundant expertise which is relatively poorly paid. Not surprisingly, scientists take another view; Professor Ian Lowe from Griffith University deplored the low salaries paid to scientists, arguing that they will discourage talented people from entering a career in research.[12] Nevertheless, the BIE report demonstrated that in recent years there has been, in raw number terms, a net inflow of scientists and engineers to Australia: a "brain gain" rather than "brain drain". Such numbers do not, however, tell us anything about the *quality* of import or export of expertise. In particular, the figures do not tell us whether or not we are experiencing a loss of young researchers who may be in their most innovative and productive years.

Research into practice

The overall picture is that a strong program of domestic research and development is vitally important to Australia's future. Universities play a central role in laying the base for this program. Australia is around middle-rank of developed countries when it comes to spending public money on research, and we have as a consequence a strong and broad foundation of scientific research. But we are lagging in terms of business support for research and the translation of research into products and practice.

In the early 1980s the Federal Government recognised this situation, acknowledging that we needed higher levels of applied research and business spending on research and development if we were to improve economic productivity significantly. There were two areas that needed stimulus. The first was research and development driven by business, much of which was conducted "in-house". The second was to improve the linkages between business and researchers to accelerate the process of converting research into application.

In the first case, the main boost was delivered by way of indirect mechanisms, such as pricing subsidies and tax breaks. These have the advantage of placing decision-making about research and development in the hands of industry rather than government. The disadvantage, from the point of view of Treasury, is that these indirect mechanisms can be open-ended, difficult to monitor and open to abuse. The three most significant measures were a tax concession of 150 per cent on industrial research and development, syndication arrangements whereby firms could transfer tax losses to research consortia, and the "Factor F" scheme, which provided subsidies for the pharmaceutical industry in exchange for investment and research in Australia. Together these measures helped lift Australian business spending on research and development from a level that was disastrous to one that is now merely mediocre.

Unfortunately, the future of these schemes has been under a cloud in recent years. They have all been thoroughly reviewed and examined, and some instances of dubious practice have come to light involving research syndicates. In the 1996 Budget, the Commonwealth announced that it would reduce the tax concession from 150 per cent to 125 per cent. It also abolished the syndication arrangements, replacing them with the R&D Start program. After considerable delay and speculation, the successor to the Factor F program was also announced in the 1997 Budget. In that Budget, covering the period when the changes came into full effect, it was estimated that industry R&D funding had fallen by 5 per cent after inflation.

The situation was improved in December 1997 with a boost to industry R&D schemes as part of an industry development package announced by the Government. The package provided additional funding and widened eligibility for the R&D Start program and for venture capital and technology diffusion. While falling short of making up the cuts in the 1996 Budget, the package should renew impetus to business-driven R&D, and also provide opportunities for universities to increase their role in bringing the results of research to commercial fruition. These opportunities will depend upon universities establishing effective relationships with business.

Most industrial research and development in Australia is conducted in-house. Australia has comparatively few instances of "spin-offs" from university research and few companies with links to public research institutions such as universities or the CSIRO.[13] A survey by the Australian Bureau of Statistics[14] found that Australian manufacturing businesses tend to look to in-house R&D and market-driven contracts for sources of information for innovation. They rate university research as of little or no importance in industrial innovation, though other recent surveys have suggested that this may be changing. The Australian situation reflects international attitudes by business towards universities. Repeated international business R&D surveys "confirm that the training of a competent, high level science workforce is the primary task that the business sector expects to be fulfilled by the higher education sector, even prior to research."[15]

The simple view of innovation that involves universities is that it is basically a linear process. In one direction - the "demand-driven" approach - the "users" have an idea or a product that needs improvement. They contract or commission research to be conducted by a research organisation, the results of which are turned into something new. In the other direction, "supply-driven", research is conducted in universities and other research organisations, the results made public, and then "users" build on those results.

Demand-driven commissioned and contract research is a common feature within the university system. It provides a direct mechanism for making available the expertise within the university to those outside, and in the process provides valuable income for the university. However, it can run into problems with academic ethics and ideals of freedom and openness, particularly if the parameters governing ownership of the research are not made clear at the outset. The international journal *Science* ran an editorial in 1996 entitled "A Cautionary Tale", describing the experiences of some university researchers who took a contract with a pharmaceutical company to undertake research into the difference between generic drugs and the company's "brand name" drug. The company was unhappy with the findings of the research, and demanded that the researchers retract a report of their results made in the scientific literature. The university did not back the researchers, and they in turn capitulated to the company's demands.[16]

While government should not be in the business of subsiding directly industry-commissioned research in universities, it does play the role of "user", or at least broker, in relation to research that might have benefits for public programs. Commissioning research has always appealed to ministers, members of the general public and public servants; they want direct answers to their questions and their focus is usually on a short-term response to an immediate need. In many cases this works out satisfactorily, particularly if the question is the sort that can be answered by straightforward application of research techniques, such as the administration of a survey questionnaire. It can also work if the commissioning body is not sure what it wants to do with the results, but wants to see research undertaken in a specific area. To this end, the Commonwealth Department responsible for higher education has commissioned dozens of research studies into various higher education issues over the past few years, though the take-up of many of these studies' findings is questionable.[17]

It is more worrying, however, when the impetus for research activity derives from political motives, regardless of the projected potential and capacity for worthwhile research. One example is the injection of large sums of money in Australia and the United States over recent years into research on breast cancer. Rather than any assessment of the research capacity of the country, or the best research strategies for dealing with the problem, significant sums of money were dedicated to particular research based on lobbying from affected families and some researchers in the field. The difficulty here is that better results will probably flow from deeper understanding of the basics of the problem than by directing large amounts of research money at the symptoms. There is also a danger that researchers will be encouraged to "dress up" proposals to appear relevant to areas of priority. Some questions are not simply answerable by high quality research, either because there is not a sufficiently broad base of basic knowledge, or because there are few good researchers working in the field. In such circumstances the question is whether it is better to support mundane research in an important area, or excellent research that may be in an area of broad priority, but not directly related to specific practical outcomes.

In the direction of "supply-driven" innovation, the focus has been on ensuring that Australian industry is aware of the useful research taking place in universities. Governments and universities have sought to encourage academics to commercialise their research and to promote proper protection of intellectual property, so that wherever possible the benefits of research flow to Australia. A salutary lesson of what can happen if research is not properly commercialised was provided by the CSF story in the 1970s. Australian researchers working at the Walter and Eliza Hall Institute for Medical Research in Melbourne discovered some proteins, called colony-stimulating factors (CSFs), which stimulate the development of blood cells. By promoting growth of blood cells these proteins proved particularly useful in helping patients recover after bone-marrow transplants. The discovery was picked up and commercialised by an American pharmaceutical company, which has reaped enormous rewards as a result. The Australian benefit has largely been the warm glow of academic recognition. Nowadays such a situation is much less likely to occur. In the case of Victorian medical research, the State government sponsored the establishment of a commercial company, AMRAD, which has first bite at any research coming out of the major research institutes. AMRAD has since expanded its portfolio in the pharmaceutical industry and extended its coverage nationally. Most universities have units dedicated to the commercialisation of their research, and have developed policies governing the ownership and licensing of intellectual property.

Around ten years ago, the Federal Government put considerable emphasis on the "commercialisation" of publicly-funded research. Public research funding bodies were asked to look at ways in which they could encourage academics to take their work to market, and funds were set aside for this purpose. Some business leaders complained that academics should not be driving the research agenda, that it should be driven by business. Academics countered by saying that business did not know what it did not know, and that short-term research was not in the country's best interests. A favourite saying of many medical researchers was that if industry was in charge of medical research into polio, we would not have developed a vaccine, but we would have better iron lungs.

In 1992 the Government declared that excellence should not be the only criterion for allocating basic research through schemes such as the Australian Research Council. It decided that "the potential of research to contribute to the needs of research users, the potential for innovation, contribution to research training and contribution to international links" were also significant factors.[18] However, it was not clear how these criteria were to be assessed, by whom, and in what proportion. The Australian Research Council (ARC) included a requirement that its panels assess "relevance" when considering applications for research grants. Reviewing this arrangement in 1993, the Industry Commission noted that it was questionable whether ARC selection panels could make "meaningful assessment based on such criteria" and argued that programs which aimed "predominantly at funding the advancement of knowledge ... should use excellence as the only criterion."[19]

There has been a growing realisation that the nexus between university research and innovation is a good deal more complex than suggested by linear models. An effective innovation system cannot be based on pulling by industry or pushing by funding bodies to alter the nature of basic research.

In practice the links between researchers and the users of research involve two-way exchanges of information. The nature of these exchanges, and the extent to which the research is basic or applied, depend very much on the specific context, including the type of industry. The pharmaceutical industry, for example, relies heavily on basic scientific research in immunology and molecular biology. On the other hand the information and data communications industry relies more on in-house basic research and applied research in academic fields such as mathematics and computing.[20]

The essence is collaboration. Just as a person's character is the result of a complex interplay of nature and nurture, effective practical application of research often involves ongoing interaction between the agendas of the researchers and the needs of the users. This is a relatively new experience both for Australian business and for academics. Research collaboration has usually meant work undertaken between colleagues within the boundaries of a particular discipline.

Barriers to effective collaboration between business and universities have been examined in detail in various government and industry reports. These have found that the most important problems arise over differences of expectations and culture. Many Australian businesses have not had experience in research and development, and find it hard to adjust to the timescales involved. Some seek applied research of a fairly mundane nature in order to make an incremental change to gain immediate advantage in the marketplace, whereas original and curiosity-driven research is more likely to be attractive to academics. The ownership and publication of research findings are frequently controversial. Competitive advantage for private business is often gained through limiting access to research findings, while academics thrive in a climate of open publication. The pricing of research can also be inhibiting; businesses have no incentive to collaborate if research can be done at lower cost in-house, while universities have sometimes lacked the accounting skills necessary to determine appropriate charges. Some businesses prefer to deal directly with researchers, claiming that university commercial arms are too bureaucratic and inflexible. On the other hand, universities have to ensure a proper rate of return on assets used. Issues of pricing and intellectual property will escalate as universities rely more on commercial income and as the "competitive neutrality" provisions of National Competition Policy are applied.

There is, therefore, a careful balance to be struck between institutional interests and entrepreneurship. Universities need to encourage relationships and collaborations without imposing overly-cumbersome restrictions. Some of the most outstanding successes in university-industry collaboration are built on informal and flexible approaches from universities. For many years Cambridge has adopted a laissez-faire approach. It makes no rigid claims on intellectual property, relying instead on individual negotiations and indirect returns from intellectual stimulation and grateful benefactors. Such an approach has attracted a considerable amount of business activity to the area, the most notable recent addition being an $US80 million research facility, announced by Microsoft in June 1997, which would be separate from the university but closely linked. Microsoft also announced a further $16 million in venture capital for local high-technology firms. A similar approach characterises the relationship between Stanford University and Silicon Valley in California. The University relies little on codified procedures, and does not seek to gain substantial direct economic return on intellectual property. There is considerable traffic between the university, venture capitalists, and the computer industry. The University benefits from endowed Chairs, high demand courses in entrepreneurship and in relevant computing fields, and from donations by alumni and business. Business benefits from access to ideas and people. Above all, the system revolves around personal networks, which are fostered by movements of people between university and the outside world.

Such situations do not translate directly into other contexts. Success requires a conjunction of venture capital, university expertise, business opportunity and an entrepreneurial environment and cannot be based on an approach which sees innovation as providing a direct or short-term source of income for universities.

Societal and technological change demands a response of higher education. It calls for teamwork and breaking down boundaries between disciplines, and between academics and other people with relevant expertise. We discussed earlier the traditionally isolated and inward-looking nature of academic work and the limited nature of academic collegiality. That theme recurs here. The pivotal event in the training of researchers is the PhD. Often the PhD involves several years of isolated study, under the guidance of a principal supervisor.[21] As Columbia University's David Damrosch has observed, "when people acculturate themselves to academic life by enhancing their tolerance for solitary work and diminishing their intellectual sociability, they reduce their ability to address problems that require collaborative solutions, or even that require close attention to the perspectives offered by approaches or disciplines other than one's own."[22]

Damrosch was describing the US experience of postgraduate research. However, the Australian situation is similar. Damrosch suggests that if postgraduate research is to remain a solitary activity, then the intellectually sociable undergraduate should be warned of this before embarking on such a course. This might at least reduce the high levels of drop-out that occur in postgraduate research. Preferably, he argues, graduate research should be a more open and collaborative process. The mentor-disciple relationship can certainly be productive, and should be retained as one of the available options, but it should not be the only option available. One particular suggestion he makes is that assessment of final outcomes could be more flexible; instead of the expected product being a single, large and often ponderous thesis report, it might be a collection of research articles written under the supervision of a number of different academics.

Damrosch is well aware that changing the nature of postgraduate research organisation will require no less than a fundamental shift in academic culture; it needs more than rhetoric or altered processes since disciplinary fragmentation runs deep in the workings of academe. It will also experience many of the same barriers we enumerated in relation to changing the methods of teaching, particularly the difficulty of finding sufficient staff motivation and time in an era of contracting budgets.

Nevertheless, while research training remains a solitary, narrow and isolated rite of academic passage, the university environment will do little to encourage collaboration between researchers, much less between researchers and the users of research results. The situation is compounded by the relatively low mobility of people between universities and industry. Contrast the much closer relationships that exist in the area of clinical medicine, where it is commonplace for university academics to have dual appointments and work both in the university and in a teaching hospital. Collaborative research and innovation are also not encouraged by most university policies for reward and promotion of academic staff. As the OECD has observed:

> Generally the greatest attention is paid to assessments made by peers on the basis of pure scientific criteria as well as to publication records (preferably in mainstream journals and related citations). These criteria are obviously not very appropriate when considering more direct contributions to innovation, either through patenting, collaborations with industry, technology transfer, or even training of scientists and engineers to be further employed in industry. In most countries, there is an increasing awareness of the need to adjust evaluation and promotion procedures and to take into consideration broader outcomes than the usual scientific outputs, but progress is slow and, in fact, none of the evaluation systems currently in place give precedence to innovation-related work.[23]

During the early 1990s the Federal Government contributed to bringing researchers and users together with the establishment of the Collaborative Research Grants Program (which matched industry money for selected projects on a dollar for dollar basis) and with the Cooperative Research Centres (CRC) Program. The CRCs foster co-operative research programs involving universities and partners from industry or other research organisations such as the CSIRO. More than $1.5 billion has been invested in sixty-five of these Centres over the past seven years in public and private funding, one dollar in five coming from industry. By most measures the CRC Program has produced some outstanding successes, though some critics claim that the Government, in its desire to see more practical outcomes, has been overzealous in establishing so many centres.

As is the case with the tax concession, there are clouds on the horizon. We mentioned earlier that governments optimistically launch major new initiatives and, usually despite the evidence to the contrary, expect them to fund themselves after a few years. So it is with the CRCs. By the time of the 1997 Budget, the Commonwealth showed its impatience with the level of commitment it had entered into by announcing a cut of $10.2 million in the program over two years and stating that it would "undertake a review on how Centres can increase the commercialisation of research activities and become more self-funding".

Greasing the wheels: organising and funding research

The principal challenge for our national research system is to prioritise research investments in order to optimise practical outcomes, while maintaining a competitive basic knowledge base in the face of constrained funding and escalating costs.[24] Clearly it is not possible or desirable to spread research resources too diffusely among Australia's forty-three institutions and thirty-three thousand academic staff. Some concentration of resources is required.

When John Dawkins, the former Commonwealth Minister responsible for higher education, brought about the end of the binary system he was well aware that he was giving grazing rights in the field of research to staff from the former CAE system. However he had no intention of providing proportionately more research money. The Commonwealth Government has never subscribed to the idea that staff, once designated as academic, should have an automatic right and expectation to undertake active programs of research. Some initial money to build up research infrastructure was provided to the new universities, but this was removed in 1994, leaving no special dispensations to this sector. In fact, the need for selectivity was acknowledged even in the pre-binary days, when universities had sole access to research money.

There are two primary ways that the government funds university research. One is by way of monies that universities direct towards research from their operating grants. This includes a component of the salaries bill for the time academics spend on research, as well as support provided by way of laboratories, buildings, libraries, administration and so on. A portion of university operating grants, known as the Research Quantum, is spread amongst the universities according to their existing research strengths, but once allocated within their overall operating grant "envelope", universities are free to allocate these funds internally as they wish. The other main way government funds research is by channelling money through the research granting schemes. There are two bodies overseeing schemes which together provide the great bulk of these grants:

the ARC and the National Health and Medical Research Council (NHMRC). While open to all researchers, within rules against "double dipping"[25], university researchers are the main recipients of such grants.

The granting schemes usually operate on the basis that the recipient is a senior researcher, whose salary is paid for by the university. He or she applies for grants to employ researchers to assist them as well as some non-salary costs to undertake specific projects, usually of three years' duration. In some areas, notably in the humanities, external grant funding is not so important, and the support of research relies more on universities freeing up staff time. The major component of university contributions to university research is therefore through the salaries of senior researchers.

No precise figures can be attached to general university funding of research, because the amount of time each academic spends on research varies greatly. However, estimates are made by the Australian Bureau of Statistics. In 1995-96, universities spent around $2 billion on research and development, of which around two thirds was from general funds, one fifth from the ARC and NHMRC, and the rest from other specific grants programs. The Commonwealth was the source for all but 11 per cent of these funds.

Over time the government has shifted more money towards the competitive granting schemes, and tightened the money available from within operating grants. In 1990 an explicit "clawback" was made, whereby money was transferred from operating grants to boost the funds allocated by the ARC and NHMRC. Since then, the granting bodies have received regular injections of extra funds, while more and more operating grant money is needed to cope with teaching pressures. Over the ten years to 1995-96, research funds provided through the ARC and NHMRC increased by 314 per cent, those through other grant schemes by 31 per cent, and the estimated general funding of research by 43 per cent.

Both the ARC and NHMRC are elite systems. They operate mainly on the basis of peer review to assess the scientific excellence of research proposals. There is no suggestion that they could or should cater for the research aspirations of all academic staff. Only a relatively small proportion of Australia's academics apply for support from these schemes, and less than a quarter of those who apply are successful. As basic research becomes ever more reliant on competitive grants, the gulf between reality and the requirement for all academics to be researchers widens. A rising third class of staff has also emerged: those who are employed on research grants. Industrially speaking, such people are usually not classified as academic staff, they are either support staff or, at more senior levels, are subject to a separate classification. Their term of appointment usually extends only as far as the lifetime of the grant. Together with the part-time and contract teaching staff, they have added to the ever-growing diversity of university staffing. To complicate matters further, some academics are employed, formally or informally, on a research-only basis, not necessarily in connection with a particular grant. Such people tend to be more successful in attracting competitive grants than those who also have to contend with teaching duties.

The older universities, particularly those with medical schools, dominate the research scene. Yet in recent years we have seen both in the UK and Australia the emergence of a clique of such universities who argue that Australia's research resources are spread too thinly across the universities. Since the abolition of the binary system, their argument goes, there are vastly more claimants to research funding. High quality international standard research requires high quality infrastructure, a situation which cannot be replicated at all universities. Those universities which have such an infrastructure should be designated "research universities" and treated separately.

As it is, the older universities already receive the lion's share of research funding. Half of Australia's thirty-six public universities were established prior to 1988; these institutions received 86 per cent of university research income in 1995. The eight established prior to 1960 received 70 per cent. However, the primary determinant of excellent research is excellent researchers, followed by access to good facilities. These may or may not be found in particular universities. It is a fallacy to suggest that research can be divided along institutional lines. Within the "sandstone" universities there are great numbers of academics who do little or no research and produce no publications.[26] Within the new universities there are islands of researchers involved in truly international standard work operating with excellent facilities. Indeed, a 1996 study found that nineteen universities were among the leading six in at least one field of research, the newer universities standing out in areas such as applied research and information technology.[27]

However there is a useful point to be made about infrastructure. By this we mean the equipment and facilities needed to undertake research, as well as basic support such as administration, rent and power. This expenditure is not funded by the research granting schemes. There is a pool of infrastructure money ($85 million in 1997) which is allocated to universities on the basis of their success in attracting competitive grants. This need not, however, be spent on supporting those grants and is generally inadequate to cover the cost of even the most direct infrastructure. The research granting schemes were never intended to pay for the full cost of the research, they are only "sponsorship" of university-driven projects. Each university is expected to pick up the tab that is needed to run the research, and the Commonwealth's infrastructure pool provided by DEETYA offsets some of this.

The trouble is, such arrangements can lead to the infrastructure for research getting out of alignment with the areas actually conducting the research. When the Bureau of Industry Economics looked at this issue[28], using data from the Australian Bureau of Statistics, it noted that expenditure on fixed R&D assets per researcher has increased, and that capital expenditure has increased as a proportion of total R&D spending. This might suggest that there is not really an infrastructure problem, but they did acknowledge that their figures said nothing about the more indirect support costs, nor did they take into account the rising cost of equipment and the shorter working life of much research equipment. Other reports, and experience "in the trenches" make it quite clear that the gap between direct research activity and the provision of proper support is very real. A government study concluded in 1995 that a reasonable amount to cover the direct costs of infrastructure, as opposed to the "deep" infrastructure such as libraries which can not be ascribed to particular projects, would be around forty cents in the dollar. The level is at present around twenty-seven cents in the dollar and could fall to as low as twelve cents by the year 2000 if one-off funding increases are not renewed by the Commonwealth Government.[29]

Within universities there are many competing demands for research support, both from established fields with competitively-awarded grants, and from disciplines which are either new or which do not do so well under the ARC or NHMRC. The competitive schemes have tended to want to fund more research with less money per project, rather than fewer projects with more money. As a result, universities are torn between accommodating broad demands for support or starving some areas to pay for research projects they have won. Such a situation can only be improved if universities are willing to be more ruthless about their allocation of research funding and if research granting bodies are prepared to pay for the full direct costs of the projects they support.

None of this supports an argument that the name of an institution should be a criterion in the allocation of research funding. In practice, of course, the "Great Eight" or "Sandstone Seven" are not as blunt as this. Their argument is based on building on strength, although this logically does not lead to any change in the competitive award of grants, and a push to have more research money allocated by way of the Research Quantum. A combination of fewer peer-reviewed grants and formulas which reward those who attract such grants is likely to lead to research being concentrated in fewer institutions. The research-strong universities would in effect have more money for research without the bother of having to compete for it through the various competitive funding bodies. Decisions about priorities and the allocation of research funds would be shifted back from the national funding bodies to the institutions, which would be driven by internal pressures rather than national interest. If the government is serious about promoting selectivity and excellence in research, it would be better off ensuring that research grants are better funded, that selectivity is driven by assessment of quality (and not by "performance indicators" which reward activity), and that the imbalance between infrastructure and grant support is not allowed to grow too large. It could do this by abolishing the separate funding for research infrastructure and requiring granting schemes to pay the full direct costs of those research projects they sponsor. Such a proposition was put forward for the UK Research Councils by the Dearing Review of Higher Education and also favoured in the discussion paper released by the Australian Committee to Review Higher Education Financing and Policy.[30]

Our attention so far has been on the competitive grants side of the funding fence. The other side, as we mentioned earlier, is the support of research through the block grant. This element is intended to cover the broader bases of research, such as those which would not be supported under grants schemes, and to pay the salaries of academic researchers. Such a diffuse mechanism owes its origin to the notion that research and teaching are combined duties of academics. The visible part of this is the Research Quantum, which was originally 6.2 per cent of operating grants, when the process was instituted some seven years ago, but has now dropped to around 4.9 per cent. The Quantum falls far short of covering all research expenditure. In 1997 it amounted to around $220 million compared with an estimated expenditure of more than $1 billion in general university spending on research, not including grant money. The point of identifying the Quantum was to enable some of the operating grant to be allocated on the basis of performance, so that it would be weighted towards those universities which attracted grants and published research.

The United Kingdom has adopted a different approach to allocating a research component of university grants. As is the case in Australia, a proportion of the university operating grant is deemed to be allocated to research, and is distributed among universities on the basis of performance. However, whereas the Australian model uses "objective" measures of publication counts and grant income to measure performance at a distance, the UK has embarked on a major exercise of research assessment. This exercise involves panels of experts examining evidence supplied by universities about the quality of research within their departments. The panels rank areas on a scale of 1 to 5, though with gradations in some of the ranks, and the Higher Education Founding Council gives a weighting to these ranks which affects the allocation of a pool of research money.

Both the Australian Research Quantum and the British Research Assessment Exercise (RAE) are different responses to the desire by funding bodies to obtain some quality assurance and performance reward for the research that is supported through operating grants and allocated at the discretion of universities.

Both approaches have some benefits in rewarding certain areas of the system. There are, however, several drawbacks; both approaches are administratively onerous[31], and the results, in terms of identifying good performance, in many cases reflect the separate quality assurance process inherent in obtaining competitive research grants. The Australian grants index, made up as it is of weightings for grant income as well as various measures of output such as publications, is a blunt tool that does not reflect quality in the way that peer review can, nor does it accommodate differences between research disciplines. The UK exercise has been criticised for failing to introduce international perspectives on quality and for not dealing with interdisciplinary research.

In a report commissioned by the National Board of Employment, Education and Training[32], Professor Paul Bourke of the Australian National University analysed and compared the two systems and concluded that an RAE-type exercise was not ideal for Australia, given its inherent expense and the relatively small amount of research money involved. He also identified problems with dealing with some areas of research and potential overvaluation of research compared with teaching. However, he also noted that the Research Quantum process was not much better.

*

Research, like teaching, is becoming increasingly fragmented. Different elements are being drawn out and funded separately or subject to competition. Elements that are more immediately useful are being "user-driven" or, better, jointly developed by users and researchers. Applied research depends on a broad base of underlying knowledge, a base which is not developed by concentrating on finding answers to immediate practical problems. With no direct "user" or straightforward commercial return, such basic research is primarily fostered by universities. Since resources for research are limited, activity must be concentrated at national and institutional levels, and some degree of selectivity is needed. This selectivity must represent a balance of societal interests with the desire of academics to develop their own disciplines.

There is a need for greater clarity about the respective roles of universities and funding bodies in influencing research selectivity. Such selectivity is inevitable: the traditional views that research needs to be conducted by tenured academic staff and that good teaching can only be done by good researchers are unsustainable. When it comes to block-funded research we need to distinguish between the task of quality assurance on the one hand, and funding on the other. They can be linked, in performance-based funding, but that can produce its own problems in perpetuating limited areas that measure well, a matter we will re-visit in later discussion.

Balancing university control over research with that of funding bodies, inevitably raises the issue of autonomy. The rationale for academic freedom and university autonomy in this area is that there should be scope for research to be conducted which is not hampered by political pressures or driven by short-term concerns. It is the process which enables basic research to be undertaken in order to provide the underpinning for economic, social and cultural benefit. Yet such autonomy is always constrained by available resources; not every academic can research what he or she likes because in any system there would not be enough money. The task becomes one of allocating a given amount of money to particular areas of research.

Moreover, some degree of systemic judgement needs to be made about selectivity. If left entirely to the universities, some may fail to be sufficiently selective, and seek to spread their resources too thinly, or else the combined results of separate selections may not add up to a desirable level of national activity. In the area of basic research, selectivity should be based on quality. What we need is a body of peers, a community of scholars, to make national judgements about the balance of activity between the different areas of research, and the support of particular research projects. Of course we have just such a body or two in the competitive granting schemes. It is essential that these schemes have a degree of autonomy in their operations for the reasons mentioned above, but it is to be expected that they would coordinate and link their work with national priorities that might be enunciated in areas of application, through support of "strategic basic" research.

At one extreme we might suggest that university operating grants be used only to employ academics to teach, and that any research would need to be supported by buying out academic time with a fully-funded research grant. The training of research students could be funded separately through scholarships. Thus, research funding could be separated entirely from teaching. The Australian Committee to Review Higher Education Financing and Policy (the West Committee) advocated such an approach in a Discussion Paper issued in November 1997.[33] While being more compatible with the trend towards contractualism with associated concepts of competition and contestability, such a proposal would be enormously disruptive. In any event there is a strong case to continue to allow universities to link teaching and research and to make some institutional decisions about the allocation of research money to areas of local priority.

Nevertheless, it is reasonable to expect that the shift from block-funded to grant-funded research will continue. Universities will need to make far clearer choices between education and research activities, and reflect this through greater diversity in the appointment and management of staff. Success in attracting competitive grants will increasingly be the determinant of basic research funding. However, it will be incumbent both on individual universities and on the grant funding bodies with responsibilities for basic research to ensure that an appropriate level of activity is undertaken in "Cinderella" areas, which may be important but not thriving under competitive systems. This may well mean that only a few universities nationally support such fields.

Outside the "curiosity-driven" basic research, the key to success lies with the ability to promote and sustain collaboration between academics and the users of research, whether they be in hospitals, government departments, or industry. This requires some fundamental rethinking of academic attitudes and work practices, which were originally developed to suit the isolated pursuit of knowledge for its own sake.

The structure and attitudes of Australian business necessitate a substantial role for governments in funding research, particularly basic research. Since this must be targeted, it is reasonable that public funds be allocated through competitive grant schemes, and infrastructure funding should keep pace. The interplay of accountability and autonomy is particularly important in this setting. Governments always seek the short-cut, whether this is in the form of cheap access to quick degrees, or the idea that they need only fund research that delivers direct answers to questions of national priority. Yet in research there must be an acceptance that the public interest is best served by keeping a sliding scale in mind - the biggest returns can come from unexpected quarters, and the priorities of users should come into play in accordance with the applied nature of the research involved. A source of funding for curiosity-driven research must be allowed to exist with minimal shaping by national priorities, although with suitable accountability to ensure the money is spent as intended. Furthermore, as this provides the platform for application of research, it must be a large source. Australian support of basic research falls far short of our capacity to undertake consistently excellent research, and while governments have proven willing to support collaboration between industry and universities, this support has been uneven. Both remain vulnerable in a climate which sees such outlays classified as public consumption rather than investment.

Research support will inevitably drive a greater separation of academic functions within universities. The pursuit of externally-funded research will both alter the nature of the academic community, as some areas will be more successful than others, and influence the balance between research and teaching.[34] The main danger is that restructuring the relationship between education and research could result in divorce. Higher education needs to be fertilised with research, and research will benefit from interaction with teaching and postgraduate research training. If there is too precipitate a move towards graduate schools and research institutes, then we could see quality education even further marginalised than it already has been. Perhaps poor teaching will have its revenge. "The British government spends very much less on research than it would spend if it were actuated by sound financial calculation", wrote Bertrand Russell in 1961, "the reason being that most civil servants have had a classical education and are ignorant of everything that a modern man should know."[35] Were he writing today, the only change he might make would be to substitute economics for classics.

CHAPTER SEVEN

Universities Learning to Manage Themselves

Readers familiar with *Alice's Adventures in Wonderland* may recall that when Alice first entered Wonderland she drank a potion which made her alternately grow and shrink in size. After growing to giant proportions, she burst into tears and found that when she shrank, she had fallen into a pool of her own tears. A motley collection of animals also fell into the pool of tears, and when they all swam to shore and climbed out, they were faced with the problem of how to get dry again.

One of the animals, the Dodo, proposed that they take part in a Caucus Race:

> First it marked out a race-course, in a sort of circle ("the exact shape doesn't matter," it said) and then all the party were placed along the course, here and there. There was no "One, two, three, and away!" but they began running when they liked, and left off when they liked, so that it was not easy to know when the race was over. However, when they had been running half an hour or so, and were quite dry again, the Dodo suddenly called out "The race is over!" and they all crowded round it, panting, and asking "But who has won?" This question the Dodo could not answer without a great deal of thought, and it stood for a long time ... while the rest waited in silence. At last the Dodo said "*Everybody* has won, and all must have prizes."

The author of *Alice*, Lewis Carroll, was in real life Charles Dodgson, an Oxford Don. A distinguished logician, he had experienced his share of Caucus Racing in one of the birthplaces of the Western university system.[1]

Our universities are long-time Caucus Racers; indeed, they have turned this activity from a small professorial event into a mass academic fun-run. The very notion that academics should conform to any structural regulations, that they should be judged on their performance, or that one academic should receive preferential treatment over another, is anathema to many.

Are Australian universities destined to go the way of the Dodo?

This book has traced some of the major pressures that have been brought to bear on higher education, and examined some of the gaps between what society wants and needs from its universities and what it is receiving. In broad terms we also know what we want from higher education in the 21st Century; it must provide for a more diverse and mobile student body in an age where knowledge is a key commodity that must be renewed throughout an individual's life.

We know, too, that universities are not going to receive larger portions of public money either to sustain themselves or to change their ways. In all likelihood they will receive less taxpayer support to conduct their operations. Like organisations in other sectors of the economy, they will embrace efficiency and quality regimes not to attract some reward money from the government as in the past with the Quality rounds, but because of the more fundamental need to survive and prosper in an increasingly uncertain world. Equally, however, it is important for people in universities to come to recognise that the prospect of less taxpayer money should not necessarily mean less money overall; it does, however, mean less reliable money and a more volatile funding climate.

If universities are to move from their traditional operating paradigm to one capable of dealing with rapidly changing circumstances they will obviously need to be well led and capably managed. It is equally apparent, given the essentially conservative and tradition-bound nature of our universities, that the management of change is itself a key task confronting the higher education sector.

On the whole, however, our universities have shown themselves to be profoundly slow to recognise the necessity to professionalise the way in which they operate. For example, until very recent years there has been little interest in students: their presence was a given, and there was little substantive attention given to the quality of university teaching or the relevance of particular courses. But this lack of interest in students was despite the fact that the basic element of a university's income base is its student load. Equally, the single largest item in a university's budget is its salaries. Yet some institutions still have little idea about trends in their staff costs, most universities have no real understanding about how to plan for future staffing, and many do not seem to be devising strategies to accommodate the fundamental changes which are taking place in the nature of academic work and the university workplace.

Reconciling academic tradition with contemporary realities

As obvious as it may be that universities need to be professionally managed in order to survive, much less prosper, many people inside our institutions find no place for the term "management" in their vocabularies. Academic unions use the term in a pejorative way when referring to University representatives with whom they are negotiating, while even some Vice-Chancellors steer clear of the term, preferring the far more lofty activity of "leadership". Indeed, a familiar response to any demand that universities should better manage themselves is the issuing of a call to arms in favour of collegial ideals and the need for leadership.

Frequently, those who invoke the call for leadership have a heroic model in mind, one which characterises the leader as the captain of a ship standing on the bridge surveying the horizon. This imagery might be attractive to those holding or pretending to high office, but it is neither helpful nor relevant to exaggerate the distinction between leadership and management. Not all managers are leaders, and effective leadership is important in managing. But that does not mean that leadership is difficult and management is easy. If management is easy, why are governments defeated for poor management or mismanagement, and why do corporations fail? Closer to home, why are universities so poor at managing staff and planning future staff needs, and why are some universities near to insolvency? And finally, why are governments - of all colours - telling universities to manage themselves better?

Instead of constructing an artificial dichotomy between leadership and management (not to mention administration), it is important to appreciate the interrelationship of the terms. It is particularly unconstructive to equate the term "management", as applied in the contemporary sense, with old-style public service administration. Management these days is very much about setting directions and guiding, that is, about being strategic in nature and intent. It is also about ensuring that what we do, and what we are accountable for, mirrors that direction. It is true that setting the guideposts for the future is difficult and that few may be capable of that articulation. In that sense, and reverting to the nautical analogy for a moment, the task of leadership is, in part, about scanning the horizon and proposing a destination. That of management, on the other hand, is about getting there. To return to Lewis Carroll, those who argue the irrelevance of contemporary management in universities are

akin to the Bellman in *The Hunting of the Snark*, who navigated with the aid
of a blank map:

> He had bought a large map representing the sea
> without the least vestige of land:
> and the crew were all pleased when they found it to be
> a map they could all understand.
>
> 'What's the good of Mercator's North Pole and Equators
> Tropics, Zones and Meridian Lines?'
> So the Bellman would cry: and the crew would reply,
> 'They are merely conventional signs!'

The aversion by many people in our universities to the notion of
management was illustrated during 1995 at a seminar being held in a
leading Australian university. A member of the Higher Education
Management Review, the group appointed by the then federal government
to look at management issues within the nation's universities, was speaking
and answering questions on a matter totally unrelated to that Review.
Toward the end of the session a member of the audience interjected
"Aren't you a member of that inquiry looking at the management of
universities?" When a reply in the affirmative was indicated the questioner
continued "Then I'm glad you are here. Because it is important for you to
understand that there is no place for management in a university."
Momentarily, the visitor assumed that the questioner was joking, but
quickly realised that this was not the case, given that no one in the
audience was laughing.

At a more substantial level, the case against "management" is that it
is seen as an unworthy activity which is inconsistent with traditional
concepts of collegiality, academic freedom and academic autonomy.
Alternatively, it is regarded as something of an unwelcome and
unnecessary transplant from the corporate world.

What is there to these concerns?

The concepts of collegiality, academic freedom and academic
autonomy derive from the operation of the university as a medieval guild.
Guilds operated on the basis of a community of masters, where students
were inducted through the initial stages of apprentice and journeyman. The
earliest universities were guilds of scholars, which developed into
institutional forms in the twelfth century. Levels of progression were
signified by degrees, from bachelor, through masters to doctorate. These

universities had certain rights conferred by church or crown, but little in the way of common property or stable location. Students could and did break away from one university and establish another somewhere else. Such migration led to the establishment both of Oxford, when students left the University of Paris around 1168, and Cambridge, when disaffected students left Oxford some forty years later.

Both Oxford and Cambridge developed distinctive federal structures based on self-governing colleges, with the role of the university as such limited to conducting examinations and the awarding of degrees. The vice-chancellor was responsible for these relatively limited university functions, and this position was filled on a rotating basis by the heads of the colleges. Colleges were run by the senior academics, the Fellows, with all being accorded equal status and power. As we have stressed earlier, Australian universities were not established along the lines of Oxford and Cambridge, either in terms of curriculum or structure; nevertheless the traditions of academic practice and governance derived from these institutions, together with the German reformations of the nineteenth century, providing the template against which were derived the myths and realities of modern academe.

We mentioned earlier the work of the American sociologist Robert Nisbet, who noted that the medieval guild-based modes of academic operation relied for their authority and standing on the concept of the university as a community of scholars united by an "academic dogma", by which he meant a set of beliefs and values centred around the pursuit of knowledge for its own sake. He also noted that universities were inherently aristocratic: power was vested in the masters, or professors, while academic freedom, tenure and autonomy represented special privileges over and above the civil rights of freedom of speech, and conditions of continuing employment. However, once this academic dogma was shaken, the practices that depended on it were under threat. And shaken it has been, by the massification of higher education, the accordance of differential status within the academic community, expectations of direct rendering of community service, and by the pressure for "useful" and "relevant" education and research. Academic autonomy and governance could not remain unchanged as society itself became more democratised and as the university became "useful" and subject to external scrutiny.

Australian universities have always been expected to be of practical benefit to the community. Yet while they were small and largely marginal to Australian business and public life, a style of academic management derived from long-standing overseas practices was able to hold sway. Until the 1960s, academic autonomy and authority were enshrined in the German model of a traditional department with a single professorial head. Universities were run on the basis of informal relationships between the professors and central administration, an arrangement which worked as long as departments were few and the interactions of the external, political and economic relationships of the university and its internal academic affairs were simple. "In the traditional framework of departmental autonomy, the real work was in the departments and central administration was a secondary function properly carried out by the Vice-Chancellor, the Registrar, some interested Professors on a part-time basis and some submissive clerks of various grades."[2] As universities grew in size and importance in the post-war period, and as they became more exposed to the changes affecting society, such arrangements could not last.

The ideals of the academic guild became impossible to sustain as enrolments grew and research perspectives came to dominate. Teaching became more the responsibility of the lower status grades of lecturer and tutor, and non-professorial staff and students began to make demands for greater representation in decision-making. Concessions were made to these demands in the 1960s and 1970s, as committees proliferated and university policies and procedures became codified. Even in the colleges of Oxford, the home of the British professorial guild, "personal discretion was out of fashion: rules must be made by committees and enforced by joint courts".[3]

The golden age of democratic collegiality, in the form of management by representative committees, lasted in Australia during the 1970s and 1980s, by the end of which period the financial crisis arising from cuts in government funding and slow-down in demographic growth began to bite. Since that time it has been ever more apparent that the basis on which traditional collegial government rested, that of a community of scholars, could not be reconciled effectively with the changes that were occurring in all organisations. Nor could it be reconciled with the desire of universities to reap the benefits of these changes by acting as entrepreneurial organisations, willing and able to grow by fitting what they did to the needs of governments, business or other sectors of the community.

The most important of these changes was the fact that money, whether public or private, no longer came without strings attached. Funds were either earmarked at the outset, or else allocated on grounds of efficiency and effectiveness. Professional management was a necessity; it was not, as some have tried to portray it, an economic rationalist fad. Academic status and power could not be held constant across all areas as some individuals and disciplines proved better able to access funding than others, and as individual performance became ever more important to institutional prosperity.

It follows from the above that the supposed dichotomy between collegiality and managerialism is as unhelpful as that between leadership and management. In reality, contemporary university management is a complex amalgam of administration, academic decision making, financial management, strategic planning and marketing, residing in a large organisation with multiple stakeholders and subject to ongoing shifts in priorities and demands. To say that an approach to such complexity is either managerial or collegial adds little. One must suspect that at times people who wrap themselves in the flags of collegiality and academic freedom do so less from disinterested motives than from a wish to protect their own turf and to avoid reasonable scrutiny.

Due at least in part to an enforced reduction in reliance on government support, higher education institutions have increasingly involved themselves with external organisations, through research partnerships, continuing education and what can be broadly termed as community service. These developments have placed considerable demands on institutions for management skills of the sort not traditionally associated with academe, including marketing, intellectual property negotiation and accurate costing and pricing of assets.

Many academics are uncomfortable about students being regarded as "customers" or "clients", or by the notion of universities providing "services". Yet the reality is that transactions do take place where academics and universities are paid for teaching students, undertaking research, providing short courses or a variety of other activities at least some of which must be tailored to whoever is paying for the relevant work. There is also a growing need for universities to be more flexible and selective in what they do, and how they go about their activities. But these demands do not sit easily with the usual collegial management practices of higher education, which typically involve extensive debate, endless rounds of consultation, detailed scrutiny by unwieldy committees and lengthy implementation schedules.

While the debating of ideas is a fundamental characteristic of an academic setting, there are innumerable committees in our universities which expend vast amounts of time and energy on matters of the most marginal consequence. Such committees, often dominated by noisy and articulate minorities, tend not to debate and resolve issues, but rather prefer to workshop often trivial matters with seemingly endless patience. And while many people in our universities view with contempt the bureaucracy of governments, our universities today still exhibit the sorts of old-style public service process tendencies which have been under relentless attack for at least a decade in most public sector jurisdictions.

Universities and the public sector reform agenda

Most Western governments have, over the past twenty or so years, sought to improve the effectiveness and efficiency of their public sector operations. Approaches have included introducing contemporary financial, accountability and management practices into the public sector, imposing cuts in the budgets of public sector organisations, and opening up parts of public service provision to private providers. Initially these reforms were introduced to government departments and agencies, but in time they broadened to influence the activities of all categories of taxpayer-funded organisations. In recent years particular attention has been focussed on the goal of requiring public agencies, under national competition policy principles agreed to by all levels of government in 1995, to compete where appropriate on even terms with the private sector.[4]

The higher education sector has not avoided the development of these trends occurring in the wider public sector arena. Universities were also directly targeted during the late 1980s by the Federal Government's program to create a unified national university system. In more recent years Australian universities have been exposed to a number of public sector-style regimes designed to improve their performance and accountability. We thus have heard a great deal about the quality agenda, strategic planning, performance indicators, benchmarking, performance-driven research funding, competition and performance management for staff.

The so-called Dawkins reforms, set out in the 1988 White Paper, ushered in some significant changes to institutional structures and relationships with the Commonwealth. These included the abolition of the binary system, the mobilisation of a program of institutional amalgamations and the introduction of the educational profiles process. Some significant steps towards reintroducing student contributions to the cost of their education also appeared in the form of HECS, the later introduction of fees for some postgraduate courses, and the advent of fee-paying overseas students. However, the government still accepted the need for continued expansion within the system and provided for this without the introduction of up-front student fees or substantial cuts to operating grants.

These developments took place within a climate which constantly tested the balance between institutional autonomy and government involvement and regulation. State and Commonwealth governments were well aware of the proper limitations of their direct involvement in university management. However, they exercised considerable influence through setting legislative parameters and using financial carrots and sticks. Examples of the former included the establishment of a national climate for industrial relations, restrictions on student intake characteristics through profile negotiations, and legislation on matters such as discrimination and occupational health and safety. The exercise of financial influence was particularly noticeable in areas such as performance-based research and the development of systems of quality assurance. For example, the allocation of monies to competitive research schemes and the development of the research quantum have had powerful repercussions for the way many institutions manage and reward their internal research efforts.

Strategic planning is now commonplace in Australian universities; at least this is true of the mechanics of planning. The Government requires publicly-funded universities to produce these documents in order to qualify for money, and they are dutifully drawn up. But with very few exceptions they are not strategic plans of the sort that scout the territory, examine new threats and opportunities, and serve to inspire staff and inform the public. Instead they are for the most part public relations exercises or cumbersome justifications for the status quo, developed by following government guidelines. Targets are often poorly developed and inappropriately applied, and indicators to measure progress are seldom clearly defined and even less frequently actually measured and reported. There is also a tendency within individual institutional plans for all targets to be seen as universally applicable. The problem with this approach is that

it takes no account of the reality that in most organisations different elements make different contributions at varying levels toward the overall outcomes of the organisation.

These problems are by no means unique to the university sector, but they are symptomatic of a situation where a process is being followed without any real understanding or commitment to the underlying intent which, in this case, is the basic and important one of planning for the future. In the words of J. Brian Quinn, Professor Emeritus of Management at Dartmouth College, "a good deal of corporate planning ... is like a ritual rain dance. It had no effect on the weather that follows, but those who engage in it think that it does ... moreover, much of the advice related to corporate planning is directed at improving the dancing, not the weather."[5] The net result is that much administrative time is wasted in tick-a-box activity and little strategic light is shed.

Perhaps more tellingly, the result is also that the strategic plans of most Australian universities look remarkably similar, when in fact there is no single garden variety of university, and when there are strong demands for differentiation and diversity across higher education institutions.

It is recognised that strategic planning does not, in itself, produce change. Sometimes the best a formal plan can do is to document change and inform others within an organisation that change has occurred for good reasons. Where flexibility is constrained, where decisions have to be made or endorsed by committees or where conservatism is written into operating procedures, formalised processes of planning can and do become tedious and constitute an active impediment to change actually occurring.

Moves towards quality assurance and performance-based funding have also been international themes with local variations, comprising audit or assessment by government agencies, peer assessment arranged by institutions themselves, or assessment by intermediate "buffer" agencies. In most countries these arrangements have not involved additional funding. Again, however, Australia has been relatively well treated with some $200m being provided over a three-year period as reward funding to grease the wheels of quality. Where these arrangements have directly influenced funding allocations they have been powerful forces for change, at least for compliance with the parameters for assessment. For example, in Australia there has been enthusiastic production of "quality portfolios" to attract the special funding associated with the three quality rounds, and the formula-based allocation of research quantum funding has been very influential in shaping institutional research strategies towards external competitive grants and maximising output measures such as publications.

Attention to performance has not been welcome to many in higher education, in part for the valid reason that the outcomes of universities, particularly the outcomes of university teaching, are not readily amenable to measurement. However, we live in the age of consumer rights and information. The various external stakeholders, such as students, the professions, and taxpayers, wish to know, and are entitled to ask, whether they are receiving value for the significant investment that is made in higher education. For better or worse, we will continue to see an increase in performance assessment, if not directly by government then through independent mechanisms such as the Good Universities Guide. It is also likely that performance-based funding will be attractive to government, a matter that we will consider in the next chapter.

In a broader sense, governments have shown an interest in how effectively universities manage themselves given the considerable taxpayer support they receive. It was, for example, concerns over institutional management which prompted an efficiency and effectiveness review of the university sector by the Commonwealth Tertiary Education Commission (CTEC), a "buffer body" set up in the 1970s to advise the Federal Government on higher education. The 1986 CTEC Review identified a number of areas which needed to be addressed by university management, many of which were subsequently taken up in the 1988 Federal Government White Paper which introduced the Unified National System. Almost a decade later, and in the face of continued demands for increased government funding, the Keating Labor government in 1995 instituted another review of university management. However, whereas the CTEC review had been undertaken by leading university representatives, the 1995 review was headed by a prominent figure from the business sector, Mr David Hoare.

The Hoare Review, formally the Higher Education Management Review, found that the implications of the changing nature of the academic enterprise had not yet been fully grasped within Australian higher education. Nowhere was this more apparent than in the handling by the sector of employment and industrial relations issues. The Hoare Report noted a "culture of mutual dependence" within universities, where university management and unions persist in blaming each other, or others outside, for a general failure to tackle major workplace and work practice issues. Enterprise bargaining, the Report suggested, had not provided the hoped-for circuit breaker, as negotiations for the most part had not been undertaken in terms of strategic considerations relevant to each institution, but rather in terms of national frameworks and the preservation of existing conditions regardless of pressures arising from changing circumstances.

The Hoare Report recognised the importance of preserving academic freedom, necessary for the free expression of critical ideas and the pursuit of independent research. It also acknowledged that the expectation of on-going or "continuing" employment was an important element underpinning the quality of university activities. However, it also observed that tenure had become an industrial issue, rather than one primarily concerned with the protection of academic freedom. The Hoare Report did not support, as some have suggested, the abolition of tenure. Rather, it accepted the need for the concept of tenure to be reformulated in terms which reflect performance of the individual as well as the budgetary circumstances and the strategic needs of individual institutions.

The forgotten groups

Because it is the tenured academics who have been traditionally seen as doing the teaching and research, universities have tended not to take as seriously as they might the concerns of two other major staff groups : academic staff holding casual or contract appointments; and the very large number of administrative, technical, professional and support staff collectively and unsatisfactorily labelled "general staff". Significantly, women constitute a large proportion of both groups.

This situation may be the less surprising given the traditional view that the professors and lecturers were "the university". But the reality is that, were it not for the two groups mentioned above, our universities simply could not function. At least half the undergraduate teaching in Australian universities is performed by contract and casual academic staff, while it is the so-called general staff who run the student systems and university computer networks, who provide the key support role in areas as diverse as building programs, marketing, asset management, and curriculum development. And, perhaps ironically, the term "general staff" also includes many of the specialist researchers, frequently qualified at doctoral level, who are directly responsible for a sizeable portion of the

WHY GOD NEVER RECEIVED TENURE AT ANY UNIVERSITY

1. He had only one major publication.
2. It was in Hebrew.
3. It had no references.
4. It wasn't published in a refereed journal.
5. Some even doubt he wrote it himself.
6. It may be true that he created the world, but what has he done since then?
7. His co-operative efforts have been quite limited.
8. The scientific community has has a hard time replicating his results.
9. He never applied to the ethics board for permission to use human subjects.
10. When one experiment went awry he tried to cover it up by drowning the subjects.
11. When subjects didn't behave as predicted, he deleted them from the sample.
12. He rarely came to class, just told students to read the Book.
13. Some say he had his son teach his class.
14. He expelled his first two students for learning.
15. Although there were only ten requirements, most students failed his tests.
16. His office hours were infrequent and usually held on a mountaintop.

research output of universities.

While the role of established academics in our institutions should not be diminished, it is important to acknowledge the team networks which sustain their activities. It is equally important to recognise, as the Hoare report did, that the boundary lines between academic and general staff are becoming increasingly blurred. This is occurring in both directions, as academics perform a range of administrative duties, while the specialist skills contributed by various "general" staff groups play an increasingly key role in "academic" areas such as the use of multi-media in course delivery and design.

While it is entirely understandable that tenured academic staff should lobby heavily to retain their liberal terms of engagement, and to secure their next pay increase on the best possible industrial terms, these are not issues of foremost attention to the growing academic underclass of casual and contract staff on whom an increasing amount of the undergraduate teaching burden is falling. Quite often these people are engaged from semester to semester, and their other conditions of employment are comparatively meagre.

Nor is there any doubt that it is this underclass of contract and casual staff on whom the burdens of change and budget compression are falling. The industrial incapacity and managerial inability of universities to address the issues of performance and employment adjustment in the context of a more volatile budgetary environment have led to an understandable pre-occupation with ensuring that universities have a level of flexibility in terms of their staffing arrangements and therefore a preference for short-term engagement. In practical terms, what this has meant is that those who are engaged on short-term contracts have found their conditions and their prospects even less stable, while those lucky enough to be employed on a continuing basis remain in most universities still very largely insulated from the changes affecting their less fortunate colleagues.

In practical terms this is a disastrous recipe. Not only is the higher education sector yet to seriously embrace the principle of performance as that underpinning ongoing engagement (as evidenced by the debate over tenure), but universities do not seem to appreciate in a strategic way the role and contribution which is being made by contract and casual staff. Not only do these people bear a pivotal role in maintaining institutional reputation by their contributions to undergraduate teaching, they are mostly young and well qualified, and include many women.

While the role of the "academic" remains central to teaching and research efforts, the further blurring of the academic - general staff boundary line is inevitable. This feature underlines the importance of teamwork between academic and non-academic staff. As the Hoare Committee pointed out, however, the development of such teamwork is not likely to be assisted if non-academic staff do not perceive their role as being valued as highly as that of their academic colleagues.

Some universities have made more progress than others in acknowledging the development needs of middle and senior managers. However, little attention is given in most institutions to the large numbers of general staff who feel trapped by their job descriptions, and threatened with extinction unless they have access to training in order to increase their skills or diversify their experience. To that extent most of our universities continue - as do other institutions in our economy - to view staff in "salary cost" terms rather than as a resource and investment.

In recent years women have become much more vocal about their circumstances in universities. While many institutions can now boast that women predominate the ranks of undergraduate programs, the gains have been more meagre on the staffing side. Women academics are still concentrated at the lower levels, with a relatively high proportion of them in casual or short-term contract employment.

The prospects for women academics have not been assisted by the ways in which universities have responded to changing budget circumstances. This has led to a severe curtailment in the availability of new opportunities. The position of women is also not assisted by the lower levels of resignation occurring in the sector, and by the potential unintended consequences of the recent abolition of compulsory age retirement. These factors, which particularly work against women, also have a broader consequence for the sector in terms of its capacity to rejuvenate and diversify its ranks.

In any case, the circumstances of women academics will not improve unless there is a sustained increase in the participation and completion rates by women in higher degree study, as well as a fresh look taken at the way in which academic careers are defined and structured.

More recent forces for change

The changes announced in the 1996 Federal Budget represented a major departure from the framework of the past two decades. Senator Vanstone, then Howard government minister responsible for higher education, stressed the individual benefits of university education and used those benefits to justify the changes to HECS, the introduction of full fees for undergraduates enrolled above approved load limits, and the expansion of fee-paying arrangements for postgraduates. At the same time, growth in government-funded enrolments has been capped and operating grants cut.

Such a new climate (new at least to Australia) has precipitated the identity crisis within higher education which was discussed earlier in the book. Hitherto there has been something of an assumption that higher education is an unquestioned public good, and along with that status universities have received substantial public subsidies for their activities. Students have been able to make choices about going on to university without incurring major financial sacrifice; conditions of employment of university staff have been nationally uniform and salary increases sustained by government through adjustments to the operating funds. Innovations in areas such as management, collaboration or teaching development have occurred by and large with the aid of additional funding.

It is inevitable that the higher education sector in Australia will experience further deregulation and we will see a progressive weaning from government support and influence. Universities are operating under changing public policy parameters, and institutions will need to turn for survival to a society which is itself undergoing rapid changes.

We are already seeing much greater attention to the possibilities for income generation through tailoring consultancy and research in ways which are attractive to those who might pay for them. This understandably causes some unease amongst those who see the university role as undertaking basic, curiosity-driven research, and amongst those who see this as yet another threat to academic community and autonomy. Others see greater interaction between universities and the external world as a source of opportunity, whereby academic research can be invigorated.

As universities have become larger they have tended to develop more centralised functions to coordinate activity across schools and faculties, and to promote the development of institutional activities such as research, teaching and fund-raising. These functions have usually been headed by senior academic staff who take on management responsibilities, sometimes to the exclusion of academic work. The rise of the so-called "Vice Squad" of Pro-Vice-Chancellors and Deputy Vice-Chancellors with specific program responsibilities has been remarkable. By mid 1997 there were more than 130 such officers across thirty-seven Australian universities. It is also true that responsiveness to outside demands, particularly from governments, has necessitated a greater degree of executive decision-making and management by non-academic staff. It is not uncommon to hear complaints from academics about what they see as unwarranted intrusion into their affairs by non-academic staff from finance departments, research offices or personnel areas, when in fact such staff are ensuring that activities are being carried out in accordance with legislative or university requirements.

Further challenges to academic icons will be posed as higher education enters an era of greater competition and deregulation. Given that institutions must become more flexible, selective and performance-oriented, and given that they are inherently labour-intensive operations, it is inevitable that we will see profound impacts on staffing.

To begin with, we will see progressively more differentiation within the academic profession. As industrial arrangements are freed up, there will be different remuneration for academics in different institutions. The need for institutions to specialise, and to respond to competitive pressures will result in greater fragmentation of academic work between teaching and research. As we have discussed earlier, the conventional expectation that all academics will encompass teaching, research and community service activities at significant levels of excellence cannot be sustained. This is not to say that teaching should be divorced from research; indeed, the relationship between the two is the essence of a university education. Rather, the balance of professional activity between teaching and research may be established or negotiated individually, as is currently proposed for example in North Dakota and in some other States of the United States. Many Australian universities have taken steps towards this goal, allowing some negotiation over percentages of time spent on each activity, but there is a long way to go from policy to practice. Such developments have clear implications for methods of hiring and the criteria for promotion.

Greater differentiation is also likely to arise as institutions incorporate the tools of information technology into academic practice. As discussed previously, development and maintenance of teaching resources will require alliances among content experts, instructional designers, software specialists and experts in intellectual property. The distinctions between academic and non-academic staff in such alliances will be increasingly uncertain. More flexible approaches to teaching will also have implications for the ways in which academic time is employed and accounted for, as lecture time is de-emphasised and more time is spent in preparation and development of course materials, contact time over computer networks, or practical work. Of course, it would be too costly in terms of time and money to develop all resources in-house: significant changes in attitude will also be required of staff as they use materials prepared elsewhere and adapt them for use in their own context.

Freeing-up the university landscape

Any freeing-up of the industrial arrangements governing academic employment needs to recognise that - even in our leading sandstone universities - many academics do not engage in research. Moreover, that across the university sector as a whole, a minority of academic staff contribute an overwhelming proportion of published output, as measured by the research quantum index. In addition, recognition also needs to be given to the fact that the interests of many individual academics undulate during their careers: it is unrealistic to expect academics to maintain uniform momentum across their teaching and research; terms of employment engagement need to be flexible enough to accommodate shifting patterns of interest over time.

The Howard government's Workplace Relations Act, taken in conjunction with funding policy changes affecting the higher education sector, provides the framework against which universities over the next several years may seek to fundamentally reappraise their industrial strategies. Whether they do so remains to be seen. Little freeing-up of the industrial rigidities across the higher education sector occurred under the Enterprise Bargaining regime, with both universities and the unions preferring to bargain on a pattern basis, that is, both sides pretending that the universities were of a common variety, and that similar productivity offsets and negotiating menu items were therefore applicable across the sector. To that extent, the higher education sector as a whole was regarded as a single enterprise. This approach, however, made it very easy for the unions to target individual Vice-Chancellors who were "courageous" enough to believe that their own university should be seen, for negotiating purposes, as a discrete enterprise.

A more flexible approach to industrial relations will lead to more differentiated arrangements for the engagement of academic staff, including some of the styles of flexible staffing arrangements already commonplace in the United States. These include the widespread engagement of adjunct staff who work in a professional capacity outside the university. We are also likely to see more diverse arrangements including, for example, engagement of some staff for a set period of teaching semesters and also funded for research, while others may be employed for, say, two teaching semesters within a year and be free to work outside the university for the remaining months. Such arrangements may be particularly attractive in enabling institutions to build links with industry and the professions and in demonstrating the relevance of their teaching. They will be even more attractive if there is a further deterioration of the salary environment.

Universities find it industrially difficult to entertain the prospect of a more flexible workplace setting. In part, this is because of the implications of new alternatives for traditional expectations regarding academic tenure. As already mentioned, the original purpose of tenure was to protect academic freedom, particularly the freedom to pursue innovative research and to teach in accordance with appropriate academic standards. The necessity of continuing employment to achieve these ends is more often being called into question, and sits uneasily in a society where most other people have to earn their ongoing employment and demonstrate performance. One might, for instance, note that much of our world-class basic research in medical science is being undertaken in independent research institutes, such as the Walter and Eliza Hall Institute in Melbourne, by researchers who are engaged on a contract basis.

Any freeing up of human resource practices inside our universities should consider the later stages of academic careers as well as hiring and promotion practices. Also, options for more flexible superannuation arrangements should be explored. The Hoare Committee recommended clearer methods of phasing retirement involving, for example, staggered retirement benefits corresponding to reduction from full-time to fractional or sessional engagement. The Committee also commented on the importance for superannuation arrangements not to disadvantage those who take a career break or those who move between industry, government and higher education during their careers. To date, Government has not responded to these issues.

Shifts towards a greater "market" influence on higher education provide incentives for institutions to compete with one another for the best students. This competition will be at both national and international levels, and will not be confined to competition amongst established universities. For example, in Australia universities currently hold a monopoly in terms of the awarding of degrees, but this is likely to be challenged as private providers of vocational education and training push out the boundaries of their activities. Governments will look to universities to mesh certain of their activities with both the TAFE and secondary school sectors in order to provide a more integrated range of lifelong education and to meet the education and training needs of industry.

At a broader level, universities will be required to digest the possible implications for their operations of the National Competition Policy agenda. The Commonwealth's Review of Higher Education Financing and Policy has the responsibility for advising the federal government on the extent to which universities might be affected by the application of competitive neutrality principles[6], although work undertaken for the Ministerial Council on Employment, Education and Youth Affairs gives an indication that a number of areas of university activity could be affected. These include: the matter of whether publicly-funded universities, as currently constructed, constitute a restricted marketplace; and the possibility of universities structurally and financially separating certain of their commercial or quasi-commercial activities (such as professional development courses, residential colleges, and bookshops) in order for them to be seen to be competing on equal terms with private providers.

This is potentially of great significance for universities as they attempt to play on a commercial field. Slaughter and Leslie, reviewing what they termed "academic capitalism" in four countries including Australia, described academics as "state-subsidised entrepreneurs", able to dabble in commercial markets without, in many cases, having to bear individual risk or pay full costs.[7]

One thing is certain. The national competition policy agenda is going to force a scaling-up of the sophistication of marketing and competition activities across the university sector. To date we have seen universities enter into competition with one another by positioning themselves in terms of their brand names, locational advantages, fee levels, or incentive systems. For example, the University of Tasmania recently offered overseas students $1,000 in order to go to Tasmania, while the University of Central Queensland (which came under some pressure over its tactics) offered a "frequent flyer points" style program in which overseas students who recruited other overseas students received prizes for their efforts. Thus, an existing student who attracted one new colleague would receive a bookshop allowance, but the recruitment of several new students might result in a free holiday in the Whitsunday Islands or at Uluru. In November 1997, the University of Melbourne placed national advertisements aimed at luring undergraduate students already enrolled at another university to complete their studies at Melbourne. "Are you sure your current university will give you the best start to your future career?" the advertisements asked, suggesting that for an extra investment "about the equivalent of an additional year's HECS payment for each year of study" students switch and complete a final year of study to earn a University of Melbourne branded degree.

To many people in higher education such practices are regarded as unseemly. But the likelihood is that universities will continue to poach one another's students. Indeed, the practice is likely to be further encouraged by the ability to charge fees for domestic students above agreed load targets, and by the additional marginal funding that has now been promised to universities to compensate for over-enrolment of HECS-liable students.

The shift to a more market-driven system of higher education, especially when accompanied by a decreasing level of taxpayer support, also would seem to encourage institutions to collaborate in a strategic way. Yet this is happening only very slowly.

To date, collaborative activities have largely been either within the research arena, or under the banner of national initiatives funded by the Government, as in the case of attempts to produce standard administrative computing packages. There have been some examples of collaboration between universities in the production of computer-based teaching packages, in the delivery of MBA courses, and in the delivery of some public health and medical courses. An example of the latter was an initiative jointly developed by the University of Queensland, the University of Sydney and Flinders University of South Australia for the introduction of a four-year graduate entry medical program, with common assessment methods and the use of practical problem-solving as a part of the learning process. This program was developed by a consortium involving the participating universities which was able to attract central government funding. However, the experience of this consortium provides an interesting illustration of the effect of local factors on attempts to standardise courses:

> As course design proceeded it became clear that local needs outstripped consortium experience. Thus from a position of division of labour, each school ended up pursuing its own agenda and goals. At one stage it was imagined that the problems to be used in the course could be shared and used in each school. However as the course details became clearer it was obvious that there was too much local individuality for this to happen. The way the years were integrated, the amount of emphasis on clinical contact and even the different geographical organisations of the schools meant that each course was developed in essence by each school alone.[8]

Despite the existence of examples of collaborative initiatives, they remain too few, and the wider possibilities in the area of sharing teaching resources and broader infrastructure are still largely unexplored.

"How not to do it" : academic staff hiring and promotion practices

Nowhere is the failure of universities to manage themselves adequately more evident than in the way academic staff are hired and promoted.

During a recent speech in London, Sir John Daniel, Vice-Chancellor of The Open University in the UK, recounted the experience of being selected for his first academic posting, in the following terms:

> It was during the fuss in 1968 that I was hired for my first job. A professor from École Polytechnique - not France's top grande école but the engineering faculty of the University of Montreal in Canada - had come to France to recruit academics to his growing department... Because of the strikes my interview took place in the bar at Orly Airport and after two beers I was hired as an assistant professor at the École Polytechnique. It was not a model of fair selection practice but I thought they made a good decision anyway...[9]

It is doubtful whether in many countries nowadays two men sitting in an airport bar could, without any other intervention, settle a university academic appointment. To be fair, however, the Sir John Daniel example also showed that a distinguished academic appointment, as his has obviously proved, can sometimes come from a lousy selection process.

The management of staff is a critical issue not just because universities by nature are heavily labour-intensive in what they do, but also because there is a reluctance at all levels inside our universities to recognise that there is a relationship between the performance of individuals and the performance of the organisation as a whole. On the academic side this reluctance derives from the traditional though sometimes convenient acknowledgement that academics may feel a stronger sense of loyalty to their discipline than to the institution which happens to be paying them.[10] It is not an argument, however, which can be sustained in respect of the many other professional, technical, administrative, clerical and other staff employed by our universities. These people, the general staff, are in no doubt that they work for the university.

Universities pay a high price for this reluctance to link the performance of individual staff to the overall performance-improvement agenda of the institution as a whole. This price is that institutions are engaged in all manner of initiatives to improve their teaching and research performance without adequately recognising that the basic prerequisite for performance improvement of the university as a whole is the talent and commitment of individual staff. Universities have thus been slow, very slow, to consider the management of staff, and the planning of staff needs, as a strategic issue.

There are some explanations for this blindspot about staffing. The growth of the higher education sector in Australia helped to shield the sector from the budget cuts affecting other taxpayer-funded sectors of the workforce. Universities were therefore able to steel themselves from encroaching budget realities by reminding themselves of their unique characteristics - the individualistic nature of academic work, the self-evident need for the community to uphold the benefits of independent scholarship and a collegial modus operandi. There was also that other favoured fallback position already discussed, namely, that there was in any case no place for management in a university.

Over the last two decades many universities, including those in Australia, have put in place quite elaborate machinery to improve the way in which they hire staff. They have proceeded in this direction not so much because of any self-realisation that their processes were poor or outdated, but because of proddings from government that changing community standards required that greater openness and fairness should attend the way in which jobs (especially those funded by taxpayers) are filled. Particular pressure was being exerted to provide career opportunities for women and other groups disadvantaged by the "boys' clubs" which traditionally had run our public bureaucracies, including universities.

Sadly, many universities still seem to have very little idea about how to hire good academic staff. Their recruitment processes do not focus on the role and duties of the job, nor upon the reason they need to make an appointment. Nor do they often consider the strategies that might be utilised to fill the position, nor indeed whether they should be recruiting the position in the external marketplace or giving opportunities for existing staff to develop.

There will be those who will dismiss these concerns by referring to the difficulties of defining the true qualities of an academic, and by pointing to the efforts which are made to ensure that academic selection panels are truly representative and inclusive of all possible interests. It is not uncommon, for example, for academic selection panels to include eight or ten, or even sometimes a dozen members. Unfortunately, panels of this size often have little shared understanding of the qualities they seek in applicants and, instead, wallow in a mire of factional wrangling. In such circumstances, the outcome of the selection process is little more than a lottery.

Let us take as an example the recruitment of a typical junior academic, to the position of lecturer. In most Australian universities it is usual for a lecturer to both teach and research. In practice, however, serious attention in many universities is really only given by the selection panel to research. There are several reasons for this, which we considered earlier in this book. First, in the context of this example it is difficult to measure good teaching; academics like to argue about what constitutes competent teaching, and the value of student opinion of teaching is either rejected entirely, or is closely contested. Second, candidates at this level usually have only limited teaching experience, and virtually none of them have either formal or even informal training in either instructional techniques or pedagogy. Third, research is seen to be measurable in the sense that a candidate who has been awarded a doctorate has proved to his or her peers that they are scholarly. This requirement for scholarship is essential for any person whose role in the university it will be to develop the intellectual potential of their students.

What this means is that selection panels frequently select an applicant for a position which is most visibly a teaching one, not on the basis of the workload to be carried as a member of the academic teaching staff, or even on the basis of serious evidence of teaching potential. Rather, what is critical is the selection panel's assessment of research pedigree.

Of course, it is the case that large numbers of accomplished researchers also make inspiring teachers, but there is no guarantee of this outcome. What the situation requires, of course, is that there be more streaming of academic staff. Many people can both teach and research, and their careers are sustained by maintaining the nexus between the two. But there are many others who are interested only in pursuing research; yet, as we acknowledged earlier, while there has been some loosening at the margins in this area, there is a reluctance to let go of tradition in most Australian universities.

Given that selection panels for largely-teaching positions tend to examine research credentials rather than focus on teaching aptitude or demonstrated potential, it is hardly surprising that most universities in Australia provide so few real career opportunities for people whose first love is teaching, and who therefore prefer to devote their careers to their engagement with students. At the present time, many universities tolerate exclusively teaching-based academic appointments only at the lower levels, and the opportunities for advancement of people with such interests - for example, by promotion to senior lecturer, associate professor or above - are meagre.

The argument against the widespread use of exclusively teaching appointments is understandable from the perspective of a concern about maintaining standards of scholarship. But it is a difficult argument to run in practice given, as already mentioned, that only a modest proportion of Australian academics contribute to the national research output.

There is at least as much to be concerned about when it comes to the appointment of academic managers such as heads of department, deans of faculty, deputy and pro-vice-chancellors, or even Vice-Chancellors. Far too often the "working" selection criteria for these positions (as opposed to the selection criteria distributed by an institution's human resources department) make it impossible for candidates from outside the university sector to be appointed. In any case, outsiders initially attracted to a position are often deterred by the nature of the selection process itself. This is especially the case for Vice-Chancellor positions, where the process oftentimes can be likened to a beauty pageant. And, as with beauty contests, rather more preference is given to immediately attractive candidates, those who make an instant impression, than to the carefully-assessed capacity of particular candidates to do the job.

What this suggests is that while the term "merit" is much debated in the higher education sector, there is a deal of evidence to suggest that many people in our universities, including a good number at senior levels, have very little idea about what constitutes merit. They also have very little idea of how merit should be assessed and, more fundamentally, about how to devise selection criteria that are a reliable reflection of the requirements of a position and thereby would provide a selection panel with what it needs to make a dispassionate assessment of an applicant's claims for a particular job.

Australian universities today are no more advanced than were most of the public services a generation ago in their thinking about, and applying, merit. In the old-style government department, the use of seniority and length of service were held to be consistent with merit-based selection. The logic was that extensive experience on the job, measured by rank and years on the job, resulted in increased knowledge and skills on the part of the employee. However, government agencies came to realise that since the increasing complexities of the modern world required the development of different roles, a global assessment of an individual's merit was problematic because some people were very much more effective in certain roles than in others.

The university sector, by and large, has been slow to appreciate this. People who are successful academics are usually assumed to have serious claims for roles which combine academic and management skills.

The problem with this thinking is that it assumes that a successful academic record (most likely, an academic research record) is a reliable indicator of success in an altogether different role. For example, this role might involve managing people or money, or some other portfolio of the university's activities, and working effectively with a range of other people.

This problem of defining merit in the context of a particular role, as opposed to a generalised manner, is one which bedevils many university selection panels. The pursuit of merit is also not assisted by selection committees which overly rely on interviews. The interview is one selection technique, and an important one, but unless a combination of selection techniques is utilised there is a very real risk that the person selected will be the best interviewee, and not necessarily the most suitable person for the job.

Universities not only have an indifferent capacity to make appointments against particular job requirements, they have a very ordinary track record in the way staff are managed. Putting aside for a moment that some academic staff do not accept that they should be "managed", most universities do not yet have in place mechanisms which will allow the performance of staff to be monitored and supported. Progress has been made in some institutions, but the number of cases reaching our industrial tribunals indicates the long path which still lies ahead. For example, no Australian university yet has in place a comprehensive system for managing the performance of all academic and general staff; some universities have no real systems at all, while most still tend to approach different aspects of staff management in a piecemeal fashion. There is also a deal of concern throughout the higher education sector that "performance management" is in fact a code language enabling institutions to rid themselves of people; on the contrary, there is little appreciation that performance management should be comprehensive in its scope, providing not only feedback and development opportunities, but also linkages between the activities of the individual and his or her school, department or faculty.

There will be some who may regard these expressions of concern as overstated. But this is not the case. There is a level of genuine disquiet on the part of many staff across our universities, indeed a degree of alienation, about the way a number of our institutions are being led and managed. Several Australian universities are in a parlous financial condition, while there are concerns across the sector about the implications of the new funding realities, and about the capacity of university managers to make sensible choices. This sense of concern is not alleviated when selection lotteries result in unsuitable door prizes in the form of bad appointments at senior levels. This is especially the case when selection exercises are undermined by the disregard of relevant evidence about the previous track record of candidates, the exertion of undue influence by either the "chaps" or the women's network, or by the insidious use of export references (the term "export reference" refers to the practice of writing a glowing though inaccurate testimonial for a colleague with the deliberate intent of the colleague being "exported" to another institution).

Governance and direction-setting

The central proposition of this chapter has been that universities, despite their distaste for such matters, need to be well run and well managed. They are large and complex organisations, still very significantly supported by the taxpayer, operating in a complex and rapidly-changing environment in which students are paying a steadily increasing share of the cost of their education. And while it is important for universities to be able to operate as autonomous bodies in terms of their teaching and research activities, it is equally important they are able to satisfy the community at large that they are operating effectively.

With that background it is less surprising that one of the key issues focussed upon by the Higher Education Management Review in 1995 was that of university governance. The findings of that group on the issue were also unexceptional, namely, that the governing body has three primary roles in a university - external accountability, strategic planning oversight, and performance monitoring.

Many universities, often against the grain of their tradition, have recognised the importance of this matter of governance, and many university governing bodies have sought in recent years to define for themselves a more strategic role. But is it not always easy. Some governing boards are still captured by the self-interests of inside members, while at times the members of such bodies fail to even recognise the basis of the growing external interest in their activities. David Hoare experienced this himself when, shortly after the release of his Committee's report in late 1995, he addressed a meeting of the governing body of the University of Melbourne. After completing his address on the role of governing bodies, he offered to take questions, the first of which was as follows:

> "Mr Hoare. You and your colleagues have said that councils should have about fifteen members. But there are forty of us. What will happen to the other twenty-five?"

Hoare replied to the effect that it was not the matter of the size of the Council which was important, but rather what the Council actually did. He added that, indeed, the role decided for the Council should inform the structure of its membership but that, in any case, with forty members it was far too large to be an effective decision-making body.

The questioner was not satisfied and indicated that "my constituents would not agree with that". Hoare retorted: "what you are telling me is that councils and senates are effectively parliaments and not really the sorts of bodies that I would see as providing direction to and oversight of universities".

Nonetheless, Hoare's message must have been digested. The University of Melbourne in December 1997 announced that its Council would be effectively halved, to 21 members, as from 1 January 1998.

Sometimes, however, it is not just the members of councils who do not seem to understand or agree about their roles. Some chancellors have been famously intrusive in the day-to-day running of their universities, while in some universities vice-chancellors have attracted similar notoriety for their attempts to blunt the legitimate probings of their governing bodies. One vice-chancellor making a personal representation to the Higher Education Management Review made much of the way he had ensured that his university's governing body had no capacity whatsoever to fetter his discretion in budget matters.

The point to be made, of course, is that while universities tend to emphasise how different they are from other organisations in the community, they are no different from either the corporate or public sector in their need for direction and monitoring, and their obligation to satisfy the community at large that they are operating effectively.

CHAPTER EIGHT

Paying the Piper

The system for funding higher education in Australia is an unsustainable hybrid. Twenty years ago things were fairly consistent: market mechanisms were not supposed to operate; public universities could not charge for what they offered, they subsisted on grants from the Commonwealth which covered nearly 100 per cent of the costs involved, and the Commonwealth took care of salary increases on a national basis.

With time, through a mixture of financial imperatives and ideological leaning, governments have introduced some market-like mechanisms into the picture. Major steps came with the allowance in the 1987 Budget of fees for some postgraduate courses, followed by the introduction of the Higher Education Contribution Scheme (HECS) in 1989[1], and full fees for overseas students from 1990. In the 1996 Budget the Commonwealth announced that it would not pay for salary increases above a minimum "safety net" level and would allow universities to charge fees to Australian undergraduate students enrolled above the levels which the Commonwealth was prepared to subsidise.

The Commonwealth also announced in the 1996 Budget that ongoing small cuts would be made to university grants, and that reductions in student load commensurate with these cuts would be expected to fall in the postgraduate area. The then Minister was able to say, quite correctly, that the cuts were relatively small, "just a nick" in her own words. However, the Commonwealth was fully aware that a salary rise for university staff was justified and overdue. By requiring universities to pay for any salary rise out of existing funds the Commonwealth was in effect imposing a larger cut. The actual amounts vary from university to university, and will depend on how many students each university enrols annually. But broadly speaking, between 1997 and 1999 Australian universities will need to find savings of more than half a billion dollars, or around twelve per cent of their total budgets, in order to meet the government cuts (around $150 million) and salary rises (around $400 million).

The system has thus been evolving towards a position consistent with the trends in the broader public sector discussed earlier. Government wishes to establish itself as the provider of a subsidy to the higher education of students, moreover a subsidy that amounts to a lesser public expenditure than applies at present and which is focussed at the undergraduate level and at postgraduate research training. It wants universities to become more entrepreneurial, responsible for their own finances and responsive to market signals. Unfortunately this evolution has been piecemeal and inconsistent.

Autonomy

Academics have long been accused of being remote from the everyday concerns of society. We have already noted the uncertain relationship of the early Australian universities with the growing colonies; while many of the professors played important roles in establishing scientific societies, influencing school curricula, and providing public lectures, they were widely perceived as being closer in spirit to the old country rather than the new. Academics have undoubtedly become more active since the 1960s, serving on government committees and (though less influentially than their overseas colleagues) appearing on television and radio to debate issues of national concern. Nevertheless, the popular image is of an ivory tower, and the term "academic" is usually used pejoratively by outsiders to mean "out of touch".

Irrelevance could be tolerated as quaint in a time when universities were seen as above and apart from society. However when higher education became available to the masses, and governments and industry looked to universities to provide the intellectual stimulus to economic growth, it became more of a problem. There has been a constant tug of war over the past five decades between universities and those who want to see more practical relevance, and most of the debate centres around the concept of university autonomy.

Autonomy basically means the ability to conduct one's own affairs. It is one of the icons of university life, a legacy in Australia from the British system. Universities are autonomous in the sense that they decide what they teach and research, how they will do it, and who will be admitted to study. At individual staff level, such freedom is tied to the concepts of academic freedom and tenure.

The justification for university autonomy rests on the assumption that university academics are better placed than outsiders to determine what constitutes a proper university education and what questions are amenable to research. Unlike teachers in schools or TAFEs, university lecturers can design their own units and teach them the way they want. Such autonomy is one of the hallmarks of a profession, and indeed we frequently hear reference to "the academic profession". However it is worth noting that some of the other distinguishing characteristics of a profession do not apply to academics. In particular, most academics receive no specific training at the university level for the teaching aspects of their profession, there is no ethical code governing their professional behaviour[2], and there is no nationally representative professional association. One of the most galling aspects of the "academic profession" to outsiders, particularly in government or business, is that accountability is often seen as a threat to autonomy.

Academic autonomy has always been constrained, both internally and externally. Internally, many decision-making processes have been opened up to varying extents to allow students some say, although some limitations on individual leeway are inevitable as courses are designed to achieve some degree of coherence and consistency. Externally, limitations may arise from the need to meet the requirements of the professions and the accountability requirements of government. The question for universities and those who use them is what level of autonomy is necessary, and should it apply across the board?

The Commonwealth Government exercises its influence on universities through the use of financial inducements; indeed it has little other scope under the Constitution. Inducements are a powerful lever, and there is great potential for the Commonwealth Government to influence the operations of universities by threatening to withhold money for non-compliance. Such influence raises concerns about balancing institutional autonomy against the need for universities to be accountable for their use of public money. This is not an easy balance. The UK Lord Chancellor expressed his frustration when he said in 1988: "surely it cannot be argued that the Government, on the taxpayers' behalf, has no right to determine how these substantial sums are disbursed."[3]

There is no reason why government, industry or whoever else provides funding for universities should not have a say in the way funds are used. In the research arena, it is often understood that funding is for specific projects and that at times the results of the research may be owned by the funding body. Institutional autonomy will often be constrained in that untied funds are becoming scarcer, though there is a difference between limiting the funds for *what* academics do, and telling them *how* to undertake their work.

In practice, the constraints placed upon university actions by accepting government money have not been unreasonable, and the forays made by Government into university activity, such as the establishment of the Open Learning Initiative and the rationalisation of distance education, have been supported by advice from within the sector. The payer of the piper has not so much called the tune, as taken advice about what tune ought to be played, and limited the repertoire. Universities that participate in the so-called Unified National System (and they need to do this to secure government funding) have to produce strategic plans for scrutiny by government officials. They also need to provide a wealth of facts and figures about enrolments and graduations. Many of these data do not see the light of day in practical form for a considerable period of time, and then their usefulness is open to question. However none of this really represents an infringement of university autonomy.

Many staff working within universities perceive the effects of recent changes in universities arising from financial stringency. They feel that this is the result of malign intervention by government, with imposed agendas of "economic rationalism" or "managerialism". However, the reality is that the pressure on funding arises less from firm ideas about higher education from the Commonwealth than a general desire to reduce government spending. There is a brutal indifference from senior politicians and bureaucrats to the inner workings of universities; they do not want to tell academics how they should go about their job, only that they should do it with less public money.

The squeeze on university funding to which we referred earlier, namely a thirteen per cent fall in discretionary teaching income per full-time student over the past thirteen years, has put substantial pressure on university operations. This pressure will continue. Nevertheless, even though universities are weakened by reliance on government, block funding at least provides some protection from uncertainty.

The prospect that the umbilical cord between governments and universities could be severed through changing financing arrangements appears very real, particularly as government has encouraged universities to charge full fees for various categories of courses. Already many universities have enrolled large numbers of fee-paying postgraduate students and fee-paying overseas students. For some, fee-paying student load amount to one fifth or one quarter of their total load, for others it is less than ten per cent. For the time being there is room for expansion in both these fields, but the longer-term outlook for overseas students is that competition will intensify as countries other than Australia offer their services, and countries such as Malaysia seek to develop their own education systems. In any fee-paying environment there is greater uncertainty for the long-term resource base of institutions.

Financing universities

There is a difference between the cost to a university of running a particular course and the income received directly for that course. If the income is less than the cost, then the course will be subsidised from the university's other activities. If the income is greater than the cost, then that course makes a profit which can be used to subsidise other activities. A university can either set its own income by determining the price of a course and charging a fee, or else the price might be determined by government. Government can fix prices either by preventing universities from charging fees, in which case they have to rely on whatever income the government deems fit to provide, or else it can say to universities: "you are allowed to charge fees, but we will reduce our grant to you by whatever extra income you earn by way of fees." The latter approach has been adopted, for example, by the UK government.

Government subsidy can be allocated either by way of grants or by scholarships. We will discuss these alternatives later. The difference between the price of a course and the amount the government is prepared to subsidise represents the share that the student is expected to bear of the cost of his or her education. This might be paid up-front, financed by loans where necessary, or covered by the government as part of its grant to the university with an expectation that the student will pay the government back at a later date.

There should be no argument that some level of government subsidy for higher education is warranted. Society benefits both materially and culturally from having a highly educated proportion of the population. There is every reason to believe that without government intervention, the level of participation in higher education would be much less than is desirable, and it would be inequitably distributed. This becomes even more important as the changing nature of the workplace demands ever greater levels of skills and adaptability from individuals, and as national wealth depends on expansion of knowledge-based industries. There is also, as we have observed, a case for government support of a spectrum of university research.

In 1974, motivated by concerns about the under-representation of students from poorer backgrounds in higher education, the Commonwealth government abolished university tuition fees. This era of "free" university education, that is, where tuition was 100 per cent subsidised by public money, lasted for around fifteen years. The situation now is that some level of government subsidy is acknowledged, at least for some categories of courses, but students are expected to make a contribution to the cost of their education. This contribution ranges from a minimum amount via HECS arrangements through to payment of full fees.

*

At present, student-related funding (the non-research part of the university operating grant and student fees) comprises, on average, around 78 per cent of university income. The table on the following page shows that the bulk of university funding is not only derived from the Commonwealth government, but that the level of unit funding is also set by the Commonwealth. Most funding, particularly that for non-research activities, is not allocated on the basis of performance.

Note that we have not separately identified HECS as a financing mechanism for universities. Rhetorically, universities and the government like to point to a decreased reliance by universities on Commonwealth grant income, particularly arising from student contributions through HECS. While HECS represents a contribution to the cost of education by students, it only notionally comprises university income. Universities have no say in determining the level of HECS, and any HECS contribution from students that is collected by universities is offset against the Commonwealth grant, so the total amount remains as negotiated by the Commonwealth. In other words, HECS is a reimbursement from students to the Commonwealth, and has no direct effect on university income. Australian public universities remain reliant on government grants for the major part of their income, ranging from around half for the older universities, which have greater endowments and consultancy opportunities, to 70 per cent or more for most of the rest.

At present the level of government subsidy for undergraduate education ranges from around one half to two thirds of the average course cost. The total cost, both Commonwealth subsidy plus student contribution, is covered by way of block grants from the Government to universities and, as noted above, students reimburse the taxpayer for covering their contributions. In the case of postgraduate education, some courses are full fee-paying, while others are subsidised in the same way as for undergraduate education.

Variation between universities generally depends on age: the older, research-based universities derive more of their income from research grants and investments, while some of the newer universities garner significant income from overseas students. Nevertheless, all public universities derive the bulk of their income from price-controlled Commonwealth grants based on student numbers.

Student-related and research-specific income sources for universities in 1996

Category	Who determines level of unit income?	How is income allocated?
Australian undergraduate students (69% of all 1996 students)	Commonwealth government. (From 1998, universities can set fees for students enrolled above the quota subsidised by government)	Allocated by way of student intake based on levels negotiated by university and government
Australian postgraduate students (19% of total)	Commonwealth government for 67% of this group	Allocated according to negotiated level of intake
	University for 33%	Fees
Overseas students (9% of all 1996 students)	University	Fees
Other (includes non-award and enabling courses) (3% of total)	Commonwealth for 28%	Student intake
	University for 72%	Fees

The mix of fees and controlled pricing is inconsistent, as is the mix of levels of government subsidy. Confusion was further confounded by the 1996 Budget decision to allow universities to charge some Australian undergraduate students full fees from 1998. Despite the Australian Vice-Chancellors' Committee's consistent support for this development in previous years, most universities were uncomfortable with this option, for reasons we will examine below, and only a few offered such places in 1998.

The present situation is the result of years of erosion of a fundamentally unsustainable position that the taxpayer would meet all costs of university education. We now have a poorly-balanced funding system which presents an awkward situation both for the universities and for the present Federal Government, which espouses a creed of economic rationalism, even if it does not follow through such a philosophy. On the one hand government is exhorting universities to act as if they were providers within a market, on the other they control and regulate most of the price signals within this market. David Phillips, a former senior government education official, made just such an observation in relation to the requirement that universities meet the cost of academic salary increases: ".. this policy has at its heart a view that the sector should be responsible for meeting growth in its own costs (above a minimum standard level). Such a policy, in the end, is inconsistent with a broader policy framework which fixes the price of the sector's main product, undergraduate teaching."[4]

There are two key questions that must be addressed when considering university funding. Under what circumstances, if any, should the government directly control the pricing and charging of university activities? And, how should government subsidies for higher education be allocated?

Tuition fees

One of the pivotal arguments in favour of allowing universities to charge fees is that it would encourage diversity. When universities are restricted to a national average income level, they have limited opportunity to provide different learning environments and opportunities for students. This is particularly the case when the funding provided by the government per student is progressively squeezed; under these conditions, staff time and resources available to pursue new approaches are limited, and the common reaction of departments and schools is to pull back to core activities, seeking efficiency at the expense of quality. To date, most universities have managed to find money either from within their budgets and discretionary income, or from government grants, to pursue innovation. This will become increasingly difficult as the government seeks to reduce budget outlays on higher education and as universities have to find funds for academic salaries.

Another point in favour of universities charging tuition fees is that it would remove the distorting effects on student entry arising from the current system. At present, each course has a limit on the number of students who can enter, a "quota", which, when aggregated across the university, depends on how many places the government is prepared to provide. There are financial penalties for consistently failing to meet university quota, and so universities go to considerable lengths to ensure that their total student load is at least at the amount funded by government. Given the uncertainties in ensuring this level, which depends not only on how many students accept university offers but also on how many students drop out from year to year, most universities aim to play it safe by over-enrolling. This has two effects. First, since 1990 universities have enrolled more students (on average by more than 3 per cent each year) than were provided for by government funding. The government achieved an "efficiency" bonus but universities squeezed themselves further. Secondly, universities are under pressure to determine entry to courses on the basis of achieving a quota rather than insisting on a minimum standard.

Some proponents of tuition fees have argued that allowing institutions to determine prices, in conjunction with structural reforms to promote competition among universities and new providers, will allow market forces to operate. In particular it will enable some institutions to offer cheaper higher education by operating more efficiently or by restructuring offerings. Such a view underlies the Discussion Paper issued in November 1997 by the Australian Higher Education Financing and Policy Review Committee (the West Committee) and is also reflected in the Discussion Paper issued by the New Zealand Government in September 1997 on future tertiary education policy.[5] On the other hand, there is a concern that if universities are allowed to set fees, the cost of higher education would rise as universities seek to pass on rising salary and other costs. Critics can point to the United States where university and college fees have been a long-standing source of friction between government and the institutions. Over the past twenty years US tuition fees have risen far faster than inflation, particularly at the high end of the market. The drivers of these increases included increasing costs, higher salaries and better conditions for tenured professors, expanding administrations, and costs of technology. They also included poor management decisions and collusions between the Ivy League players whose fees tended to set benchmarks for the other institutions.[6] In more recent times competition between institutions has been enhanced, collusive arrangements prohibited, and tuition increases have been more modest.

Some also argue that the ability to charge fees will establish a provider-client relationship between universities and students, making universities more attentive to student demands and needs, and students more assertive about demanding quality. Certainly, many of the current fee-paying postgraduate students and overseas students have been assertive about their expectations of quality in return for the fees they pay. However, such provider-client signals will be diluted to the extent that many students will not pay the fees themselves, but rather be subsidised partly or entirely by families, employers or from other sources.

Some degree of heightened attentiveness to student needs already occurs, as universities seek to fill their quotas without lowering standards by competing for the best students. Service and quality relationships are also not determined solely by financial considerations: most academics have professional concerns to achieve quality. But the main difficulty with this claim about quality from competition is that many, if not most, students do not make a dispassionate, informed judgement about the quality of different universities when they choose to enter higher education. Undergraduate students first and foremost are looking to enrol in particular courses, such as engineering, law, or environmental science, but when similar courses are offered by different universities, prestige and status do play a major role. The more prestigious universities, which are generally those older research-based universities, enjoy a head start which lessens the need for them to invest in expensive marketing strategies or to pursue students with lures of high quality teaching. As Simon Marginson from the University of Melbourne puts it:

> They do not need to become more efficient, cheaper or more responsive to win support. They do not expand, which would reduce their positional value. Instead the waiting lists become longer. This creates a further excess demand

for high value positional goods. But the market is not contestable. "Quality" cannot be diluted. The established institutions are underwritten by decades of powerful investment and the long slow accumulation of reputation and cultural authority. As the newer universities have found, the leading universities in each State, which long enjoyed a monopoly or duopoly, are not easily augmented or displaced.[7]

Many of the newer universities have only been in existence for a few years, and their ability to develop distinctive missions has been limited by the averaging tendencies of the current system, which both protects them from the need to establish genuine differentiation and also limits their ability to "undercut" the established institutions. The race may be handicapped, but positions can change, particularly if the older universities allow sustained indifference to the quality of teaching to affect the status of their degrees. In fact, Professor Alan Gilbert, the Vice-Chancellor of Marginson's own university, has been active in highlighting the threat to established universities of "virtual" organisations which could operate more cheaply and flexibly across national borders.

Nevertheless, it is certainly true that the more prestigious universities will be able to charge a "status premium" for their degrees, which, if used properly, could enable them to entrench their advantages in attracting certain types of student. Why would this be a problem? After all, such differences already exist within the Australian higher education system; the best performing school leavers already aim to go to the major urban universities to study medicine, law and the like. Two difficulties have been put forward; firstly that the less prestigious, particularly the regional, universities could become non-viable in unprotected competition, and secondly that exacerbating positional advantage could worsen social inequity as students with access to more money have preferential access to the best universities, which in turn gives them better access to high-paying careers.

The first observation to make is that status and prestige is an important variable, but not the only one. Students pick which university they want to go to on the basis of many criteria. These include, in addition to the status and prestige of the university, the availability of a particular course, financial considerations, perceived attractiveness of the degree in the job market, location, flexibility in delivery, quality of teaching and learning, access to high quality staff, and so on. An undergraduate school leaver will base his or her decision on different criteria to those of a graduate in the workplace who is seeking employment-related skills. Likewise, those seeking vocational preparation will choose differently from those seeking a general education.

Second, we should note that the segmentation of the current fee-paying market, in non-research postgraduate study and overseas students, has not fallen along the lines of traditional status and prestige. Looking at national data for 1995, the national university non-fee income pie was divided 48 per cent to the nine universities established prior to 1960, 20 per cent to the nine established between 1960 and 1986, and 32 per cent to the seventeen established since 1986. However the total income from fees was divided 43 per cent to the pre-1960 universities, 17 per cent to the 1960-1986 universities and 40 per cent to the post-1986 universities. Clearly, the newer universities have been able to stake a significant claim in the current fee-paying field; this holds true at both the undergraduate and postgraduate level.

We might also observe that opinions seem to be divided about the likely reaction of the privileged universities. Marginson, as cited above, argues that they are likely to wish to protect their positional advantage. This would mean that they would not seek to greatly expand their numbers, but might instead seek to "poach" the top performing students from other universities. Others have claimed that the privileged universities will grow in size at the expense of the others. Professor Michael Osborne, The Vice-Chancellor of La Trobe University, wrote that " ... acute overcrowding is also one of the likely effects of the so-called 'voucher system' which permits holders to enrol at the university of their choice. For without some enrolment quota based on physical and staffing capacity the temptation on the part of 'prestige' institutions to indulge in excessive enrolment to generate resources will be irresistible."[8]

Certainly the enthusiastically entrepreneurial approach of at least one sandstone university to the introduction of undergraduate fees would seem to support Osborne's view over that of Marginson. This included the option of enticing students who had undertaken most of their studies at another university to pay a fee to complete their degree at the sandstone university, thus buying the "brand name". However, at present most universities, including the older and better resourced institutions, are operating at fairly high rates of usage of their facilities, at least within the limits set by current academic practice. Major expansion would require new land and buildings, or a major investment in distance education, which has not been their forte. Such expansion could not be financed from voucher income, and would be subject to control by government. It is unlikely, therefore, that an unchecked expansion of older universities would occur, even if they had the desire to do so. It might also be observed that under the current system, the top performing students can already go to the institution of their choice. One final point is that privileged universities are likely to charge a higher fee, and so the additional cost would be a factor to be taken into account even by the top students.

One solution to the problem of relative advantage for the asset-rich older universities over the newer institutions is for the government to introduce a charge on assets, including buildings and land. In this way, universities which had been favoured in the past by generous allowances of land, often in prime central positions, would be expected to provide some return on these assets. In addition, such a charge would encourage institutions to use their assets more efficiently, and would put them on a more equal footing with private providers who have to factor in the cost of infrastructure in their prices. The introduction of an infrastructure charge was recommended by the West Committee in its Discussion Paper. It has also been closely considered since 1992 by the New Zealand Government, which indicated in its September 1997 Green Paper that the issue was connected to the question of ownership of university assets and the introduction of a competitively-neutral market. This not only required the removal of factors which advantaged public providers (such as the absence of a need to consider the cost of their capital) but also the removal of disadvantages faced by the public institutions. Such disadvantages include restrictions imposed by the Government on the use of assets - for example in relation to the sale of university land - and on pricing. In other words, a capital charge regime would need the Government to assign far greater freedom to universities to use their assets as they see fit and to charge fees which take into account their capital costs.[9]

There are obstacles in the way of capital charging, even setting to one side the broader issue of tuition fees. Practical factors include questions about charging for non-publicly-funded assets, balancing Commonwealth, State and local government interests, administrative complexity, adjusting for historical imbalances, and determining appropriate mechanisms to avoid inflating prices and to achieve desired efficiency gains. One might also consider the likely reaction of universities which already have to bear the cost of maintaining heritage buildings and collections.[10]

A further complication with tuition fees arises when capacity to pay becomes a factor in university admissions. Thus, within a particular course there might be a mix of subsidised and non-subsidised students. Under current arrangements, postgraduate level courses are either full fee-paying or all students are subsidised. At undergraduate level, from 1998 the government has allowed universities to charge full fees to some students, namely those enrolled above the quota funded by government. This allows for the unpalatable situation where students who are less qualified may be able to buy their way into a course. Whatever the criteria used to determine eligibility for subsidised placement, allowing additional students to enrol outside those criteria represents a situation where those with the ability to pay have an advantage. Uncomfortable with this situation, many universities have chosen not to pursue this option in 1998. Nevertheless they will watch closely the outcomes for those universities which have chosen to admit such students.

Of course, the principle that money can buy better service applies widely outside higher education. We accept it in relation to health care, where those who can afford top private health cover do not have to wait as long for health care and receive better service, while a minimum standard is provided through the public system. Yet we have been conditioned to expect a uniform level of service for university education, and the thought that money could buy some advantage greatly worries many people. On the other hand, there is an equity issue involved in the current situation, where merit is often measured by school performance, and school performance is not entirely independent of parental income. Those students whose parents can afford to send them to the top private schools generally produce better grades, and more often go to the prestigious older universities. If there is a positional advantage to going to such universities, within specific disciplinary areas, then why should such students or their parents not pay a premium? Of course, one would not expect that a university would accept anybody who was willing to pay; they would need to balance minimum standards against the desire to take the student's money.

Yet it is one thing to suggest that students who go to more prestigious universities should pay fees, and quite another to propose that those who can pay fees should obtain privileged entry. In the prestigious

American fee-paying universities, selection of students is an intensive process, based on school grades, individual testing, recommendations from school counsellors, and various other strategic factors that the university wishes to take into account. These would include regional considerations or students' financial backgrounds. However, once a student is deemed ineligible to enter, they cannot ask to be accepted if they are prepared to pay extra. It is worth noting that applicants already know the institutional fees up front, so institutions are largely selecting from a pool of people who can afford the flagfall, or who are eligible for government or other assistance.

However, in the Australian system, where course entry standards are determined on the basis of how many subsidised places the Government makes available, which students are supposed to be admitted on a full fee-paying basis? Presumably there would be few students who wish to enrol at a sandstone university and pay full fees for the privilege, when they already have a subsidised place in a closely similar course at another institution. The catchment, therefore, would be students who just miss the "cut off" for a particular course, and who wish to enter on a fee-paying basis. Imagine, for example, a student who wishes to study Engineering, for which he or she needs to be in the top 5 per cent of the school leaver cohort. If the student leaves school in the top 6 per cent, he or she might be let in on a fee-paying basis. If the student scores brilliant marks for the first year, should he or she be allowed a subsidised place in second year, or should fees continue to be required, while another student who barely made the cut-off and performed poorly continue to receive a subsidised second year place? The Opposition spokesman for higher education commented that he would not want to be operated on by a surgeon who bought his way into a medical degree. Presumably this was a rhetorical device; after all, no matter what method of entry is employed, presumably students still have to pass the appropriate examinations. The issue is really one of fairness and consistency.

For these reasons, a hybrid system of fully-subsidised places and full-fee places within particular courses is unattractive. If fees are to be charged at all, they should be charged uniformly. The question then becomes one of finding appropriate levels of subsidy.

The principal advantages of a fee-based system would be that universities would operate at a level which reflects the demand for what they offer, that standards would not be unduly affected by the need to achieve a certain quota, and that greater diversity in university offerings and operations would be possible. The disadvantages include the possibility of greater cost to the student and the taxpayer, and possible weakening of the position of the less well-endowed and prestigious universities.

Whether these advantages and disadvantages are realised depends not only on whether or not fees are charged, but also the extent of government subsidies and the ways in which such subsidies are allocated.

Government subsidy

We will assume here that HECS arrangements will continue to be available to students in subsidised courses to allow them to defer their contribution. We will also assume that government subsidies will always roll in the HECS component, with that component being returned to the public purse through the tax system or up-front.

It is possible that HECS might be separated from government subsidy in that students might have access to a HECS option in full fee-paying courses. Under such a system, HECS loans could be extended to a wider range of students, and charges set at a level which enable the government to recoup administrative costs and the risk of default. Such a proposal was advanced by Bruce Chapman of the Australian National University in an appendix to the West Committee's Discussion Paper. Chapman proposed extending HECS more widely than at present, including to students enrolled in TAFE. However he noted that the higher the level of debt, and the lower the level of expected income, the greater was the possibility of HECS debt remaining unpaid over a person's lifetime, thus jeopardising the scheme. While such a scheme could be constructed to be fully-funded over time, it would involve new short-term costs for the government which would be politically unpalatable and inhibit the extent to which it could subsidise students in appropriate courses. At the time of releasing the West Committee's Discussion Paper in November 1997, the Government stated that it "had no intention of introducing ... HECS for TAFE."[11]

As David Phillips has pointed out, government subsidies will always be limited in overall size, and so the question becomes one of rationing.[12] In a particular year the government might either decide it is prepared to spend a fixed amount of money on higher education or else it might decide it had a fixed number of places it was prepared to subsidise. There are essentially three options: one is *regulated grant provision*, where the government apportions grants between a specified set of institutions in return for a minimum level of enrolments; another is *student-based*, where subsidies are allocated via the students in the form of a fixed entitlement or through scholarships or vouchers; the third is *open tender*, where institutions bid either for a specified number of places or for a pool of money. These approaches could be used in combination.

Regulated grant provision

The current situation for publicly-funded higher education is based on the first option; indeed this is the model that is consistently used in the publicly funded higher education systems of other countries.

The most obvious way to do this is to base the amount of the grant to each institution on the number of students, usually expressed in full-time equivalent terms. An alternative would be to allocate at least part of the grant on the basis of some indicator of performance, as is the case for some research funding. Such an alternative has the attraction of consistency with moves to ensure public sector focus on outcomes by rewarding those universities that do well on certain indicators. Indicators of performance might be based on drop-out rates, student progress and credit granted, rates of course completion, graduate employment measures or surveys of student satisfaction of courses.

In any system of resource allocation, attention needs to be paid to the administrative cost of the process. The reliability and validity of the measures used and the impact of the system on the activity being funded are also factors that demand scrutiny. The intention of performance-based funding is to reward recipients for performance in specified areas without unduly compromising other areas that are deemed valuable.

If assessment is based on a national set of indicators along these lines, administrative costs need not be prohibitive as much of the data is already available. There are, however, problems in precise definitions and measurement. Ideally, a system would be based on detailed assessment of quality and performance based on measures tailored to each institution, but this would increase complexity and cost. In the United Kingdom, both research and teaching are assessed by an expensive and ambitious program of institutional visits, which provide a set of scores for each university. The research score is used to allocate research funding, but there is greater reluctance to use the teaching scores in this way.

There are also significant concerns about the distorting effects of allocating funding on the basis of performance indicators. The present system based on student intake has the advantages of administrative simplicity, together with statistical accuracy, and its impact is to encourage universities to maximise enrolments levels. The downside of this is that universities could try to cram more students in, and devote less attention to standards and to their students' educational welfare. If universities were penalised for high drop-out rates, they might be tempted to lower standards to retain students; if they were funded according to the production of graduates, they might be tempted to lower standards of examinations. If they were funded according to immediate job-placements of graduates, they might be accused of promoting short-term vocationalism. Such concerns may underplay the value placed on standards by academics and institutions, but universities have in the past shown themselves to be extremely willing to comply with funding signals. Indeed, that is the whole point of performance-based funding.

Nevertheless, the possibility of rewarding institutional performance is appealing to government, and hybrid systems based on a mixture of student intake and performance indicators might be adopted on the grounds that they introduce at least some benefits while diluting the methodological problems. Concerns about favouring some institutions which have natural advantages could be overcome by applying the performance measures only to a specified bonus which would be framed in terms of meeting institution-specific goals. If the bonus is not earned it would revert to the government rather than being diverted to another university. This approach has been adopted in some States in the USA.

If performance-based funding were to be introduced, it would need to be developed in terms which recognise institutional diversity, and so would be based on performance against targets agreed between each university and government. Universities might select from a national menu of indicators and establish targets which they are to achieve in return for extra funding. This need not represent the so-called Matthew effect[13], where those who are already advantaged are further rewarded. Performance-based funding can be based on improvement, so that those who meet agreed targets are equally rewarded, even if this improvement is from a different level.

One option that has been put forward on several occasions is that government funding should be allocated on the basis of credits awarded or some other measure of student progress. This will undoubtedly raise the hackles of those who believe that academics will throw aside concerns of quality in pursuit of money, and promptly lower examination standards. However, advocates argue that the government should not be subsidising students who are uncommitted to their study, and that the taxpayer should adopt the same approach as is taken by many employers who pay the fees of employees undertaking work-related education, that is, fees are covered once the subject is passed.

Government grants could operate either in an environment where universities determine the price through charging fees, or where prices are controlled by government. If an institution charged fees that were higher than the level of the government grant, including a standardised HECS component, then the gap would need to be funded either by institutional scholarships or by the student, possibly by way of a loan scheme. Government grants might be adjusted for fee income, as is the case in the United Kingdom, or might be based on guarantees from the institution that a defined number of students in specific areas would not have to pay fees.

One other point relating to grant-based subsidies is that they generally do not take account of an individual student's circumstances. The Commonwealth has taken a broad-brush approach to specifying eligible intakes, in the past insisting on a minimum target for school leavers or for those entering higher education for the first time. However, finer tuning is left to the universities. Students undertaking second or even third undergraduate degrees can receive taxpayer subsidised places, as can those who perform badly and take several years of study before dropping out.

The benefits of regulated provision are that institutions can operate in a more stable environment, and it is a relatively simple scheme to administer. The drawbacks are that the advantages of market-based competition are not achieved, it does not take account of individual student eligibility and, in the case that government controls price, institutional diversity is discouraged.

Student-based

Under this option, students would either pay up-front (perhaps by taking out a loan) and seek subsidies from the government to reimburse them; alternatively, and this is the model usually countenanced in Australia, students would be allocated a certain amount of public funds to finance their education. Institutional funding would then "follow the student". Allocating resources this way would introduce a more direct market-like arrangement into the funding of higher education. A question arises in such schemes as to whether scholarships or vouchers should be provided to institutions outside the existing public university system. This would certainly be in line with broader principles of public sector reform, and was raised as an issue, but not answered, by the Australian and New Zealand Discussion Papers on higher education.[14] Contestability - allowing other players to compete to provide services - is necessary to allow the benefits of competition to be realised. It is a fundamental plank of the National Competition Policy and a key component of reforms to vocational education and training. But while it might be argued that suitably accredited private providers should be eligible to receive government scholarships, there is the additional complication posed by the growing possibilities of global higher education. Should an Australian government subsidy, and HECS arrangements, be available to an Australian student who wishes to undertake a fee-paying undergraduate course at a US or British university using distance education?

There are essentially two possible models for student-based funding. One is to ration subsidies through the issuing of a limited number of scholarships or vouchers, the other is to provide a universal entitlement through what has been termed a "learning account". In both cases, the rationing of public funding is a key issue.

Rationing vouchers or scholarships

A voucher or scholarship could be allocated to prospective students either before or after they have been accepted by an education institution.

If allocated *before* enrolment, the government would need some method of ranking applicants. A standardised test for all intending university applicants was recommended by a recent study of selection methods for Australian universities. The intention was to remove the distortions on schooling and course selection caused by the use of the school leaver score, or TER.[15] Senator Amanda Vanstone, the former Federal Minister responsible for higher education, noted with approval innovations in some areas to move away from the "tyranny of the TER", meaning that instead of relying on the single school leaver score, some courses use the methods mentioned earlier for American universities, which rely on interviews and other approaches to assessing student suitability.[16] While more diverse selection methods are undoubtedly desirable, nationally standardised testing of all applicants would have significant administrative and resource implications, and would not be well suited to an environment where there is greater flexibility in university entry and articulation.

By linking funding to such testing, the funding agency would in effect be making judgements about the suitability of candidates for university study, something which has usually been left to universities to decide. While school results are at present the prime determinant for school leavers, universities also make decisions about mature-age entrants on the basis of credit granted for previous study, or for expertise they have acquired in their time since school, which is often tailored to the particular course. For example, entry to a performing arts course may be based on auditions or portfolios. This can only further complicate proposals for allocation of scholarships.

The alternative would be to allocate vouchers or scholarships to students *after* they had been accepted for enrolment. Since it is inevitable that there will be more applicants than available vouchers, some students would miss out on subsidies, which would influence their decision about continuing with study. There would be what the New Zealand Government termed in its Green Paper, a "wash-up" of enrolments as students chose between institutional offers or chose to discontinue study. The disadvantages for institutions in terms of resource uncertainty, and for both institutions and government in terms of administrative burden, are obvious.

Learning Accounts

The learning account model has received considerable attention in recent years. In the aftermath of the Report of the 1997 National Committee of Inquiry into Higher Education (the Dearing Report), learning accounts "have moved to the top of the student support agenda" in the United Kingdom.[17] The West Committee's Discussion paper also promoted the concept.

In essence, a learning account is a consolidated account held by an individual into which funds, either public or private, are placed for education and training. An account might be issued to a person on leaving school. The account could be credited with a government grant, by contributions from the prospective student, parents or employer, or by funds lent to the student. The individual would then decide which combinations of education and training would suit him or her best, drawing on the account funds as needed.

Such a system has the virtue of encouraging people to make their own decisions about education and training, and by placing the funds in an identifiable account it makes the resource implications of such decisions explicit. The account would operate in a commercial climate, where institutions set their own fees against which prospective students weigh the costs and benefits of particular educational choices. Both the West Committee and the former Minister for Education, Peter Baldwin, proposed learning account models for financing a "seamless" postsecondary education, so that students would use their accounts to finance mixtures of VET and university education as appropriate.[18]

Learning accounts recast public subsidies as a universal rather than a selective entitlement. As such, public subsidies are spread more widely across the potential student population and so it follows that either the government will incur greater costs, or subsidies will be rationed. Rationing, the only practical option, would be through a combination of restricting the duration of subsidy, in terms of years of study or particular programs (for example excluding postgraduate study), and limiting the amount of subsidy for each person. Even assuming the obstacles to achieving a "seamless" tertiary education system could be overcome, the implementation of learning accounts would require substantial administration, and complex transitional arrangements would be required to cater for those who are not school leavers and who have had some previous education and training.

Learning accounts also raise the question of whether or not the full amount of public funding should be allocated up-front, the concern being that people of school-leaver age may not be in the best position to manage long-term finances and determine their educational needs. This would be of particular concern if a student exhausted their lifetime public subsidy for tertiary education quickly, as might happen for example if students were allowed to use their public subsidy to cover the full cost of fees for a course, thereby avoiding making a personal contribution.

Open tender

A third method for allocating public subsidies is by way of opening a set number of places, or dollar amount, to tender. Universities would bid for these places or dollars, in competition with other providers if appropriate, and bids would be assessed by the funding agency. Such an approach is already being used for in-service teacher education in some States and for vocational education and training.

Such an approach may have advantages in defined areas, where a funding agency is able to make meaningful judgements between the bids of different institutions in relation to specific program goals and costs. After all, there is no doubt that Australia needs knowledge-intensive industries, and more qualified people to service them. We need more graduates with skills relevant to high-technology manufacturing and information technology. This point has been reinforced by various reports to government on the state of our manufacturing and IT industries.[19] Why then should the government have to increase places across the board in higher education? Do we really need more graduates in archaeology, dance or medicine? Why can the government not simply purchase extra places in defined fields?

Of course it can, and undoubtedly will look closely at the proposition in some cases. However, a widespread extension of tendering would be counter to the trend towards shifting decision-making about course selection from central government or institutions to students. It would also go against the grain of traditions of institutional autonomy in deciding which students enter various courses. Such a proposal would be opposed on the grounds that it is too narrow and that it would drive down courses to "the lowest common denominator". This would only happen if the selection process concentrated on the cheapest bids, and did not take into account educational or regional outcomes. One might also observe that the application of tendering within higher education is also likely to be limited by the administrative costs involved, particularly if the allocation of tenders is able to be appealed.

*

The funding of universities is clearly a complex business. Policy makers find themselves faced by a funding Hydra; as soon as one head is lopped off, another grows to create problems.

While it is widely accepted that some share of the cost of higher education should be borne by or on behalf of the student, and some by government, there is no definitive way of determining which parts of higher education should be subsidised, or what balance there should be between government subsidy and individual cost. These matters are left to the political process.

However, in settling such questions, governments should be consistent and coherent in their policy formulation. If universities are expected to operate as providers within a market, to meet their own costs, become more diverse and selective about what they do and to adjust their offerings and pricing in response to student demand, it is hard to see why they should be constrained from charging appropriate fees for what they have to offer.

A system based on fees is likely to prove attractive to government, and is consistent with the philosophy of market-based provision of services. More cynically, one attraction to government would be that blame for levels of service would be attributed to institutions, as fees would not be directly linked to government grants. Within a fee-paying system, the key question is how to allocate government subsidies. As a general rule, we would suggest that for a proposal to have any likelihood of success it would need to have the following characteristics:

(a)   the overall cost and debt burden on students should not be significantly increased for newcomers to higher education;

(b)   student contributions should be financed by HECS mechanisms;

(c)   an open-ended commitment of funds by government should be avoided (for example in setting subsidies at a proportion of fees that are determined by universities);

(d)   complex changes to the tax system should not be involved;

(e)   clear and logical ways of directing subsidies to mature-age students as well as school-leavers should be provided; and

(f)   administration costs for both government and institutions should be manageable.

One model that would have the virtue of simplicity in the sense that it is nearest to the current situation and the least disruptive, would be to allow institutions to charge fees within more or less the current arrangements. Thus, government grants could be provided to public universities in exchange for a minimum student load. The grants would amount to the current average levels for various courses, minus the HECS contribution. Institutions could then set fees, and the difference between the fees and the base subsidy would represent the amount needed to be covered by the student via HECS or other mechanisms, although HECS would be capped by government. Some students may have a smaller HECS burden than at present if an institution is able to charge lower fees. Others may charge high fees which result in the same HECS burden that currently exists plus an additional amount to be funded by the student. It would be expected that in the latter situation the institution would operate suitable scholarship programs, and equity enrolments may be one of the performance criteria in allocating government grants.

Such a system would remove the current inconsistencies in fee-charging at the undergraduate level and promote greater diversity, on the other hand it lacks the attraction of contestability, in that only a defined set of public institutions would participate. In practice, any system will have flaws. The existing system has the virtues of simplicity and stability but the vices of uniformity and subjection to government cost-cutting policies. A market-based system will encourage diversity and responsiveness, but has the potential to lead to greater instability and higher student costs, as well as inequitable access.

*

Many people within higher education institutions, and many students, believe there is not much wrong with universities that a sustained dose of extra funding would not fix. However, it is highly unlikely that we will see a reversal of government parsimony. If the system needs money, then extra funding will either have to come from the student, or on his or her behalf by an employer or the family. At the very least, institutions will need to find greater efficiencies by lowering unit costs. Some universities

have sought to do this by winding back across the board, so that contact times and opportunities for interaction between staff and students have been reduced, with a consequent effect on quality. It is better if universities concentrate on those areas which are most attractive to students, which generate the most enrolments. Of course, some areas may need to be preserved which have smaller enrolments but which have particular strategic importance for the institution or for government. However, most Australian universities have a large number of subjects with low enrolments that represent a burden on their budgets.

Such an approach might seem inconsistent with the need to offer students greater choice. One of the most straightforward ways of increasing choice, and one which also serves to satisfy the desire of individual academics to teach in areas of their own interest, is to increase the number of optional subjects that may be studied as part of a course. However, such an approach is likely to generate a high level of unit cost, and has also been criticised on educational grounds that it either fragments the curriculum or simply allows students to pick more subjects that suit their narrow preferences.

An alternative to increasing the number of optional subjects is for universities to examine ways in which units of study can be shared between courses, particularly in areas relevant to generic skills that the university wishes to inculcate in its graduates. Such approaches also can have educational limitations if they are extended too broadly; the American Association of Colleges and Universities found that "distributed" subjects can result in students being unmotivated, subjects being poorly taught and a general lack of overview arising from decentralised responsibility.[20] Another option for broadening student curriculum choice includes the use of double degrees, which have proved particularly popular in recent years. Universities can also look to more systemic ways of increasing student choice, for example by using more flexible modes of delivery to allow options for the time and place of study, or by using better structured transitions between courses, including credit recognition for study undertaken elsewhere. Again, a balance must be struck between expanding student choice, achieving educational objectives, and being able to provide sufficient financial support.

While there is no magic recipe for achieving university efficiency, the imperative remains that an institutional perspective must be taken on matters of flexibility and resource management. In a stable or growing environment, large organisations can operate without really knowing what their activities actually cost. They can draw up their budgets on a year-by-year basis, they can hire staff on a permanent basis, and they need not consider one area a higher priority than another. In an uncertain environment they must operate on a forward-looking basis, anticipating threats and opportunities, knowing the sustainability of their activities and being able to identify and jettison activities which are of a low priority when they are not able to support them.

We have come a long way from the conception of the university as a collection of independent senior academics, who could run an institution on the basis of often undocumented agreements, bluster and appeals to tradition. Vice-chancellors have evolved from being part-time fund raisers and university advocates to the equivalent of chief executive officers. The clear need for centrally-articulated objectives and institutional management has not arisen from an innate love of managerialism; after all, the "perpetrators" are themselves senior academics. Rather, it has arisen from the necessity of dealing with change and financial uncertainty in a large organisation.

*

No discussion of funding and autonomy of Australian universities, or indeed of universities anywhere in the Western world in recent years, could be complete without some consideration of quality and accreditation.

Concern with quality is the natural successor to the international higher education agendas of rationalisation, amalgamation and cost-cutting. The centralised approach to higher education in the United Kingdom contrasts with the more market-driven attitudes that prevail in the United States. Again, we have ended up somewhere in-between.

In the United Kingdom the debate centres around the concepts of assuring quality and, importantly, standards. Oddly enough, for a country whose higher education system is steeped in traditions of university autonomy, there are more concerns heard in the UK than in Australia and the United States about the need to ensure that degrees mean the same thing across different universities. The Americans are more relaxed about the notion that a degree from a State University may not mean the same as a degree from an Ivy League institution. Contrast this with the concerns expressed by Roger Brown, the Chief Executive Officer of the UK Higher Education Quality Council:

> If we, as an academic and professional community, cannot define and protect some measure of comparability, then we are laying ourselves open to a number of dangers ... the academic community will break up and standards will be established and protected by individual institutions or groups of institutions in response to what they see as being the requirements or needs of their particular bit of the 'market'[21]

In some ways, institutional autonomy is what drives governments' concerns about quality. In some countries, notably some of the European countries, governments have greater control over the curriculum, though perhaps not to the extent of that exercised over the school curriculum by Napoleon's minister of education, who boasted that he knew, at any given hour, exactly what was being taught by every teacher in every school in France. However if the government has little or no say in what is taught and researched, universities must expect the price of autonomy to be accountability, and that accountability will go well beyond providing proper financial statements.

This might appear to be an expression of mistrust by government. After all, the university system should be based on academic authority, and the maintenance of professional academic standards is the glue that holds the disciplines together. Some recognition of this is, of course, given by the Australian and UK governments in that their national quality systems have been based on assessments made by sages from within the sector, and the measures by which each university is to be assessed are set by the university itself. Indeed, the generally accepted view is that in any such system there should be, for reasons of clarity and legitimacy, a separation between funders, providers and accreditors, with quality assurance something that should be "owned" by the universities, but independent of their operations. In the UK for example the funding councils are government-run, while the Higher Education Quality Council is owned by the universities (as revealed by Roger Brown's comments), but not beholden to any one of them. Things are a little more complicated in New Zealand, where the New Zealand Vice-Chancellors' Committee is responsible for accreditation in the form of approving new courses in New Zealand universities, but an independent Academic Audit Unit exists, funded by the universities, to oversight quality matters.

The need for some sort of system for assuring quality, if not uniform standards, is well accepted in Australia. As in all evaluations there is some tension between the desire of those being evaluated - to see it as something which is designed to be encouraging and lead to improvement - and that of the evaluator, whose task may be to assess and make summary judgements about performance. The two agendas are improvement and accountability. We will sidestep to some extent the volumes of literature that have been written on this dichotomy in the quality debate, and suggest that the improvement aspects are largely an internal responsibility. It is the accountability dimension which is clearly the driver for external quality assessment.

Internally, institutions monitor various measures of performance, review their structures and activities, and examine individual performance at times of appointment and promotion. We have briefly considered some of the external scrutiny of quality earlier in this book. At the government level, there were three "quality rounds" of assessment at the overall institutional level, as well as measurement of various indicators such as the opinions of graduates, drop-out rates, employment of graduates and so on. Non-government assessment in the form of the *Good Universities Guide* and similar publications, draws on these publicly-available measures as well as other measures to provide information for prospective students. These guides frequently provoke controversy, at least from those universities who are not rated as highly as they would like to be. A third form of quality control comes from professional accreditation of courses, which in some cases involved quite detailed scrutiny of course structures and content by professional groups.

In the research arena, excellence of projects is assured as well as it can be by a process of peer review, and by scrutiny of past performance when making judgements about future support. At an institutional level, the government bases at least some research funding, and a good deal more than is the case in most other countries, on "performance" measures such as counts of publications and grants earned.

We have moved from the tendency prevalent some years ago to seek institutional league tables. Publicly at least one cannot point to an overall measure of one university against another, although this is unavoidable when funding (for example for research) is allocated on the basis of some sort of performance measures. A more sophisticated understanding is emerging that quality is highly variable between different areas within different universities, and that we can at best only catch a blurred glimpse of quality by using numerical measures of performance.

The national quality assessments that were undertaken in Australia in the early 1990s did not satisfy many observers, either within the sector or outside. They were brief, aimed at the whole university rather than its component parts, and generated a great deal of paperwork and compliance but shed little light. Ideally, or at least ideally from the point of view of an external stakeholder with unlimited funds, the funders of higher education would like to be assured of quality on the basis of the best possible method of assessment. Unfortunately the best method of assessment is for external peers, preferably from overseas, to come and visit for an extended period of time and focus their attention on a particular department or discipline rather than a whole institution. Something of the sort was attempted in the UK in the case of research, as we examined earlier. Realistically it is not an option if we want some sort of up-to-date measure of quality across the whole sector on a regular basis.

Universities can safely assume that governments and the public will want some sort of reassurance about quality in the future. It is consistent with the reformulation of government as a purchaser of services that it develops a focus on outcomes and value for money. If we are to have an independent system, as opposed to a reliance on professional standards by academics and institutions, it should allow for and actively encourage diversity. This inevitably means that it will be complex and spread out over several years, and will not and should not provide a simple ranking of universities, however much that may be desired by the various "stakeholders".

Allied to the notion of quality is that of accreditation, or the formal recognition by an independent body of the status of an organisation. This is a responsibility of the relevant State or Territory government, who oversee legislation that prohibits unaccredited organisations from offering higher education. We have already noted the data from The Australian Council for Private Education and Training to the effect that in 1997 State accreditation bodies had approved forty-nine private institutions to offer some 186 higher education programs. These programs lead to awards including those at diploma, graduate certificate, graduate diploma, bachelor, masters and doctoral levels. The chairman of ACPET spoke out in 1997 against the perceived conflict of interest involved in accreditation procedures whereby accreditation panels comprised members from industry and public universities, including a representative of the AVCC. His proposed solution was to call for a private national regulatory body to avoid duplication and "inconsistent quality standards."[22]

The issue of accreditation is gaining in importance as new providers are looming on the horizon. It is consistent with National Competition Policy that these providers be allowed to compete, including for students subsidised by government, provided they are suitably accredited. It would seem necessary that some form of national coordination exist if accreditation is to lead to access to Commonwealth funding. On the other hand, the possibility of international providers extending educational services into Australia poses deeper problems, both in terms of quality assurance and formal recognition of status through accreditation by State governments or national funding bodies. These issues have yet to be addressed.

One rather depressing prospect was put forward by Glenn R. Jones, an American higher education entrepreneur, who has been instrumental in driving some of the commercial distance education brokerage arrangements in US higher education:

> Because US higher education accrediting bodies are non-governmental, some of their agency officials believe the US could become the center for accrediting higher education programs worldwide.[23]

He also offered the prospect that international accreditation might be better effected through some global alliance of providers. Not surprisingly, he had a candidate in the form of the Global Alliance for Transnational Education (GATE), an organisation founded by Jones in 1995 to develop quality assurance for electronically-delivered courses worldwide.

CHAPTER NINE

Poisoned Ivy

Australian universities over recent years have sought to heed the demands of government and the broader community to lift the quality and relevance of their teaching and research, to reach out to the external world, and to modernise their methods of operation. Our universities have begun to internationalise their perspectives and their curricula, and to diversify their funding sources. Also, a small but influential proportion of academic staff are working with their technical and specialist colleagues to explore the potential of information technology to enhance the teaching and learning platform supporting our mass system of higher education. In the process, signs are emerging that our universities are beginning seriously to consider the needs of students as customers and clients.

These changes have been significant, yet it is also relevant to note that in two ways they have been secured in relatively benign circumstances. First, the commitment of successive federal governments to grow the higher education sector has helped to shield universities from the chilly budget winds which for at least a decade have been blowing across other parts of the taxpayer-funded landscape. And second, government has been prepared to offer financial inducements to universities to encourage them to renovate their systems or secure compliance with new policy regimes.

By international standards the funding cuts to Australian universities, at least those cuts implemented prior to 1998, have been mild. They also have been evident mainly in terms of reduced funding levels for undergraduate teaching. The cuts to date have been seen either as the first phase in the weaning of universities from their hitherto almost complete reliance on public subsidy, or as a specific attempt to pressure universities to overhaul at a more fundamental level their approach to undergraduate education.

Many people inside the university system have resisted the legitimacy of either proposition: they have clung to the hope that the requirements of a mass higher education system with diverse and complex needs could be met by simply scaling-up traditional academic practices. In any case, such people have consoled themselves with the fashionable view that any decrease in Commonwealth funding was a matter of profound regret and self-evidently illustrative of the philistine attitudes of politicians to education in general, and university education in particular.

There is some validity in this response. It is the case that there has been something of a longstanding ambivalence by government in Australia towards our universities. And from a national strategic perspective it is regrettable that governments over the years have displayed such an uneven capacity to recognise the potential contribution of universities to future economic and social development through the formation of intellectual capital.

But universities themselves have to accept at least some of the responsibility for this state of affairs. The role of universities as incubators for the professions has come to be taken largely for granted. But over the years universities have been widely seen as relatively impenetrable and self-absorbed organisations operating mostly outside the mainstream of public policy and without particular attention to the implications for themselves of the significantly changing circumstances and priorities of government.

There is little doubt that our universities have become more outward-looking and commercially savvy over the past decade. But there remains something of an assumption on the part of many university insiders that the changes which are occurring are taking place only at the margins. On that basis, universities have been able - at least for the moment - to cling to the assumption that they will be able to cope with the future by extrapolating from the past and without compromising idealised academic values. This has encouraged a culture of incrementalism.

Such a culture might suit those whose experience in leading and managing universities has been largely one of presiding over an assured pattern of funded growth. But these circumstances no longer apply. Governments are repositioning themselves as purchasers, rather than as patrons, of higher education. The needs of those attending our universities also are changing. Institutions will continue to cater for the career front-end group entering undergraduate programs directly from school. However, large-scale and rapid changes in the labour market profile, together with an increased emphasis on performance, will require education providers to focus more on the needs of those requiring reaccreditation and retraining as well as other lifelong learners. These various groups will have diverse needs and institutions will need to respond flexibly, in competition with other providers.

Competition has been seen in relation to research for many years. Over the past two decades this has intensified, as the balance between research funded through university operating grants and through competitive project grants has shifted toward the latter. Even though this competition is limited, it is already producing pressures on universities, particularly upon the tradition that all academics should both teach and research. University research based on academic departments and the solitary training of researchers will have to adjust to demands for problem solving that is multidisciplinary in nature and so requires teamwork. Teamwork will not only be among researchers, but with people inside and outside the university who have an interest in the outcomes of the research.

Such demands on academic work will intensify as commercial pressures for efficiency and specialisation are expanded. The heroic image of the professor who combines the virtues of expert teacher, master of an academic discipline, administrator and leader, and whose authority is paramount, is crumbling before the tide of change.

The forces of globalisation and information technology are radically reshaping the teaching and learning environment, while the prospect of open competition in the higher education marketplaces is likely not only to fragment the existing university system, producing major variation in the type and quality of institution, but also to produce enormous change in the ways universities are managed, in the nature of academic work, and in a more differentiated approach to academic careers. Institutions will need to adapt to these changes, while government needs to ensure that market forces do not entrench social inequities by restricting access to higher education.

These forces are immense and obvious. That they are makes it the more surprising that some would prefer to encourage the perception that business is as usual, and that changes can be accommodated incrementally.

For those who see universities as simply the custodians of academic traditions, the Ivy has been poisoned. The goals which these traditions were established to serve are not worthless. Society needs people to be educated in a climate of open inquiry, and it needs to develop an evolving base of knowledge that is not driven only by short-term considerations. But these goals need to be achieved against a background of constant change, where those who pay for the services of universities demand high standards of efficiency and performance.

Universities, to many the embodiment of conservatism and inertia, have only one choice in the face of this new environment. They can redefine themselves to operate successfully at the forefront of change, or they can remain as they are, and be overwhelmed.

Notes

Chapter Two: Drifting into Trouble

1. Carnegie Council (1980)
2. Report of the Joint DEET/HEC Working Party, *Review of Funding of Student Residences*, September 1991.
3. Barcan (1988), p. 67
4. Dates for the foundation of the universities are those of the passing of the relevant Act. In most cases the first intake of students occurred two years later.
5. Lord Bowden (1965), p. 37
6. Smith and Crichton (1990)
7. William Bragg continued at Leeds University the work on x-ray crystallography he had undertaken at Adelaide between 1886 and 1908, and went on to receive a Nobel Prize. See Moyal (1986), ch. 11
8. Greenwood (1960), p. 237
9. Murray (1957), p. 29
10. Martin (1990), p. 113
11. Richardson (1972)
12. Williams (1990)
13. Rowe (1960), p. 22
14. Willett (1972)
15. Some of the reduction was caused by the transfer of CAE courses to universities, however it is clear that there was an overall reduction in per capita funding to universities over this period.
16. Vanstone (1996)
17. The thinking behind the efficiency dividend is that organisations generate savings as they become more cost-efficient. Since they should have become more efficient (regardless of whether or not they actually have done so), there are savings which should have accrued. In the case of publicly-funded organisations, so the argument goes, the taxpayer is entitled to a share, or dividend, of these savings. Hence the government has a rationale for introducing ongoing cuts to the budgets of public organisations.
18. Since the reduction in Commonwealth places has been focussed at the postgraduate level, funded undergraduate places will increase by around 4,000 between 1997 and 1998, but total places will decrease by 6,730
19. The impact on demand for undergraduate places arising from demographic factors was assessed using Australiian Bureau of Statistics data in the Discussion Paper released by the Higher Education Financing and Policy Review Committee in November 1997 (p. 108). It showed that over the next fifteen years, demand would rise significantly in the Northern Territory, Queensland and Western Australia; rise moderately in New South Wales; remain stable in Victoria, South Australia and the A.C.T.; and decline in Tasmania.

20.   The NSW University of Technology was established without a Faculty of Arts. Throughout the 1950s it steadily built up a profile in this area, but degrees were awarded through the University of New England. The Murray Committee Report made it clear that if the institution aspired to be a "real" university, then it would need to award its own Arts degrees and to have a Faculty of Arts. This was accomplished in 1960.

21.   Wilkes (1965), p. 26

22.   "The People's University" was the title of a 1989 history of the South Australian Institute of Technology, one of the antecedents of the University of South Australia, which was established in 1990 (Aeuckens 1989). The same term provided the heading for the first chapter of the 1985 history of the University of Queensland (Thomis 1985).

23.   Nisbet (1971), p. 21

Chapter Three: The Purpose of a University

1.   Connell (1993), p. 10
2.   Higher Education Council (1996)
3.   This point is made in Marshall and Tucker (1992).
4.   Walshok (1995), p. 5
5.   Medawar (1984), p. 29
6.   Newman p. xxvii
7.   Flexner (1930)
8.   Kerr (1963)
9.   Snow (1962). The two cultures referred to by Snow were science and literature, literary analysis being a dominant force within the humanities. He added later that a "third culture" of the social sciences had emerged.
10.   Leavis (1962)
11.   Adams (1988) and Becher (1989)
12.   Damrosch (1995)
13.   ASTEC (1991)
14.   DEET (1995), Table A7.1
15.   Andrich and Mercer (1997), p. x
16.   Rosenman (1996)
17.   Auchmuty (1959), p. 18
18.   Philp (1964), p. 16
19.   Dawkins (1988), p. 7
20.   Boyer (1990)

Chapter Four: The University Identity Crisis

1.   Australian Council for Private Education and Training, submission to the Review of Higher Education Funding and Policy.

2.   Davis (1996), p. 308

3.   This type of statement is often hotly contested by the Federal Government and the relevant department. They point out, correctly, that if funds for buildings and research are included then total grants per student are only around 2 per cent less in 1996 than they were in 1983. If you compare total grants to planned student numbers, then in fact the ratio is 4 per cent more in 1996 than it was in 1983. All of this does not help universities, who cannot spend capital and research money on teaching staff, and who have to teach actual students, not planned numbers.

        The percentages quoted here are derived from the Australian Vice-Chancellors Committee tables of May 1997. Operating grant funding in 1983 was $3.1 billion for 255 thousand full-time students (or $12,143 per student) and in 1996 the figures were $4.6 billion for 437 thousand eft students (or $10,594 per student). This represents a 13 per cent drop in per capita funding. The figures are in constant prices and included superannuation funds in 1996.

4.   Slaughter and Leslie (1997)

5.   Painter (1996)

6.   Hood (1989), p. 90

7.   Cunningham et al. (1997)

8.   Bowden and Masters (1993), p. 33

9.   The following description of the development of the national competencies process is taken from Lundberg (1995), pp. 26-31

10.   Lundberg (1995), p. 118

11.   Humphrey (1997)

12.   Golding, Marginson and Pascoe (1996), p. 19

13.   ibid. p. 34

14.   Lundberg (1995) p. 126-131

15.   Pennington (1997)

16.   *The Australian*, April 2, 1997

17.   *The Australian*, November 5, 1997

Chapter Five: Teaching: From Side Show to Main Game

1.   Tutorials are a legacy of the British system of linking students with a senior mentor. In Oxford and Cambridge, the tutor-student relationship occurred at the college level, and tutorials consisted of detailed assessment by a tutor of a student work, for example reviewing a student essay on particular texts. As Australian universities have not adopted the college model of university structure, and tutorials have been a university function. The nexus between tutors and students is less personal. In the era of mass higher education, tutorial class sizes have risen, to the point where students are often faced with, in the words of Professor Michael Jackson of the University of Sydney, "a steady diet of lectures more lectures, and further lectures called tutorials, and even more expensive lectures called multi-media".

2.   Connell (1993), p. 7

3. Desmond and Moore (1992), p. 26
4. ACER(1996, 1997). The results of the Course Experience Questionnaire always need to be interpreted with caution. They report only the statements of those who graduated, not those who dropped out, the questionnaire is undergoing continuing refinement, and response rates are variable. However, even allowing for such qualifiers the broad statements about feedback represent a breadth of graduate opinion, and should be disturbing to those concerned with the quality of education in our universities.
5. see for example, Connell (1993), p. 491-2
6. Some universities do make student evaluations of teaching available to management. There are legitimate grounds for concern if this leads to a simple-minded reward/punishment system that encourages teachers to maximise their student ratings across the board without taking into account higher goals. Some students are quite happy being spoon-fed, particularly if that is what they are used to at school, and some resent being asked to think more actively, to solve problems, to work in groups, to use computers etc. As with any other "performance indicator", the focus should be on the word "indicator". However, none of the above justifies the widespread view that because indicators are not total measures, students should have no line of feedback past the teacher.
7. Martin (1996)
8. *Campus Review*, July 23, 1997, p. 11
9. Ballantyne (1997)
10. The American Association of Higher Education on-line discussion group devoted to matters of educational technology group, AAHESGIT, which has a large international membership, devotes considerable space to this issue. It is clearly a problems that transcends national and sectoral boundaries.
11. *Campus Review*, September 28-October 4, 1995, vol. 5, no, 38, p. 28
12. Slaughter and Leslie (1997), p. 236
13. op. cit. p. 114
14. Institution of Engineers (1996), p. 34-5
15. Boyer, Altbach and Whitelaw (1994), Table 24
16. Anderson et al. (1997), p. 73
17. Williams (1965)
18. See for example Martin (1997), p. 77: "It is also clear that in the best schemes the workplace and the university are seen as equal partners contributing to the development of vocational practice. Both parties are involved in the planning of the overall experience and in the monitoring and guiding of day to day development."
19. Damrosch (1995) notes that there are often good reasons for opposing unfettered student initiative; how many first or second year students really know enough to formulate a quality program of study? But he also drily mentions that it is "not that professors are opposed to anarchy on principle ... they can live quite comfortably with "organized anarchy" so long as they get to be the anarchists." (p. 171)

20. Rumble (1997)

21. Since we are concerned in this chapter with the "how" rather than "what" of teaching, we have not included government activity in the areas of attempted national standards in course length and naming, or credit recognition and transfer. We merely note for now that these initiatives have generated much activity but little progress.

22. See *Campus Review* August 24-30, 1995, vol. 5, no. 33, p. 5

23. Professor Don Anderson, quoted in *Campus Review,* August 31-September 6, 1995, vol. 5, no. 34, p. 36

24. *Campus Review,* August 17- 23, 1995, vol. 5, no. 32, p. 2

25. Baldwin (1997), p. 46

26. Baldwin (1997), p. 47

27. The Open Learning Initiative was not "full" open learning. While being more flexible about entry and subject choice, it fell short of opening up all aspects of higher education (the "how", "when" and "where" of entry, study and assessment).

28. The Federal Government denied that the OLA had anything to do with meeting unmet demand on the cheap, though such an agenda was occasionally let slip (Williams, 1995). It has certainly shown less interest as unmet demand has abated.

29. Pritchard's comments were reported in *Campus Review* Vol 6, No 46, Nov 27-Dec 3, 1996, p. 6

30. Yetton and Associates (1997), p. x

31. *Seeing Things are They Really Are,* interview with Peter Drucker, in *Forbes,* 10 March 1997

32. Noam (1995)

33. Davidow and Malone (1992)

34. See L. Gubernick and A. Ebeling, *I got my degree through e-mail,* Forbes, 16 June 1997

35. Laurillard (1996)

36. Massy and Zemsky (1996)

37. *Chronicle of Higher Education,* November 17, 1997.

38. Writing in 1968, D.S. McMillan remarked on the use of television by the University of New South Wales. "The University is now satisfied that this method has an important place in future university teaching and may well replace large lecture groups entirely, leaving staff available for seminar and discussion sessions."

39. Ashworth (1996)

40. Bates (1997)

41. The vice-provost for information systems and computing at an Ivy League American university has stated that undergraduate distance learning programs would be more difficult to justify at Ivy League prices. At the elite private universities "the one thing that they sell is that the people sitting next to you are smart people. Universities haven't yet figured out how to recruit a comparatively talented pool over the Internet." (*Chronicle of Higher Education,* June 20, 1997, A20)

Chapter Six: Research: Making it Count

1.   The growth of the PhD has been particularly astonishing. This award represents the pinnacle of university education and is given on the basis of a piece of original research, assessed by external experts and usually the outcome of several years of intensive work. The first Australian PhD was awarded in 1949, in 1995 there were 2,432 PhDs awarded and more than nine times that number enrolled in PhD studies. The original intent was to open the door to a career in research, but over time it has come to be expected of all academic staff as a prerequisite for certain levels of promotion, and, in perception if not in fact, even serves as a requirement for entry to the senior ranks of some professions.

2.   *Australia's Science and Innovation System: Background Information* presentation made to the 14th meeting of the Prime Minister's Science and Engineering Council, September 1996

3.   Porter (1990)

4.   *Science* v. 276, 16 May 1997, p. 1011

5.   Comroe (1976)

6.   Medawar (1984), p. 36

7.   This example was cited by Medawar (1984) as the best example he knew of "the apparently useless bringing in the goods"

8.   Definitions of the different categories are rather imprecise, and interpretation of particular instances is left up to the universities in their reports to the ABS. The percentages given should, therefore, be treated as a rough guide.

9.   Bureau of Industry Economics (1996)

10.   Almost half comes directly from government, more comes by way of tax concessions of various sorts to business R&D

11.   Strategic Industry Research Foundation (1995)

12.   Lowe (1997)

13.   Twomey (1993) cited a study which surveyed 310 small to medium sized manufacturing exporters, finding that only 8 per cent had links with public research institutions. He also noted that in 1992 less than fifteen enterprises spun-off from Australian universities, whereas, for example, the University of Cambridge averaged 35 spin-off enterprises per year since 1975 and the Chalmers University of Technology in Sweden has averaged 18 per year since 1965.

14.   Australian Bureau of Statistics (1995)

15.   OECD(1997), p. 10

16.   Zinberg (1996)

17.   The Evaluations and Investigations Program (EIP) goes back to 1979. Over this period, it has supported a large number of studies, most in the nature of investigations rather than evaluations. Many of these studies have been surveys of opinions and attitudes on various subjects of interest to the Department. A great deal of research into the same or related issues is also undertaken by

universities or by bodies such as the Higher Education Council. This is not to say that the EIP program has been superfluous or a waste of money, indeed the authors are privileged to be involved in an EIP project themselves, looking at media and virtual universities. Rather, the question is one of contrasting the availability of information with the take-up of that information. It is far from clear that many, or indeed any, of the EIP studies have been influential in policy development at either university or government level.

18. These principles were outlined in the 1992 White Paper on science and technology.

19. Industry Commission (1993), p. 25

20. A recent article in an on-line magazine in the Economist group has suggested that the pace of change and competition in the data communications and IT industries is such that the companies involved cannot afford the risk of undertaking even their own basic research programs. Citing the break-up of AT&T, which has led to the separation of its eminent research arm, Bell Labs, the article suggests that a major shift is happening, with research giving way to development (*No More Blue Sky* D.Comm Magazine May 1997).

21. Cullen et al (1994) report the results of a survey of students at the Australian National University in the early 1990s. The majority of students had one principal supervisor (27 per cent had more than one, a figure that varied between disciplinary areas but was always less than 40 per cent). While most students were happy with their supervision, only 18 per cent reported they received critical assistance from other students in the department, and less than 6 per cent reported such assistance from students outside the department.

22. Damrosch (1995), p. 148

23. OECD(1997), p. 15

24. This formulation is adapted from Byerly Jr and Pielke Jr (1995), who applied it in the context of science and technology.

25. For example, researchers from the CSIRO or the Institutes of Advanced Study at the Australian National University already have access to government research funds, and so need special dispensation to apply. ARC grants almost all go to university researchers, while significant NHMRC funds go to hospitals and independent medical research institutes.

26. A 1990 study showed that nearly one in five academics from the pre-binary universities reported that they had not published a single journal article in the past five years (Ramsden 1992).

27. Turpin et al. (1996)

28. Bureau of Industry Economics (1996)

29. Higher Education Financing and Policy Review Committee (1997), p. 134

30. Higher Education Financing and Policy Review Committee (1997), p. 165

31. The administrative burden of the research grants system is hidden in that most of it is borne by the universities rather than the Commonwealth department. Some argue that the ARC and NHMRC represent large bureaucracies and are an inefficient way of allocating basic research. Yet administration of these schemes consumes only around two per cent of the funds involved, a level of support that is only grudgingly provided by the relevant government

department. A study commissioned by DEETYA in 1996 found that if allowance was made for the time academics spent in peer review, the cost of assessment became a sizeable proportion of the actual grant amount. However, describing peer review as an "opportunity cost" overlooks the fact that it provides, as a "spin-off", opportunity for interaction, information sharing and improvement of research proposals. Peer review, the cost of which is largely met by the universities, is thus a legitimate part of academic research activity.

32.   Bourke (1997)
33.   Higher Education Financing and Policy Review Committee (1997)
34.   Slaughter and Leslie (1997)
35.   Russell (1961)

Chapter Seven: Universities Learning to Manage Themselves

1.   Martin Gardner, in his *Annotated Alice*, notes that the term "caucus" derives from the United States in reference to a meeting of the leaders of a faction. He suggests Carroll was referring to the propensity of committees to run around in circles, but does not suggest a university connection with the Caucus Race. However, Carroll, as an Oxford Don at Christ Church, with Conservative sympathies, also wrote a poem parodying concerns by Liberals about the majority of Conservatives on the Hebdomadal Council of Oxford. In *The Elections to the Hebdomadal Council* he wrote:

> To save beloved Oxford from the yoke
> (for this majority's beyond a joke)
> We must combine, aye, hold a *caucus*-meeting
> Unless we want to get another beating

2.   Willett (1972)
3.   Kenny (1997), p. 51. Anthony Kenny is a former Master of Balliol College, Oxford. He wrote of the lively but relatively civilised tensions between the junior members of college and the elderly dons, many of whom were dismayed by the demands for participation by outspoken radical junior members. In 1976 junior members pushed to join the College's executive committee. This was opposed by many of the senior members not because they were against democracy in principle, but because "we all felt that, given the truculent attitude of left-wing JCR committees, junior member participation at that time would be a recipe for fruitless argumentation and endless posturing." Nevertheless, junior members were admitted. "The structure of governance thus set up remained in force for more than a decade. Towards the end of my own time as Master I was able, in rather different circumstances, to persuade the Governing Body to remove junior members from the executive committee and return to the system in which the government of the College was restricted to its Fellows."

4.   In 1992 the Commonwealth commissioned an independent inquiry into competition policy in Australia, with particular emphasis on areas outside the *Trade Practices Act*. The inquiry, chaired by Professor Fred Hilmer, reported in 1993. The recommendations of this report were adopted in essence by Commonwealth, State and Territory Governments in April of 1995, when they endorsed a set of principles, agreed to implement legislation, and established national bodies to oversee the implementation of the program. The thrust of these reforms was to promote competition by changing structural barriers and privileges which unfairly advantaged public sector agencies, provided that these changes do not compromise the public interest. A key principle is that of "competitive neutrality", which requires the elimination of any net competitive advantages that publicly owned businesses enjoy simply as a result of their public sector ownership.

5.   Peters (1994)

6.   See note 4. The Discussion Paper released by the Committee in November 1997 strongly favours the introduction of a competitive market to tertiary education, and the establishment of competitive neutrality through such mechanisms as the introduction of an infrastructure charge and the removal of impediments to the entry of new providers to the Australian system.

7.   Slaughter and Leslie (1997), p. 203

8.   Bower (1997)

9.   Daniel (1997)

10.   We referred earlier to an international survey of professorial staff, undertaken by the Carnegie Foundation for the Advancement of Teaching (Boyer, Altbach and Whitelaw 1994). This survey found that 67 per cent of Australian respondents indicated that affiliation with their academic discipline was very important to them, but only 22 per cent felt the same way about affiliation to their university. Similar percentages applied to the UK respondents. US professors indicated stronger ties both to their academic discipline and to their university. University affiliation was lowest for German academics, who have a long tradition of wandering between institutions.

Chapter Eight: Paying the Piper

1.   HECS is way of requiring students to contribute to the cost of their education by accruing an interest-free debt (though indexed to keep pace with inflation) which can be paid up-front, with a discount, or paid back via the taxation system. At present payments cut in at 3 per cent above a minimum threshold, rising to 6 per cent once a maximum threshold is reached. Such a system does not represent a lifetime burden on graduates, and avoids the financial disincentive of imposing an up-front charge on students, which would be a particular deterrent to those from poorer backgrounds.

       HECS debt was originally imposed at a flat rate for all courses. By 1996 this meant that on average students were responsible for meeting around one quarter of the cost of the course, though this varied depending on the actual course costs. Arts students on average contributed more than one third of their course costs, because Arts courses were cheaper to run, while medical students contributed around one eighth the cost of their education. Major changes were made in the 1996 Budget: the government lowered the threshold at which tax repayments cut in, from around $28,500 to $20,700, and also lowered the threshold at which maximum repayments were to apply. The level of HECS charge was changed from a flat rate to a three tier system, based on the subject cost and expected graduate earnings. The rate of HECS charge was also increased, by around one third for students in the lower band, by 90 per cent for those in the middle band and by more than 120 per cent for those taking subjects in the top band.

The effect has been to increase significantly the level of debt which students will have on graduation, and to force them to repay more of it sooner.

2.   Such a code has been proposed for members of the national academics' union.

3.   cited in Russell (1993), p. 10

4.   Phillips (1997), p. 228

5.   Higher Education Financing and Policy Review Committee (1997) and Creech (1997)

6.   Larson (1997). Larson had this to say about collusion between Ivy League institutions: "For years a group of America's most influential schools traded data on tuition policies. Penn, Harvard, M.I.T., Princeton, Brown, Columbia, Cornell, Dartmouth and Yale shared information about future tuition rates and fees, agreed never to grant aid solely on the basis of a student's academic merit, and met to negotiate how much need-based financial aid should be offered to individual students accepted by two or more of the member institutions. Ostensibly the goal of this "Overlap Group," dismantled in 1991 after a two-year federal anti-trust investigation, was to equalize the amount of money a given student's family would be required to contribute and thus keep price from clouding the student's decision. In practice, by liberating schools from price competition, the arrangement may have allowed them to boost tuitions to artificially high levels and, thanks to imitation by others, drive up tuition throughout the country."

7.   Marginson (1997), p. 162

8.   Professor Michael Osborne, in *Campus Review*, Vol 7, No 20 May 28-June 3, 1997, p. 13

9.   Creech (1997), section 6

10.   Professor Ingrid Moses, the incoming Vice-Chancellor of the University of New England, complained in a paper delivered to an OECD conference on universities and regional needs that regional universities such as hers found themselves in the position of cultural custodian of many heritage buildings and collections, but without additional funding to undertake the task. "Having just taken up the position of Vice-Chancellor of a regional university which is richly endowed with heritage buildings and collections I (nearly) despair", she said. She took responsibility for "the academic culture and commitment to (be) responsive to community needs .. but I cannot take responsibility for those

places and collections which are held in trust." (*Campus Review* July 30 - August 5, 1997, p. 5)

11. Media release from the office of Dr Kemp, Minister for Employment, Education, Training and Youth Affairs, November 12, 1997

12 Phillips (1997), p. 229-230

13. From the New Testament, Matthew 13.12: "For whoseoever hath, to him shall be given, and he shall have more abundance: but whosoever hath not, from him shall be taken away even that he hath"

14. Higher Education Financing and Policy Review Committee (1997) and Creech (1997)

15. Pascoe et al. (1997)

16. The former Minister's comments were made in an address delivered on 5 August 1997. She highlighted the fact that the TER score was not a good basis for selection for courses, as it was no indicator of the degree of difficulty of courses, and it had various gender and social biases.

   It is certainly true that TER scores are not a striking predictor of success at university. Generally speaking, those in the upper three per cent of school leavers, as measured by TER, do better than those around the ten per cent mark, but no direct relationship exists. However, the distortion of course entry arises from the need to screen out applicants in popular courses, so it will always be impossible to relate entry standards to intellectual difficulty in any systematic way between courses. Furthermore, a distinction needs to be made between the inadequacy of the TER as a measure of the likelihood of success at university and its reflection of the equity biases inherent in secondary schooling. Even if universities had a perfect and intensive method of interviewing and selecting those school leavers most suited to university study, it is unlikely that gender and social biases would be overturned. This is partly the reason why the impact on equity of changes to university systems (such as changes in fees and charges or equity policies) have had relatively little impact on the equity profile of university students or graduates. The make-up of universities remains largely dominated by the middle and upper social groups, many from private schools, and this is particularly the case in those courses such as law and medicine that are hard to get into. It is true that more women have gained entry, but this reflects changes in secondary schooling more than changes introduced at university level.

17. Tony Tysome, "Will we be able to bank on learning accounts?" *The Times Higher Education Supplement*, October 10, 1997, p. 8

18. Higher Education Financing and Policy Review Committee (1997) and Baldwin (1997)

19. The report of the Information Industries Taskforce (the "Goldsworthy Report") recommended in July 1997 that the Commonwealth issue 15,000 vouchers for additional places in information and communication technology-related courses, redeemable at "approved institutions". This is not an open tender proposal, rather it allows funding to follow the student to whichever institution succeeds in attracting an eligible student. The details of such a scheme, including how such places would relate to existing negotiated places

within university profiles, were not elaborated in the report.

20. Linda Rosenman from the University of Queensland (1996) reviewed various options for increasing the range of options available to students in a study funded by the Evaluations and Investigations Program. The AACU findings were reported in that study.

21. Brown (1997), p. 127

22. *Private Training Chief Hits "Monopoly"* in *The Australian*, 25 June 1997

23. Jones (1997), p. 120

References

Adams, Hazard (1988) *The Academic Tribes*, Second edition. Urbana: University of Illinois Press.

Aeuckens, Annely (1989) *The People's University*, South Australian Institute of Technology.

Anderson, Don, Robert Arthur and Terry Stokes (1997) *Qualifications of Australian Academics: Sources and Levels 1978-1996*, Department of Employment Education Training and Youth Affairs Evaluations and Investigations Program 97/11, AGPS, Canberra.

Andrich, David and Annette Mercer (1997) *International Perspectives on Selection Methods of Entry into Higher Education*, Higher Education Council Commissioned Report No. 57, September. AGPS, Canberra.

Ashworth, K.H. (1996) *Virtual University Could Produce Only Virtual Learning*, Chronicle of Higher Education, September 6, p. A88.

ASTEC (Australian Science and Technology Council) (1991) *The Demand and Supply of Scientists and Engineers in Australia*, NIEIR Report, Occasional Paper 18, Canberra.

Auchmuty, J.J. (1959) Australian Universities: the Historical Background, in *The Humanities in Australia* (A. Grenfell Price, ed.), Angus & Robertson.

Australian Bureau of Statistics (1995) *Innovation in Australian Manufacturing 1994*, Catalogue No. 8116.0

Australian Council for Educational Research (1996, 1997) *The 1995 (1996) Course Experience Questionnaire*, Graduate Careers Council of Australia, August 1996 (June 1997).

Baldwin, the Hon. Peter (1991) *Higher Education: Quality and Diversity in the 1990s*, AGPS, Canberra

Baldwin, the Hon. Peter (1997) *The Lighthouse: Towards a Labor Vision for the Learning Society*. Privately circulated discussion paper, April.

Ballantyne, Roy, John Bain and Jan Packer (1997) *Reflecting on University Teaching: Academics' Stories*, Committee for University Teaching and Staff Development, AGPS, Canberra.

Barcan, Alan (1988) *Two Centuries of Education in New South Wales*, Sydney, NSWU

Press.

Bates, Tony (1997) *Technology, Distance Education and National Development*. Paper presented to the 18th ICDE World Conference, 29-31 May 1997. Penn State University.

Becher, Tony (1989) *Academic Tribes and Territories: Intellectual Enquiry and the Cultures of Disciplines*, Society for Research into Higher Education, Open University Press.

Bourke, Paul (1997) *Evaluating University Research: The British Research Assessment Exercise and Australian Practice*, National Board of Employment, Education and Training Commissioned Report No. 56, AGPS, Canberra.

Bowden, John A. and Masters, Geofferey N. (1993) *Implications for Higher Education of a Competency-Based Approach to Education and Training*, DEET Evaluations and Investigations Program. AGPS, Canberra.

Bower, Adrian (1997) *Co-operation Among Three Australian Medial Schools in Designing Radical Medical Curricula*, Journal of Higher Education Policy and Management, vol. 19, no. 1, pp. 15-19.

Boyer, Ernest, L. (1990) *Campus Life: In Search of Community*, Princeton The Carnegie Foundation for the Advancement of Teaching.

Boyer, Ernest L, Philip Altbach and Mary Jean Whitelaw (1994) *The Academic Profession: An International Perspective*, The Carnegie Foundation for the Advancement of Teaching.

Brown, Roger (1997) Learning from the HEQC Experience in *Standards and Quality in Higher Education*, (J. Brennan, P de Vries and R. Williams, eds.), Higher Education Policy Series 37, Jessica Kingsley Publishers.

Bureau of Industry Economics (1996) *Science system: international benchmarking*, BIE 96/2 AGPS, Canberra.

Byerly Jr, R. And R.A. Pielke Jr. (1995) The Changing Ecology of United States Science, *Science*, vol. 269, p. 1531-3.

Carnegie Council (1980) *Three Thousand Futures: The next twenty years for higher education*. Final Report of the Carnegie Council on Higher Education Policy, Jossey-Bass.

Connell, W.F. (1993) *Reshaping Australian Education 1960-1985*, Australian Council for Educational Research.

Creech, the Hon. Wyatt (1997) *A Future Tertiary Education Policy for New Zealand: Tertiary*

Education Review Green Paper, September, Ministry of Education

Cullen, David, Margot Pearson, Lawrence Saha and R.H. Spear (1994) *Establishing Effective PhD Supervision,* Department of Employment, Education and Training Evaluations and Investigations Program. Canberra, AGPS.

Cunningham, Stuart et al. (1997) *New Media and Borderless Education: A Review of the Convergence Between Global Media and Higher Education,* Department of Employment, Education, Training and Youth Affairs, Evaluations and Investigations Program, in press.

Damrosch, David (1995) *We Scholars: Changing the Culture of the University,* Harvard University Press.

Daniel, Sir John (1996) *The Mega-Universities and the Knowledge Media,* London, Kogan Page.

Davidow, W.H. and Malone, M.S. (1992) *The Virtual Corporation,* Harper Collins.

Davis, Glyn (1996) Making Sense of Difference? Public Choice, Politicians and Bureaucratic Change in America and Australia in *New Ideas, Better Government,* (P. Weller and G. Davis eds.), Allen & Unwin.

Dawkins, the Hon. J.S. (1988) *Higher Education: A Policy Statement,* AGPS, Canberra.

Department of Employment, Education and Training (1995) *Australia's Workforce 2005: Jobs in the Future,* AGPS, Canberra.

Desmond, Adrian and Moore, James (1992) *Darwin,* Penguin Books.

Flexner, Abraham (1930) *Universities: American, English, German,* Oxford University Press.

Golding, Barry, Simon Marginson and Robert Pascoe (1996) National Board of Employment, Education and Training. *Changing Context, Moving Skills: Generic Skills in the Context of Credit Transfer and the Recognition of Prior Learning,* AGPS, Canberra.

Greenwood, G. (1960) National Development and Social Experimentation 1901-1914. In *Australia: A Social and Political History,* (G. Greenwood Ed.), Angus and Robertson.

Higher Education Council (1996) *Professional Education and Credentialism,* National Board of Employment, Education and Training, AGPS, Canberra.

Higher Education Financing and Policy Review Committee (Mr Roderick West, Chair)

(1997) *Learning for Life: A Policy Discussion Paper*, AGPS, Canberra

Hood, Christopher (1989) Rolling Back the State or Moving to a Contract and Subsidiarity State? In *What Should Government Do?* (P. Coaldrake and J.R. Nethercote eds) Hale & Ironmonger, Sydney.

Humphrey, S. (1997) *Mature Focus on the Old Question*, Campus Review, May 7-13, p. 8.

Industry Commission (1993) *Research and Development: Overview*, AGPS, Canberra

Information Industries Taskforce (A. Goldsworthy, Chair) (1997) *The Global Information Economy: The Way Ahead*, Department of Industry, Science and Technology, July.

Institution of Engineers (1996) *Changing the Culture: Engineering Education into the Future*, (Peter Johnson, Chairman), Canberra, The Institution of Engineers.

Jones, Glenn, R. *Cyberschools: an Education Renaissance*, Jones Digital Century Inc., Colorado.

Karmel, Peter (1997) *Submission to the Review of Higher Education Financing and Policy*.

Kenny, Anthony (1997) *A Life in Oxford*, John Murray, London.

Kerr, Clark (1963) *The Uses of the University*, New York, Harper & Row.

Larson, Erik (1997) *Why Colleges Cost Too Much*, Time, Vol. 149 No. 11, March 17.

Laurillard, Diana (1996) *Use of staff time resources in teaching*, UK Open University, October.

Leavis, F.R. (1962) *Two Cultures? The Significance of C.P. Snow*, Chatto & Winders, London.

Lord Bowden (1965) The Universities, in *Tertiary Education in Australia*, (J. Wilkes, Ed.), Angus and Robertson.

Lowe, Ian (1997) *Clever country or bleak backwater: how science careers affect Australia's future*, address to the National Press Club, March 19, 1997.

Lundberg, David (1995) *A Fair Choice: Post-Compulsory Education Structures and Networks*, DEET Evaluations and Investigations Program 95/12. AGPS, Canberra

Marginson, Simon (1997) The Limits of Market Reform: Positional Competition in Australian Higher Education in *Australia's Future Universities*, (G. Harman and

J. Sharpham, eds), University of New England Press.

Marshall, F.R. and Tucker, M. (1992) *Thinking for a Living: Education and the Wealth of Nations*, Basic Books, New York.

Martin, A. (1990) *Menzies and the Murray Committee*, in Smith and Crichton (1990).

Martin, Elaine (1997) *The Effectiveness of Different Models of Work-Based University Education*, DEETYA Evaluations and Investigations Program 96/19. AGPS, Canberra.

Massy, William and Robert Zemsky (1995) *Using Information Technology to Enhance Academic Productivity*, Educom, American Association for Higher Education.

Medawar, Peter (1984) *Pluto's Republic*, Oxford University Press.

Moyal, Ann (1986) *A Bright and Savage Land*, Penguin.

Murray, Keith (Chair) (1957) *Report of the Committee on Australian Universities*. Commonwealth Government Printer, Canberra.

Newman, John Henry (Cardinal) (1947) *The Idea of a University*, Longmans Green and Co. New York.

Nisbet, Robert (1971) *The Degradation of the Academic Dogma*, Heinemann, London.

Noam, Eli (1995) *Electronics and the Dim Future of the University*, Science, v. 270, 13 Oct. 95 pp. 247-249.

OECD (1997) *Managing Science Systems: In Search of Best Practices*, DSTI/STP/SUR(97)10

Painter, Martin (1996) *Economic Policy, Market Liberalism and the "End of Australian Politics"*, Australian Journal of Political Science, v. 31, no. 3, p. 287-299.

Pascoe, Robert, Avril McClelland and Barry McGaw (1997) *Entry Methods Into Higher Education, Part 2 (Australia)*, in press

Pennington, David (1997) *Submission to the Review of Higher Education Financing and Policy*

Peters, Tom (1994) *The Tom Peters seminar. Crazy time call for crazy organisations*, London Macmillan.

Philp, Hugh, R.L. Debus, Vija Veidemanis and W.F. Connell (1964) *The University and its Community*, Ian Novak, Sydney.

Phillips, David (1997) Competition, Contestability and Market Forces, in *Australia's*

Future Universities (G. Harman and J. Sharpham, eds), University of New England Press.

Porter, Michael (1990) *The Competitive Advantage of Nations,* London, Macmillan Press.

Ramsden, Paul and Ingrid Moses (1992) *Associations between research and teaching in Australian higher education,* Higher Education, vol. 23, no. 3, pp. 273-295.

Richardson, S.S. (1972) A Role and Purpose for Colleges of Advanced Education, in *Australian Higher Education: Problems of a Developing System,* (G.S Harman and C. Selby Smith, eds) Angus and Robertson.

Rosenman, Linda (1996) *The Broadening of University Education: An Analysis of Entry Restructuring and Curriculum Change Options,* Department of Employment, Education and Training Evaluations and Investigations Program 96/12. Canberra, AGPS.

Rowe, A.P. (1960) *If the Gown Fits,* Melbourne University Press.

Rumble, Greville (1997) *University structures and labour markets in the twenty-first century: the interactive university.* Paper delivered to the International Conference "What Kind of University?" London, U.K., 18-20 June.

Russell, Bertrand (1961) *Education and the Social Order,* London, George Allen & Unwin.

Russell, Conrad (1993) *Academic Freedom*, Routledge, London and New York.

Slaughter, Sheila and Larry Leslie (1997) *Academic Capitalism: Politics, Policies and the Entrepreneurial University,* Johns Hopkins University Press, Baltimore and London.

Smith, F.B. and Crichton, p. (Eds) (1990) *Ideas for Histories of Universities in Australia,* Canberra ANU.

Snow, C.P. (1962) *The Two Cultures and The Scientific Revolution,* Cambridge University Press, New York.

Strategic Industry Research Foundation (1995) *Benchmarking Australia's R&D Costs and Skills,* Report to the Department of Industry, Science and Technology.

Thomis, Malcolm (1985) *A Place of Light and Learning: the University of Queensland's First 75 Years,* University of Queensland Press.

Turpin, T. et al (1996) *Patterns of Research Activity in Australian Universities,* National Board of Employment, Education and Training Commissioned Report No. 47,

AGPS Canberra.

Twomey, Paul (1993) *Creating economic growth through enterprise generation and industry research partnerships: the role of the post-secondary education sector,* DEET Evaluations and Investigations Program. AGPS, Canberra.

Vanstone, the Hon. Amanda (1996) *Relieving the pressure on higher education,* Australian Quarterly, vol. 68, no. 4, pp. 1-8.

Walshok, Mary L. (1995) *Knowledge without Boundaries,* Jossey-Bass.

Watts, Donald (1997) A New Approach to Higher Education Financing and Policy, in *Australia's Future Universities,* (G. Harman and J. Sharpham, eds), University of New England Press.

Wilkes, J. (Ed.) (1965) *Tertiary Education in Australia,* Angus and Robertson.

Willett, F.J. (1972) Special Problems of the Older Universities, in *Australian Higher Education - Problems of a Developing System,* (G.S Harman and C. Selby Smith, eds), Angus and Robertson.

Williams, B. (1990) *Status and Conditions of Employment at the University of Sydney 1850-1985,* in Smith and Crichton (1990)

Williams, Helen (1995) *Curriculum Conceptions of Open Learning,* PhD Thesis, Queensland University of Technology.

Williams, H.S. (1965) The Technical Colleges, in *Tertiary Education in Australia* ,(J. Wilkes ed.), Angus and Robertson.

Yetton, Philip and Associates (1997) *Managing the Introduction of Technology in the Delivery and Administration of Higher Education,* Evaluations and Investigations Program 97/3 AGPS, Canberra.

Zinberg, D.S. (1996) *A Cautionary Tale,* Science, vol. 273, 26 June, p. 411.

Index